SPIRITUALITY IN
MANAGEMENT

SPIRITUALITY IN
MANAGEMENT

MEANS OR END?

S.K. CHAKRABORTY
DEBANGSHU CHAKRABORTY

OXFORD
UNIVERSITY PRESS

OXFORD

UNIVERSITY PRESS

YMCA Library Building, Jai Singh Road, New Delhi 110 001

Oxford University Press is a department of the University of Oxford. It furthers the
University's objective of excellence in research, scholarship, and education
by publishing worldwide in

Oxford   New York

Auckland   Cape Town   Dar es Salaam   Hong Kong   Karachi   Kuala Lumpur
Madrid   Melbourne   Mexico City   Nairobi   New Delhi   Shanghai   Taipei   Toronto

With offices in
Argentina   Austria   Brazil   Chile   Czech Republic   France   Greece   Guatemala
Hungary   Italy   Japan   Poland   Portugal   Singapore   South Korea   Switzerland
Thailand   Turkey   Ukraine   Vietnam

Oxford is a registered trademark of Oxford University Press
in the UK and in certain other countries

Published in India
by Oxford University Press, New Delhi

© Oxford University Press 2008

The moral rights of the author have been asserted
Database right Oxford University Press (maker)

First published 2008

ISBN 13: 978-0-19-569223-5
ISBN 10: 0-19-569223-3

Typeset in GoudyOlSt BT 10.5/13
by Sai Graphic Design, New Delhi 110055
Printed at Rajshri Photolithographers, Delhi 110 032
Published by Oxford University Press
YMCA Library Building, Jai Singh Road, New Delhi 110 001

For

Nandini/Laboni

May she epitomize Bharat's ideal of womanhood

'They imagine that desire and enjoyment are all the aim of life,
and they are the prey of a devouring, a measurelessly
unceasing care and thought and endeavour
and anxiety till the moment of their death.
[*The Bhagavad Gita*, XVI–11]

Threefold are the doors of Hell—desire, wrath and greed:
therefore let man renounce these three.
A man liberated from these doors of darkness...
Follows his own higher good and arrives at
The highest soul-status.
[*The Bhagavad Gita*, XVI–21, 22]

Contents

Preface

The one unambiguous and unanimous lesson from Bharatvarsha's (i.e. India's) tryst with spiritual religion is: first to discover the Divine within, and then to manifest It without. And, consequently, to be Blissful to oneself and to others. This keynote rings consistently in all the streams of Bharat's 'core culture' comprising Hinduism, Jainism, Buddhism, and Sikhism. Sufi-Parsi mysticism, though originating in Persia, also resonates with the same note as the 'core culture'. This common mandate is woven into all the roles and functions humanity and society should perform—in principle.

Now that even business organizations and management literature have begun to show interest in Spirituality, it is in some respects quite encouraging. Yet, it has been deemed important to re-iterate the above essence. For, it would be erroneous to create a kind of 'secular' or 'business' spirituality. Such branding may relegate Spirituality too to an instrumental status for gratifying sensual, hedonistic goals. This book, therefore, offers critical insights into some of the authentic v. pseudo concerns in recent engagements with Spirituality. It aspires to stimulate serious and honest interest in spirituality. It is well to be conscious that the *zeitgeist* of the present times has turned upside down the dictum we had learnt in our boyhood: 'If wealth is lost, nothing is lost; if health is lost, something is lost; if character is lost, everything is lost'. Today the overriding mantra seems to be: 'If character is lost, nothing is lost; if wealth is lost everything is lost'.

As for the contents of the book, the chapters are largely independent pieces. However, the connecting thread of Spirituality strings them together. Some cross-referencing has been done. Hence, the reader could begin anywhere without incurring loss of meaning. Each chapter has received nourishment from the authors' experience garnered through continuous and thorough involvement with members of secular organizations throughout India, and at times in the West also. Such experience, stretching across a period of almost twenty five years and nearly eight thousand participants, has accrued from intensive Workshops conducted for three or two whole days each time. Each group of participants (twenty to thirty) is exposed to one, two, or three modules of conceptual and experiential learning. The contents of these modules are organized around several foundational concepts, theories and processes of Yoga–Vedanta (Y-V) psycho-philosophy. Throughout the text numerous real-life, contemporary examples of spirituality-in-action illustrate the principles highlighted in the volume. They first 'become', then 'do'.

Interpretations of organizational issues addressed below are set against the wider canvas of Indian culture—both past and present. The future depends critically on how we evaluate these antecedents. Especially, if her past essence is spurned, the future too might reject her. Therefore, this book has not shied away from touching on a few controversial issues. Superficial politeness has been avoided while dealing with them. Falsehood and opportunism of a disconcerting degree afflict large sections of Indian intelligentsia. This is bringing no good to any quarter; rather irreparable harm is being done.

Truth or Wisdom of the Spirit has always been possessed by persons of *tyaga* (abnegation). The history of the human race proves this fact irrefutably. But the decisive drift of the human mind since the 18th century has been towards *bhoga* (hedonism). The more the better. Overloaded with matter, crushed under its weight, typical 21st century minds cannot recognize their incapacity for Truth, for Spirit— even for clear thinking. Fragmented, vested 'truths' in endless succession are creating bewildering chaos. Yet, the much-derided superstitious ancient mind had left a virgin Mother Earth for succeeding generations. The enlightened scientific mind has, however, since the 18th century, been bequeathing to us a groaning Mother Earth. It is this vital Truth which awaits its hour in the new discourse on Spirituality in business, technology, management and much else. Once this begins to happen, stock phrases like self-actualization, achievement motivation etc. will carry theoretical meanings and practical implications altogether superior to those implied even in the seminal writings on these topics. Only then could man, instead of business, become the 'measure of all things.'

Another angle to the theme of this book. The centralized and volatile, rights-driven and conflict-creating urban culture of the present is hostile to Spirituality. This is an issue of paramount principle. Whether such a state of affairs can be undone, sooner or later is no question. It is the decentralized and stable, duties-inspired and cooperative grass root culture of organic times (at least in Bharatvarsha) which had produced the long line of spiritual giants- the *rishis*. There are disquieting signs that the 'don't care, except bottom line' attitude of business and commerce is trying to make an ally of even Spirituality as a technique for its own ends. Pray, let us be sensible enough not to fiddle with the priceless legacy of the *rishis*. This perspective too should exert a sobering influence on the new-born glamour-child called 'business spirituality' (much like 'business ethics') in the scorching lap of despotic economism.

Months after completing this manuscript, and during the third revision of this preface, we perchance came upon these words of Swami Vivekananda (spoken in reply to the welcome address by the Maharaja of Khetri): '...Whoever tries to bring the past to the door of everyone, is a great benefactor to his nation' (*Complete Works*, vol. iv, p. 324). This was an immensely gratifying retrospective endorsement of what this book has attempted.

The authors thankfully acknowledge the following Journals for the inclusion of our papers published by them, with appropriate modifications and/or extensions, for this book—

* *Journal of Organizational Change Management* (Vol.17, No.2, 2004) –for Chapter 3
* *Management Review* (Vol.18, No.2,2006) (IIM-Bangalore) – for Chapter 4
* *International Journal of Social Economics*, September 2007 – for Chapter 7
* *Vilakshan* (Vol.3, Issue 2, 2006) (XIM-Bhubaneshwar) – for Chapter 6
* *Vedanta Kesari* (December, 2006) – for Chapter 8

The authors are also grateful to Mrs. Paushali Chakraborty for continuous help in transferring the handwritten chapters on to the PC with alacrity and dexterity.

Kolkata   S.K. CHAKRABORTY
October 2007   DEBANGSHU CHAKRABORTY

Introduction

A small beginning was made when our first book, drawing upon Indian psycho-philosophy (primarily Yoga-Vedanta) for running secular organizations, was published in 1985 (Chakraborty, 1985). Yoga-Vedanta (Y-V) psycho-philosophy is widely recognized as the route to the highest peak of spirituality within the comprehensive range of what is generally called Hinduism. Y-V has always been universal, free as it is from identification with any single founder-prophet or ecclesiastical outfit. For this very reason Y-V is non-dogmatic, non-proselytizing and all-tolerant as well. Again, there is very little dependence on a personal God in Y-V, especially in Rajyoga and Advaita Vedanta. So the door is open here even for an atheist to peep into the courtyard of Spirit—if she or he wishes. It is noteworthy that Buddhism, Jainism and Sikhism, though derived from or associated with the names of their respective founding *avatars*, are also all-tolerant. Their birth in the womb of Sanatan Hindu religion maybe the most probable reason for this positive but rare characteristic. Children are different from their parents. But that does not eliminate the fact of the parent-offspring relationship.

Be that as it may, it was then a plunge into uncharted waters. Intuitive conviction in the perennial worth of such insights and processes, especially in the Indian cultural context, was the only empowerment behind the effort. Words like values, ethics, spirituality, yoga etc. were then hardly heard in the realm of management. Since then much water has flown under the bridge. Quite a bit has been spoken and written on these topics over the last two and a half decades or so. Many others have joined hands in exploring this territory. Yet, so long we have been reticent in talking about Spirituality so directly and abundantly. But now academics are beginning to deal with even this topic by quantitative research techniques. This book is an effort therefore to put the subject in its proper perspective. Spirituality is too sacred and ineffable to be approached along conventional intellectual tracks. Here *proof follows faith.* The common gospel 'what cannot be measured cannot be improved' may apply well in the sphere of physical objects and processes. But it is a folly to pursue this approach in the spiritual domain. The mother's love for her child cannot, and should not be expressed in quantitative terms. And this is true of spiritual practice as a whole. Of course, the effects of progress in this direction can be sensed, felt or observed.

A popular posture of today is: Yes, spirituality may have something of use to offer; but it must first clear rigorous scientific tests to be able to claim trust and faith. Such a stand has to be questioned on the following grounds:

(a) The assumption that modern sci-tech alone is the master of truths, forgets that all the Ultimate Human Truths had been intuited several thousand years ago in the ashrams, tapovans, and mountain caves.

(b) The devastating results associated with 'rigorously tested' sci-tech theories and techniques over the last three centuries or so lurk just a little below the surface glitter—global warming to high-tech terrorism, existential vacuum to cyber porn etc. (see Chapter 5). How can such a regimen of 'rigorous tests' then sit in judgement over spirituality? It should be the other way round.

(c) The assumption is that spirituality is all airy-fairy, offering nothing as universally precise and true as H_2O for water, lacking any process of verification and so on. We should then listen to Sri Aurobindo on this score (Sethna, 1997):

'I must remind you that I have been an intellectual myself and no stranger to doubt. I think I can say that I have been testing day and night for years upon years more scrupulously than any scientist his theory or his method on the physical plane.'

Besides, the following pages are not a 'Spirituality Made Easy' venture. The book tries more to inform and inspire one towards authentic spirituality in management and other secular pursuits, not so much to teach or research it. There are persons better qualified than us to play the teacher-mentor role. Nor is it a scholarly treatise which can meet the exacting standards of academics specializing in philosophy or psychology. The readership for this book is that of practitioners in business and other fields. The authors bring here the experience of almost three decades of intensive exposures of several salient concepts and processes to nearly 10,000 such people, representing the multi-cultural mosaic of India.

From the spiritual viewpoint, 'pious poverty' has been found to be more common than 'holy affluence'. This seems to hold true at all levels—from the individual, familial, organizational, to the national and global levels. Spirituality is a state for 'subjective realization'. This is the reason for coining the phrase 'human response' (Chakraborty, 1985) in lieu of 'human resource'. Unless this all-important principle is held fast, spirituality as an end, solving or preventing on the way the ills that sorely afflict us today, will remain elusive. Spirituality is not a field for 'objective research'. Physicists of real mettle have already admitted that so-called 'objective' research is impossible for human investigators even in the material sphere. Organizations of all kinds and society at large need leaders and members who are able to concentrate, whatever spare energy and time they can manage, on 'realization' of the Spirit. The case for academic research is but marginal, and secondary. Frankly, academics themselves might do well to devote much more of their relatively ample time to spiritual 'realization' within, than to do 'research' without for career goals.

Next, the word 'secular'. It recurs in the text as an unavoidable foil to 'spirituality'. And this juxtaposition is necessary too. The word secular has, therefore, been explained below according to five popular English dictionaries—

The New Collins Concise Dictionary (1982):
1. Of or relating to worldly as opposed to sacred things.
2. Not concerned with or related to religion.
3. Not within the control of the church.
4. An education having no particular religious affinities.
5. Not bound by religious vows to a monastic or other order.
6. Occurring or appearing once in an age.
7. Lasting for a long time.

The Concise Oxford Dictionary (1990):
1. Concerned with the affairs of this world, not spiritual or sacred.
2. (Education) not concerned with religion or religious belief.
3. Not ecclesiastical or monastic, not bound by a religious rule.
4. Occurring once in an age or century.
5. Lasting for or occurring over an indefinitely long time.

The Chambers Thesaurus (1999):
1. Temporal.
2. Worldly.

3. Lay.
4. Non-religious.
5. Non-spiritual.
6. Profane.

The New International Webster's Pocket Dictionary (2001):
1. Of or pertaining to this world or the present life, temporal, worldly, contrasted with religious or spiritual.
2. Not under the control of the church, civil—not ecclesiastical.
3. Not concerned with religion, not sacred.
4. Not bound by monastic vows, opposed to secular.

The gist of all these explanations is that spirituality is a sacred existential state. But the secular realm is solely material and sensual. Nevertheless, the varied agencies managing business and other secular functions can perform more exalted, honourable and wholesome roles by honouring the spiritual impulse for piety and holiness over the drive for success and reward. In the process, nothing actually remains secular; everything becomes spiritual. But, as the following typical event indicates, we are as yet far removed from such saving convergence.

The Management department of a premier Indian University had organized a three-day Conference on spirituality in organizations in early 2007. A Western University had partnered it. One of the Indian presenters had been allotted thirty minutes in the morning plenary session of the second day. The audience was about one hundred strong, including academics from the West as well as the East. The other three presenters were all from that Western University, including the chairperson. The Indian presenter spoke directly to the audience—no power point or video shows. His key question was: What is the true motive underlying the sudden spurt of interest in spirituality in business organizations? The management cupboard is already full of skeletons from the recent past: T-group, sensitivity training, behavioural labs, MBO, transactional analysis, PPBS, TQM, BPR, ERP, business games, business ethics, Six Sigma, ISO and so on. The 'tool-making animal' that man is, he seems now ready to turn spirituality too into yet another 'tool' for the business of profit or other kinds of secular success. This is a sort of hijacking. The other three presentations did not evince interest in such prime issues. Rather, through brain-teasing series of packaged power-point slides, the theme of spirituality was turned into an intricate intellectual maze—boxes, curves, loops, arrows and all that in full measure.

Shakespeare's words seemed to come alive: '... a tale told by an ..., all sound and fury, signifying nothing!'

Interestingly, in the two subsequent concurrent sessions also, both the presenters and coordinators were again from the same Western University. The grapevine has it that as a condition for some aid by a UN agency, a Western University had to be taken as a partner. It was, however, evident from the post-plenary question-answer interval that the listeners could not relate sensibly to any of the presentations, except the one by the Indian speaker. For, practically all the questions were directed towards him.

Another curious aspect of these Western presentations was the frequent assertion that 'spirituality is in, but religion is out'. Why not then argue, with but a slight inflection: 'science is in, but technology is out'? The over-zealous sci-tech movement of the last four secular centuries in the West had reacted strongly against Church-dominated religion and politics. This conflict has never been true of India. In any case, the West threw away the 'baby' of spirituality too, along with some 'dirty water' in the 'bath-tub' of religion. Now it seemingly wants to reclaim the 'baby' *without* the 'bath tub'. What will then hold the 'baby'? Of all cultures Bharat's experience should be remembered in this regard: spirituality has always been the core of religion. One cannot get a ripe mango without its outer skin or inner seed. Swami Vivekananda had it right: 'Religion is Realization.' This can be nothing else but spirituality. Realizing with certitude that one's true Self is a constant, luminous, bliss-in-itself perfection, and not just the murky, fickle, sensual body-mind self—this is religious spirituality or spiritual religion.

It will not be out of place to mention also that the current attempt by the West to take the lead in spirituality too could be a component of its globalization strategy. It is evident by now that one of the requirements of this strategy is to engineer a mono-cultural humanity in a uni-polar world. The great irony and contradiction in this is: nations which insist upon individuality at the personal level, are out to deny individuality to national cultures other than their own! The reasons for this are by now obvious to those who can see below the surface glitter.

The other side of the big canvas reveals steeply rising existential misery and ecological hopelessness. The more economics and business, finance and commerce, science and technology tend to promise happiness and peace, the more the latter seem to elude us. With a hub of life no more secure than exploding lust for money and fame, most professionals in every kind of organization are engaged in self-deception. The orchestrated din of hyperboles like paradigm shift, radical transformation, holistic development, attitudinal metamorphosis, emotional quotient, intellectual capital, human development index, communication revolution etc., is uprooting them from the basics of 'right living'. Even 'spiritual quotient' is beginning to ring in the mouths of people who should know better for example, monks. Instant gratification—from one-minute manager to two-minute noodles, from instant coffee to instant *samadhi*, from enjoy now to pay later, from annual final accounts to quarterly final accounts—all these go ill with 'right living', including personal and organizational ethics.

However, among those few who are able to ascend and observe from beyond the orbit of success-driven secular management, spirituality is perceived as the *remedial response* to the techno-economic intoxication, or 'technoxication', now overwhelming us. But when secular outfits, especially business academies and entities, begin to dabble in spirituality, the medicine itself may soon become impotent. For the present, the epicentre of spirituality-for-business is a place which seems to have 'the body of a giant with the brain of a child', and which has 'the mania for repeating a little too much the praise of money.' Both these characterizations were intuited by Romain Rolland, the great French litterateur-savant, and an authentic bridge-maker between the East and the West (Rolland, 1927, 1930). Rabindranath Tagore too (in a letter to CF Andrews on 25.12.1920) had lamented: 'These ... people believe in their wealth which can only multiply itself and attain nothing.' (Tagore, 1920)

The first international conference on Ethics in Economics and Business (Tokyo, 1996) had offered a corroboration of this cultural conditioning. During a plenary session one western academic of high standing had gleefully announced: 'Business ethics has already become big business in my country!' We had the mortification of listening to her brazen confession. This indeed is reducing the end to means. Spirituality is unlikely to escape a similar fate in such hands.

The world, India in particular, should therefore exercise prudence to avoid the ultimate mistake of using the high end of spirituality to serve the low end of profitability or other indices of secular performance. The higher must not be pressed in the service of the lower. Humankind does not deserve this sort of technoxicated reductionism. The tail should not wag the dog. With a few honourable exceptions, Indian academics tend to be generally more gullible in this regard than their European or other Asian counterparts. Given the millennia-old, unbroken Bharatiya tradition of spirituality-as-a-life-process, such conformity to 'imported' negative wisdom is regrettable. It may be confessed that we of the present, especially the bulk of rootless literates and well-offs, are unworthy of this heritage. Amongst all the cultural legacies of this world, India's heritage to date has shown relatively the least discrepancy between precept and practice, particularly in its dealings with cultures and lands beyond its geographical boundaries. Yet, Indian intellectuals are usually defensive, with no independent standards of judgement.

What we should admire, however, about the technoxicated quarters is their huge reserve of civic discipline. One important consequence of this is that, for centuries some of these countries have been managing themselves with just two or three political parties. But in India we get parties at the drop of a hat. This reflects dangerous egoistic indiscipline, endorsed by our constitution. Therefore, we seem to land up with the worse of both the worlds, losing out on both our good stuff and theirs. Surely, the West sets the standards in technology, finance, etc. for India. But equally certainly, Bharatvarsha has to set the standards in Spirituality for the world.

Here is another important angle to the issue of spirituality in secular management and administration. It is emerging at a time when one of the most ubiquitous phrases in circulation is 'human resources development' (HRD). The corridors of government and business are abuzz with HRD. There can hardly be any greater insult to humanity, and also to the English language, than calling 'human being' as 'human resource'. We had drawn attention to this affront almost two decades ago (Chakraborty, 1989). Now that spirituality is being discussed so openly and frequently, and often flippantly, we feel the phrase HRD or HRM must go. The word 'resource' smacks of nothing else but material means for manipulation to yield apparent utility. Exploitation and disposability are the very essence of resource-orientation. *Amritasya putrah's* (children of Immortality) of the world, as our *Shwetashwatara Upanishad* beckons (verse 2.5) cannot be mere resources to be used up. Spirituality and HRD cannot even be room-mates, far less bedfellows. The Director of one of the IIMs had recently (April, 2007) forecast that the heads of HRD function would henceforth be like rockstars! God may know what he meant! In a spirituality-informed secular organization, however, the Head of the personnel function would have to be a steady polestar for 'human being development' (HBD). The climax about HRD was heard by us some fifteen years ago. An omniscient (hyper-secularist) academic had boomed in a seminar: 'The mother is a resource, for she yields milk for the baby'! This masterpiece, uttered with great panache, shows the depth to which secularist reductionism can sink.

Lastly, our three-decade quest for Spirit-centered values and ethics has been leading us to four types of authors:

- 'researchers'
- 'scholars'
- 'thinkers'
- 'realizers'

Researchers were of little help. A rare scholar or two could emit some speck of light now and then. Many thinkers did transmit wide shafts of light. It is the realizers alone, however, who have provided us with *unshakeable, experientially as well as universally valid, Truths*. Therefore, although the second and third groups of writers have been referred to below, it is the fourth group which has been the steady anchor for this book.

Contrary to the presumptuous belief that the ancient mind was primitive and animistic, the ultimate, all-time Truths were all realized in the ancient *ashrams* and *tapovans*. The very conditions and environment the modern city-centric mind has been creating is making these saving Truths incomprehensible to itself. Moreover, the frenetically centrifugalized and incoherent modern temper is also incapable of realizing holistic Truths. In fact, it is distancing itself fast from them. From error to error is its privilege. But the irony is—the modern mind is too vain to admit its infirmity. Modernity is selling technical progress while buying existential poverty. This is the backdrop against which spirituality is explored in this book.

The Appendix below presents a complete picture of the content and pedagogy adopted by the authors while sharing sacred principles with management practitioners in business and other secular organizations. Management students have also been covered. This sequence and format have been crystallized after an initial trial-and-error of about five years in the early 1980's. The 3-Module pattern (3+2+2) of seven days shown below now stands on a fairly strong and proven experiential base. Spirituality, though not explicitly mentioned, no doubt remains the keynote in all the corporate Workshops and post-graduate courses.

APPENDIX
[Contents Outline of the Three Modules]

WORKSHOPS ON VALUES AND ETHICS FOR HOLISTIC EXCELLENCE

MODULE–1: **Foundation Module**

Day 1

Time	Topic	Faculty
9.15 a.m.–10.45 a.m.	Values, Skills and Ethics (Vignette: Cloak and Dagger)	SK Chakraborty SKC
10.45 a.m.–11.00 a.m.	*Silent Tea Break*	
11.00 a.m.–12.15 p.m.	Dynamics of Psychological Forces (Vignette: Dr. Anand Shukla)	D Chakraborty DC
12.15 p.m.–1.00 p.m.	Quality Mind Process (QMP)	SKC
1.00 p.m.–2.00 p.m.	*Silent Lunch Break*	
2.00 p.m.–3.30 p.m.	Case Studies (Individual Reading and Group Work) a) Smart Excellence b) Whither Systems?	
3.30 p.m.–3.45 p.m.	*Silent Tea Break*	
3.45 p.m.–5.15 p.m.	Presentation of the cases and discussions [Evening Readings and QMP Practice]	

Day 2

Time	Topic	Faculty
9.30 a.m.–11.00 a.m.	Art and Science of Work (Vignette: Rationalization)	DC
11.00 a.m.–11.15 a.m.	*Silent Tea Break*	
11.15 a.m.–12.30 p.m.	Giving Model of Inspiration (Vignette: But for a Cause)	SKC
12.30 p.m.–1.00 a.m.	QMP	DC
1.00 p.m.–2.00 p.m.	*Silent Lunch Break*	
2.15 p.m.–3.45 p.m.	Case Studies: a) A Promise to Honour b) The Mess	
3.45 p.m.–4.00 p.m.	*Silent Tea Break*	
4 p.m.–5.30 p.m.	Presentation and discussion of case studies [Evening Readings and QMP Practice]	

Day 3

8.30 a.m.–10.00 a.m.	Moral Law of Cause and Effect	
	(Vignette: Oblivion)	DC
10.00 a.m.–10.15 a.m.	*Silent Tea Break*	
10.15 a.m.–11.15 p.m.	Higher SELF and Lower SELF	
	(Vignette: Vijay and the Old Man)	SKC
11.15 a.m.–12.00 noon	Work and Its Secret	
	[Swami Vivekananda: Audio Cassette]	
12.00 noon–12.30 p.m.	QMP	
12.30 p.m.–1.15 p.m.	*Silent Lunch Break*	
1.15 p.m.–2.30 p.m.	Case Studies:	
	a) Fast or Slow?	
	b) National Electricals Limited	
2.30 p.m.–3.30 p.m.	Presentation and discussion of case studies	
3.30 p.m.–3.45 p.m.	Valedictory	

MODULE–2: Leadership and Followership

Day 1

9.15 a.m.–10.30 a.m.	Some Values Keynotes:	
	Wisdom Leadership	SKC
10.30 a.m.–11.45 a.m.	Quadrant I	
	(Impersonal Love)	DC
11.45 a.m.–12 noon	*Silent Tea Break*	
12 noon–1.15 p.m.	Quadrant II	
	(Leadership Discipline)	SKC
1.15 p.m.–2 p.m.	*Silent Lunch Break*	
2 p.m.–3.30 p.m.	Self-study and Group Work	
	a) ITC Explosion	
	b) JRD Dismissed	
3.30 p.m.–3.45 p.m.	*Silent Tea Break*	
3.45 p.m.–4.45 p.m.	Presentation and Plenary Discussions	
4.45 p.m.–5.30 p.m.	Quality Mind Process (QMP)	SKC
	[Evening Readings and QMP Practice]	

Day 2

9.15 a.m.–10.30 a.m.	Power and Ego in Leadership Roles	SKC
10.30 a.m.–11.45 a.m.	Quadrant III	
	(Excellence in Teamwork)	DC
11.45 a.m.–12 noon	*Silent Tea Break*	

12 noon–1.00 p.m.	Quadrant IV	
	(Excellence in Followership)	SKC
1.00 p.m.–1.30 p.m.	QMP	DC
1.30 p.m.–2.15 p.m.	*Silent Lunch Break*	
2.15 p.m.–3.45 p.m.	Self-study and Group Work:	
	a) Followers and Leaders	
	b) I Am The Mother's Appointee	
3.45 p.m.–4 p.m.	*Silent Tea Break*	
4 p.m.–5.30 p.m.	Presentation and Plenary Discussions	

MODULE–3: Stress Management and Integrated Personality
Day 1

9.30 a.m.–11.00 a.m.	Controllable and Non-Controllable Stress	DC
11.00 a.m.–11.15 a.m.	Silent Tea Break	
11.15 a.m.–12.30 p.m.	*Dwandwa, Nirdwandwa, Samatwa*	
	and *Pancha Kosha* in relation to stress	SKC
12.30 p.m.–1.00 p.m.	QMP	SKC
1.00 p.m.–1.45 p.m.	*Silent Lunch Break*	
1.45 p.m.–3.15 p.m.	Individual Study and Group Discussion	
	a) White Powder, Red Colour	
	b) The CEO of a Private Sector Company	
3.15 p.m.–3.30 p.m.	*Silent Tea Break*	
3.30 p.m.–5.00 p.m.	Plenary Session	
	[Evening Readings and QMP Practice]	

Day 2

9.30 a.m.–11.00 a.m.	Manifestation of Stress and its Remedies	DC
11.00 a.m.–11.15 a.m.	*Silent Tea Break*	
11.15 a.m.–12.30 p.m.	5 Pillars of Module 1 and Integrated Personality	SKC
12.30 p.m.–1.00 p.m.	QMP	DC
1.00 p.m.–1.45 p.m.	*Silent Lunch Break*	
1.45 p.m.–3.15 p.m.	Individual Study and Group Discussion	
	a) The Ganga	
	b) Readings from Swami Akhilananda	
3.15 p.m.–3.30 p.m.	*Silent Tea Break*	
3.30 p.m.–5.00 p.m.	Plenary Session	

[All the concept sessions, case studies and vignettes mentioned above are drawn from *Culture Society and Leadership: Spiritual Perspectives* and *Human Values and Ethics: Achieving Holistic Excellence* by the above authors. Both have been published by the ICFAI University Press, 2006.]

Values for Spirituality in Organizations
Some Common Doubts and Problems

THE PRELUDE

In 2001, there was much talk about 'secular spirituality' at an ethics conference in Budapest. Unethicality was sweeping across secular endeavours as never before—this the organizers accepted. Hence it was strange to hear that the ultimate remedy, spirituality, too might be diluted and deformed to suit secular objectives. Since the secular world-view does not admit of anything higher than the material and sensual immediate (see chapter 1 for the dictionary meanings of 'secular'), it has the inherent tendency to violate *dharma* or ethics. Spirituality is concerned, on the other hand, with the quest of the supra-material, supra-sensual pure essence of one's being, nay, of the One such essence of all creation. Since, ethico-moral or human values are an essential pre-requisite for this discovery and contact, spiritual ambition, in principle, prevents or reduces the downward pull of the secular. Therefore, it would be correct to speak of: *spiritualized secularity*. It is a truth of Bharatvarsha's (i.e. India's) perennial tradition that truly there is nothing secular, everything is spiritual. For example, eating food is not just about calories, proteins, fats, carbohydrates, etc., but really an offering of love and gratitude to the Divine or Supreme within one's body-temple. Snow-clad mountain peaks, silent caves, deep forests etc. are treasured for spiritual fulfilment, not for secular adventures like skiing or trekking or camping.

We believe that the flowering of *human values* in a person is the starting point for his/her Spiritual unfoldment. And only such unfolding persons can make for a spiritualized organization i.e., a courageous organization where spirituality is the end, not a means. Let us, therefore, reproduce below some typical questions raised by five groups of senior managers during a week-long Workshop on 'Values-System and Organizational Effectiveness' conducted by us in early 1993—

- In today's world of interdependence and networking, is it practicable not to compromise one's values in day-to-day decision making?
- When society at large operates in ways that are contrary to one's values, can values-transformation be a matter only of the individual?
- Is it possible that one's pursuit of higher values may result in a high degree of individualism whereby organizational performance is jeopardized?
- In a competitive scenario, when competitors adopt unfair means, one player maintaining high values makes it very difficult for it to stay in the market and survive. In this situation what should or ought to be the course of action in the terms of values?
- Values are threatened due to degradation in the social system. What is the remedy available at the moment?
- Is there any dichotomy between the development of science/technology and the cultivation of values?
- Standard of living, consumerism, employment and economic growth are interconnected. How do we establish a balanced relationship among the four through an acceptable values-system?
- How should we go about identifying and evaluating the core values, and what are the different sources from where we may draw upon them?

The above typical set of concerns remains valid to this day, thirteen years later. In an informal discussion on values with a recently-retired Chairman of one of the best-known multinational companies of India, the question posed to the author was: 'Do you mean by ethics in business: matters like giving and taking of bribes, and other forms of corruption? If so, then there will be little interest amongst managers about the subject. Values must contribute to business success, only then they will be willing to listen. These values must reflect the norms that rule a changing society'. Passionately he added: 'Who is to decide what are the right values? They are all relative.'

These are all forceful, hard-headed questions from practical people. Simple, straight answers to them are not easy to offer. But we may attempt to explore each more deeply for the several unstated issues imbedded in them. The long-term principles involved need first to be isolated from the enveloping clouds of the immediate. Equipped with a clearer perception of the principles, one may then return to the sphere of the practical. Each actor is then free to choose the course of action his or her conscience deems to be the best, assuming that he/she understands that Spirituality is his/her basic and inalienable *human* right.

COMING TO GRIPS

It is being recognized today, at the highest level of thinking, that the strategy for managing the earth-system as a whole, with sole concentration on the measurable and the quantifiable over the last three or four centuries, has led to an endless series of fragmented decisions which are now culminating in the real prospect of global breakdown. Man's assumed birthright to exploit Nature for material gain has been the dominant value underlying this process. And industrial enterprises, feeding on technological innovation, have served as the primary instruments for unfolding this overarching value. Over the next one hundred years, not just the next corporate-plan horizon, this aberration should therefore become an issue of principle for business enterprises. At bottom it is an ethical question in the realm of man-Nature relationships. If exploitation of one individual by another be treated as unethical, why not exploitation of Nature by man (especially when it is spurred by greed, not need) be regarded likewise?

The other principle of capital importance centres around the issue: is the *human being for industry-technology*, or is industry-technology for the human being? The mainstream bestsellers in management literature seem to subscribe to the first version—almost like letting the tail wag the dog. Yet, a little reflection will suggest the second version to be correct in principle.

But this correct version of man-technology relationship leads us to an even more profound question of principle: what is the model or vision that will allow the human being to be the *master*, not servant, of industry-technology? Here again the correct, though not popular, answer is: the Spiritual, the Pure Consciousness, the Divine model of man. This model/vision is as intrinsic and inalienable from the employee in industry as it is from the citizen in society Though not yet realized as such, its misconceived exclusion from serious consideration constitutes a denial of the very core of humanness, as distinct from other living species. India's poet-sage Rabindranath Tagore (1861–1941) and mystic-philosopher Sri Aurobindo (1873–1950) have both educated us, from the highest reaches of world-affirming cosmic perception, that the secret intent of Nature is to press forward, through the human form, to her sublimest, unalloyed Divine manifestation.

As a corollary to the above, one more relatively down-to-earth principle emerges: the imperative for each one of us is to reconcile, to narrow the divergence between 'doing' and 'becoming'. The domain of *doing* is ruled by division, separateness, fragmentation. The governing law of *becoming* is union, relatedness, and holism. *Doing* is gross, *becoming* is subtle. To 'do' we need *skills*, to 'become' we need *values*. Skills are *external*, values are *internal*. Skills are necessarily applied through the medium of values, If values are out of joint, skills get used for manipulative, destructive purposes—be they skills of communication or of portfolio management, of capital budgeting or of performance appraisal. And finally, as values become out of joint, times also turn out of joint (á lá Shakespeare).

For the present, the last principle we may highlight is that of the distinction between 'desired values-as-ends' and 'desirable values-as-means'. Once more it appears that the bulk of sociological work deals with values as desired end-states only. They may range from a new TV or a new car every three years to a paid family holiday each year, from freedom of decision-making from day one to fancy designations, and so on. Since the *normative* outlook is absent, all such desired end-state values, which seem to be showing galloping proliferation, are commonly accepted without batting an eyelid—all in the name of motivation, attraction, retention and the like. Similarly, market-share growth or innovative products, high price earnings ratio or corporate image are popular end-state values for industrial enterprises. 'Anything that works' seems to be the gospel here. Yet, for both sets of such values, the actual process of accomplishing or achieving them is continuously imbedded in a network of 'desirable values-as-means'. 'How I achieve or obtain what I want to' has to be the keynote of values-driven management. If the 'what' needs modification or even abandonment for upholding the generic, high-quality values-as-means, in a spiritual frame of reference, then the courage to do so should be consciously cultivated. Of course, mere mechanical rulebooks, or codes of conduct, or intellectual exercises are unlikely to suffice for this objective.

A few years ago, in course of conversation with the abbott of a monastery in Western India, former President Abdul Kalam had expressed his deep yearning for the revival of his country's great destiny by pointing out three specific imperatives:

- *punya neta*
- *punya atma*
- *punya adhikari*

How could these triple conditions be met?—he asked the abbott. Now, *punya* means holy, and is cognate with the spiritual, not the secular. And *neta*, *atma*, and *adhikari* mean leaders, citizens and managers/teachers/

administrators respectively. (*Kalam*, 2004). Here we have a panoramic canvas which puts individual career or corporate ranking into its humble, little corner.

RESPONDING TO THE ISSUES RAISED
PRESSURES TO COMPROMISE

It is a cruel irony of social existence that networks of vice seem to form and thrive more readily than those of virtue. And the more society moves in the direction of materialism, the more this syndrome appears to flourish. Besides, the characteristic of group solidarity amongst virtuous people usually seems to be much weaker than amongst the vicious ones. Therefore the response to this challenge should be in terms of methods which would make it possible to increase the number, membership and strength of 'virtuous' groups.

The most important determinant of the countervailing power of virtuous groups would be the unflinching sincerity of their members. If hypocrisy afflicts such groups also, then there is not much hope even in this direction. Just as much as self-interest binds together vicious networks, so should higher social and spiritual interest bind the virtuous networks Virtuous networks will need nurturing by self-controlled people who believe in a higher cause, and not by opportunists aiming at their own fame and power.

All this will not obviously eliminate compromises overnight. Yet no better approach, in principle, seems to be available.

INDIVIDUAL VS. SOCIETY

Much of management writing having been nourished by sociology, social psychology, social anthropology and the like, its readers seem to have become conditioned to treat society as an entity distinct from individuals. So we talk and write freely about changing or improving society first, hoping that better individuals will then be its offsprings. But this is a wrong perception, a false hope. Society is the sum of individuals—always.

Societies are transformed by individuals changing themselves first. Transformation agents cannot wait for society or organizations to change. Remember our Buddhas and Christs, Mahaviras and Lao Tses. Such personalities do not mirror or project the current values or norms of society. Rather, they reassess them, and then go on to develop a new or revised framework which *reiterates* the same perennial and wholesome human values. This has been true all the time. As the Sanskrit aphorism goes: *ekam sat, vipra bahudha vadanti.* That is, Truth is always the same and one, sages only speak of it variously.

Thus, values-transformation has always been triggered at the individual level—however small or limited its scope, initially. In other words, self-inspired courage and fortitude are required in the pilgrimage of values—both as end-states and as means. Profound, subjective, personal impulses are required. And they will be unselfish, e.g., Buddha or Vivekananda. Too much expectancy about supportive cues from the social environment will tend to postpone, time and again, the hour of take-off. Reciprocity from others cannot be guaranteed. So, to specify this as a precondition would lead to a guessing game where none risks the first move.

INDIVIDUAL VS. ORGANIZATION

Viewed broadly, if the cultivation of higher values strengthens human virtues like gratitude, caring, work-ethic, honesty, forgiveness, helpfulness, humility and so on, we see no reason why they should not improve organizational effectiveness. For, usually colossal energy leakage occurs in organizations due to the low level or even lack of such healthy human values. Team-work, coordination and communication become the major casualties. Therefore, efforts spent on keeping alive and strengthening these noble sentiments in human networks will produce individuals who shall not be narrowly individualistic. Egotistic individualism is a major scourge in most organizations. It is this disease which concerted programmes on human values have to combat.

Yes, there can be a rare case where an individual is so stubborn, for example, in respect of honesty, that he refuses to bribe a high-level person for securing a license or something else even for his organization. If the organization too insists on getting its desired value-as-end, it may then shift this individual out and put a more pliable one in his place. But if the individual himself has reached a high level of spiritual commitment, and the organization too is unrelenting, he may call quits. The more frequently this kind of 'individualism' surfaces, and the society is kept informed about it, the better should be the prospect of human values returning into management. This, in turn, should pave the way for spiritually-oriented organizations with healthy bottom-lines—in the long run surely.

SURVIVAL AT STAKE

The crux of the issue here lies in the singular focus on quantitative end-results as measures of performance and success. The entire economic super-structure is anchored solely in the ground of physically or monetarily measurable goals. The qualitative aspects continue to slip through the fingers like water. Economic plans, enterprise plans, stock exchanges, and even learning systems are increasingly getting trapped in more sophisticated measurement schemes. Business journals publish annual reviews of corporate performance by ranking companies in terms of sales value, asset figures and so on. Executive compensation is often linked with market-share achievement or higher price-earnings ratio or something similar. Thus, the whole system conspires to inflict a blindness which sets aside everything but short-term measurable results. Long-term chivalry and honour die at the altar of short-term gladiatorism and predatoriness. The contemporary rhetoric of development and globalization is doing nothing to get to the heart of this grave problem.

The real solution in this critical sphere consists in launching a vigorous movement for mandating the explicit criterion of an ongoing cross-checking between desired end-state-values and desirable values-as-means. All corporate ranking and other similar systems should develop parallel parameters for values-as-means. Considerable creative caution will be needed in this endeavour. We have to avoid indulging again in an over-enthusiastic quantification spree within a territory which is intrinsically qualitative, normative, e.g., in what seems to be now going on, in the name of scientific research, with respect to 'transcendental meditation' and TM Sidhi programmes. Similarly, the growing fancy for 'spiritual quotient' is an imposition of so-called objective investigation on a field beyond its means and scope.

Whatever help the world's religous or spiritual, sacred or philosophical literature can offer in reviving this lost consciousness of cherishing and taking pride in the quality of means, must be sought openly and freely. Secular organizations cannot afford any more to live in arrogant isolation. True, this is a long-term task. But the labours for this re-education must begin now. It will be an act of faith by the present epoch, for which the future generations will be grateful to it.

But until the time such renewal of *spiritually acceptable means-oriented consciousness* becomes widespread, what can a victim dc in the face of unfair means used by others? Whether one can readily see or accept it or not, the true response lies in developing a sound philosophical perception of life and existence. This effort is worthwhile in its own right. For, as such a perception matures into deep feeling, one begins to treat higher values as their own justification, not as tools for something else. Again, awareness about the inevitability of the ethico-moral cause and effect chain also grows. This is often spoken of as 'poetic justice', or 'the day of reckoning', or the 'law of karma'. With the strengthening of this conviction, the victim who practises fair means gains more power and patience to sustain his own convictions about *desirable values-as-means*, while being sure that the predator's deviousness will not pay in the long run.

Finally, we receive the repeated assurance from those who have moulded their own lives on such values that, if one's motives are really pure and intentions absolutely sincere, the unseen but real and helpful Supra-human powers ensure that one is not let down. There are however no instant, objective proofs of these experiential realities. One should experiment with them for oneself and experience their truth from within.

This is what T.S. Eliot (1886–1965) had to say on the 'theory of Karma'—

'For every ill deed in the past we suffer the consequences; For sloth, for avarice, gluttony, neglect of the Word of God, for pride, for lechery, treachery, for every act of Sin.

And all that was good you must fight to keep with hearts, as devoted as those of your fathers who fought to gain it.'

Social Degradation

This issue has been responded to above in point (2). The essential remedy is to develop the habit and the insight to grasp that the individual is the *cause*, society the *effect*. Each person has one's own zone of discretion (ZOD) —however small it might be. Yet, honest introspection into one's own ZOD is often a neglected or an ill-developed capacity in the majority of us. Each one is clever at detecting violation of values by others, not knowing that this often could be a projection of one's own distortions. Humility regarding one's self-image, which can stimulate introspection, needs to be practised systematically. Religious and spiritual literature can be of great help to the earnest soul. Perhaps too much surficial arrogance now rules our intellectualized, skills-dominated mentality. Let us be sensitive to this phenomenon,

The other point to note for the conscientious person is that, while with determination there is hope and probability for the individual to reconstruct his/her own values, this is not so for the whole society. Shall he/she, therefore, wait for the day when society attains a higher level of desirable values? How has society got degraded in the first place? So, how will society itself be so uplifted? By what magic, what formula? Hence, however helpless each one of us may feel, there is no remedy for this dilemma except each one commencing his/her own lonely journey. *Ekla chalo re*—as Rabindranath Tagore had sung. (Oh man! you've got to march alone).

Others will join in, sooner or later. It is a little wave which swells into a breaker. But that cannot be a pre-condition.

IMPACT OF SCIENCE AND TECHNOLOGY
'Sci' is the root word for science. It means splitting, breaking up, segmenting. When this proclivity, underlying the scientific temper is extended by technology into the domain of our material existence, human mentality begins to suffer from increasing fragmentism. This phenomenon turns out really to be more lethal than it outwardly seems because it parades on the stage of society in the tantalizing garb of progress, higher standard of living, and the like.

We have to realize that *fragmentation of human consciousness*, accelerated by sci-tech, is a prime cause for widespread fall in the level of human values in our lives. For, clearly, while it may have raised agricultural productivity or increased human longevity, in a more vital sense it has destroyed the golden maxim for higher values: 'simple living, high thinking'. The opposite has been taking place, lately at a furious pace: 'complex living, low thinking'. A non-stop exteriorized life-style, 'with no time to stand and stare', offers no scope for welding together our splintered consciousness into its original state of wholeness.

While sci-tech is accelerating splits within man, and between man and man, it has also been grievously aggravating the man-Nature split. This three-fold assault on wholeness has been going on for the last three centuries, and cumulative evidence suggests that the centralized industrial sectors are more prone to erosion in the standard of practised human values than the decentralized agrarian sectors. For, like the unseen, dark side of the moon, the dangerous side of technological innovation is the scope it offers to the unbridled indulgence of greed and passion in endless ways It is very easy to titillate the lower human instincts for commercial success, but much more difficult to cultivate or restore noble emotions.

There is perhaps too much of bragging about the help science is supposed to have rendered to mankind in getting rid of alleged irrational superstitions. It was a safer, sacred world when the elements of Nature like the sun, water, wind, sea and river were worshipped as gods or goddesses or supra-human forces presiding over human existence, It was a holistic, systemic consciousness—though not formulated intellectually or mathematically, yet felt in the heart with emotions. If Nature was 'used', it was only for 'need', not 'greed'. For instance, in India, for millennia, the river Ganga has been adored as 'Mother Ganga'. In this emotionally powerful personification lies the true secret of ecological preservation and sanctity. Even today, before bathing in this river, or while crossing over it on a bridge, people join their palms on the forehead as a mark of adoration, gratitude and affection for 'her' bounties This is superior sacred rationality, compared to the scientific secular rationality which treats the river as a 'water resource'. Conservation of the Ganga can be better achieved by the revival and spread of this sacred attitude.

CONSUMING VS. LIVING

We have been highlighting the negative consequences of the standard of living, consumerism and economic growth gospels of our times. But such dangers go by default in our thoughts concentrated upon the 'brave, new, twenty-first century world'.'

A clinching argument often made for these gospels, especially in a country like India is that, without a systematic pursuit of them there 'is little hope for the swelling ranks of our poor and unemployed. A hard look at this argument, however, may prompt its demolition.

Automated, capital-intensive, heavy as well as consumer goods industries have, over the decades, been reducing the rate of growth of new employment while the employable population has been increasing at a high rate. Even a cursory glance at the metropolitan cities of India will demonstrate this— streets and pavements all swarming with humans in endless streams. Add to this the package of new-model economic growth—consumer durables for high life-style, breweries, airlines, 5-star hotels, holiday resorts in pilgrim spots, discotheques, fast-food chains, video parlours, etc—they are the most prominent symbols of a modernized society.

We feel that this model of economic growth, with its two wings of voracious consumerism and strident life-style, is not only not generating much-needed incremental employment, but also causing an erosion of both desirable values-as-ends and values-as-means. In the loud din and intricate web of economic planning and technological upgradation, the true model of man has been completely lost sight of. *The Spiritual/Divine model of man being the only valid vision, localised, decentralized, need-oriented (not greed-motivated) strategies for socio-economic development have a better chance to provide the true answer to mounting unemployment.* Of course, the whole world has to learn to think this way. Call centres and IT can do little.

A country like India, caught in the whirl of globalization, the way it is presently conceived and executed, cannot do much in isolation. But this does not mean that she should not be constantly warning the globalizers that ultimately human values must rest in *sensible localization* and not *senseless globalization*. We should remember that dinosaurs have not survived. As the world-system is driving itself towards a man-made dinosaur-like entity, through technology-led 'gobblization', it is likely to become a piece of unsustainably complex, life-sapping mechanism . The question of where we should draw the line between *global consciousness* and *local convictions* needs all the concentrated energies of pure, intuitive minds—not just the powers of calculative, rational minds. The latter are usually as superstitious as tribal minds. Industrialized tribalism is scarcely any better than forest tribalism. In fact, it is Bharat's forest-dwelling *rishi* who had given the call, '*shrinvantu vishwe amritasya putrah*'. This is global consciousness at its highest – calling the whole of humanity as children of Immortality.

WHERE TO DIG FOR VALUES?
This task is rather easy, provided we do not suffer from the hubris that all wisdom belongs to our times, and the bygone days were all saddled with superstition. The Sermon on the Mount, the *vinaya* and the *sheela* of Buddhism, the *daivi sampat* of the *Gita*, the *shreya* of the Upanishad, the *shabad* of the Sikhs, the *adab* of the Sufis and many more—all cover a common ground of human values with clear spiritual moorings. Their perennial relevance stems precisely from the fact that they originated in states of spiritual intuition or vision, not from mere intellectual speculation. No matter what we conventionally may think in our temporary spells of disillusionment, spiritual religion will remain the final resort for true human values

But we feel this is not the main task. The crucial responsibility is that of living our lives on the basis of these core values And each generation as a whole has to practise them anew and afresh for itself And this is where, much as we may frown upon them, rites and rituals, myths and ceremonies have their functional role. Unlike science and technology, as Arnold Toynbee had once observed (Toynbee, 1987). there is nothing cumulative and linear in the values dimension of human existence. But modem mis-education has made us blind to this supreme fact. All of it is brain-culture now, no heart–culture. The culture of emotions is a distinct process, and is as serious and arduous as that of the intellect. Yet we have no place for it in the present scheme of human development.

ISSUES OF CHARACTER
The casual dismissal of bribery and corruption as practically a non-issue in the realm of values for organizations is disturbing. This is a symptom of insensitivity and glibness in the managerial mind about issues of character and conviction.

If bribery, by practice, has to-day become the society's norm then, as the Chairman seems to have suggested above, the corpus of values should incorporate and legitimize it. If value-as-means question those business practices which can lead to accelerated profits or market shares, such concerns are then merely of academic interest. If by crooked means the owners can turn a manufacturing plant into a sick unit, and compel the employees to quit, leaving them high and dry after years of service, and then use the property for real estate business that fetches much higher returns, values-as-means should be kept at bay. Integrity of purpose is conceded, without realizing that minus integrity of character, the purpose itself often becomes questionable—even though there is strong commitment to it.

Integrity of purpose is not sufficient. *The purpose itself must possess integrity,* Honesty of purpose is one thing, *honest purpose* another. While sharp and clear dividing lines may not exist about this matter in every case, yet to use exceptions to claim that values are all relative is clever sophistry, an open invitation to chaos in human society. Clearly, the bulk of transgressions in the sphere of values are understood as such by the players. Yet they are repeated like fouls in a football match to score a goal, hoping that the referee's whistle shall not blow.

Greed, impatience, temptation, competition, one-up-manship—all of them trigger such moves. (For good measure, our one-hour conversation was liberally interrupted with the Chairman's words, in response to telephone calls, on bridge and beer, cocktail and golf and dinner—and the spending of a huge sum of money for his trip to Delhi by a company of which he seemed to be the non-executive Chairman). To the question 'who is to decide which values are right?' we must reply: 'Buddhas and Christs, Tolstoys and Einsteins, Tagores and Gandhis'. All of them had accepted and declared the indispensability of spiritual consciousness in humans.

CONCLUSION
Swami Vivekananda (1863–1902), often remembered as the 'patriot-saint of India', had once intuited this metaphor: 'the world is a moral gymnasium' (Vivekananda, 1969). Of course administration in government, research in universities, management in business are all venues in this vast gymnasium where the imperative for everyone is to build and strengthen one's 'moral muscles'. For, this is a *pre-condition* for the sprouting of one's spiritual core. Only by directing ourselves towards this superordinate goal can we salvage our self-destructive modern society. By this we can also leave behind for posterity an earth-system to be proud of—for its emotional purity and sacred

richness. Like in learning to swim or to ride a bike, the plunge has to be taken with faith and courage. Too much intellectual quibbling or quantitative pre-conditions can explode the whole process even before take-off.

Sri Aurobindo (1872–1950), however, surpasses Swami Vivekananda, by furnishing a still more rigorous and ultimate view of Spirituality. For Aurobindo 'high intellectuality', or 'lofty idealism', or ethicality-morality', or 'religiosity'—alone or in combination—do not, by themselves constitute Spirituality. They may often, however, be its concomitants, valuable adjuncts. Spirituality then, according to him, is an awakening and aspiration to know, feel and contact a greater Reality beyond body-life-mind—a Being (or Soul or Spirit or Self) that permanently inhabits our own being and the Universe (Aurobindo, 1973). This is a tall order for those who are talking to lightly about Spirituality. Still, it should be sobering to be informed about the unvarnished truth. More about all this in Chapter 3.

Spiritual Psychology for Leaders

L eadership is a 'soft' field. It turns even more so when it begins to be looked at from the 'Spiritual' perspective. So, every idea or view presented below is not expected to be acceptable to all readers. A little taste for spirituality might however help.

The 'transformational' angle to the leadership process has been with us for nearly thirty years. James Burns had propposed this viewpoint in a well-known study on leadership (Burns 1978, pp. 19–20, 427). He has argued that 'transactional' leadership is characterized by a 'swapping', or a 'trading', or a 'bargaining' motive in an exchange process between a leader and the led. It lacks durable engagement between the two sides. They 'use' one another mutually—so to say. Transformational leadership, on the other hand, involves the mutual 'raising' of both sides to higher levels of motivation and morality. Mahatma Gandhi has been cited. Mention also occurs about 'transcending' leadership, but it is not explained, nor does the index include it. Similarly, 'spirituality' also does not figure in the index (ibid., p. 5).

Burns, a political scientist, has elaborately formulated his ideas against the canvas of managing nations and peoples, not business. Therefore, he proceeds to 'fashion a general theory of political leadership'. He does speak of 'mutual stimulation and elevation' among leaders and followers. But his 'transformational' leader is assigned the role of 'recognizing and exploiting' the wants, ungratified needs, demands, crushed expectations, etc. of followers or potential followers. Then he is supposed to go beyond all this and engage the whole person in a moral process (ibid., p. 4). Consciousness arousal has also been interpreted in terms of the ability to 'discern signs of dissatisfaction', grounded in the 'seedbed of conflict'. At the same time, there is a mention about followers' 'true' needs. But all such expressions do not match with notions like 'higher purpose', 'true needs', etc. No indication is available about the character of such 'true' needs. It is pertinent here to refer, for example, to Aldous Huxley for a statement about the 'true need' or 'end value' for a human being. 'The last end of man, the ultimate reason for human existence, is unitive knowledge of the divine Ground' (Huxley 1985, pp. 36–7). Burns' choice of the political backdrop has precluded such real, spiritual transformational ideas. But if it is sought to include spirituality as an element in the holistic treatment of transformational leadership, then formulations like those of Huxley cannot be left out. Such articulations are materially different from the end-values mentioned by Burns himself, for example, liberty, justice, and equality (Burns, op. cit., pp. 36–7).

Bernard Bass and his associates appear to have linked Burns' political theory to the sphere of managing business. A noticeable difference in their approach from that of Burns is the use of some tools and methods of empirical research. Burns' work is qualitative and conceptual, whereas that of Bass and others tends towards quantification (Bass 1985, p. 123).

But even the index of the later Bass-Avolio book does not show any entries for spirituality or transcendence or consciousness. Only one entry appears for 'ethical standards', and the text does not elaborate it (Bass and Avolio 1994, p. 64). Four years later, however, we see that, terms like 'ethics', 'character', 'transcendence' etc. have been incorporated in the exposition of transformational leadership (Bass 1998, p. 175). This later effort has sought a more deep-structure basis for transformational theory in the classical Socratic and Confucian traditions. One can read into such efforts the continuing trend towards greater 'softness' or 'subjectivism' in the development of leadership theory. This chapter attempts to extend this engagement to its Spiritual potential.

SPIRITUALITY-BASED ASSUMPTIONS AND DEFINITIONS

This extension towards the *deep-structure subjective*, as against the superficial objective, for leadership needs support and direction from the corpus of classical spiritual psycho-philosophy of India. There are at least three main reasons to glean some major insights from this literature. Its chief characteristics are as follows—

(1) They have formed the bedrock of a highly durable and sustainable civilization, one which has been non-aggressive and non-acquisitive in its relationships with Nature and other cultures.
(2) They constitute a living tradition to this day, as exemplified by the leadership of Swami Vivekananda, Mahatma Gandhi, Vinoba Bhave (and many others like them of whom the world may not be aware).

(3) This tradition has been built on the parallel and complementary development of both 'philosophical aims' and 'psychological methods' to fulfill them. Hence the compound phrase 'psycho-philosophical' is used above. The most profound of such psycho-philosophical pairs is that of *Yoga-Vedanta* (Y-V).

Vedanta is the philosophical base of Oneness (*Advaita*). *Yoga* is the psychological process which accelerates and stabilizes the experience of this Oneness, this union. It may be marked that the Y-V framework is not affiliated to any individual name. This insures against the dangers of diabolical charisma or institutional dogma. For the same reason, it gets closer to transcendence than other viewpoints. There are of course several other spiritual approaches within the *sanatan* Indian tradition itself (e.g. *Kundalini Yoga* in *Tantra*, *Vipassna* in Buddhism, *Preksha Dhyana* in Jainism). Other world cultures must also be having their own disciplines.

Very briefly, Y-V *ontology* posits the following—

- The Infinite, the Eternal, is the foundation of the finite, the changing.
- The 'whole' comprises both the infinite and finites.
- The individual's manifest empirical 'self' is an outer instrument of action, disconnected from the transcendent 'Self' within. So, the typical human person is not experientially holistic, though essentially he/she is.

Complementing the ontological position, Y-V *epistemology* holds the following—

- The faculty of mental reasoning, though higher than vital instinct, is insufficient for knowing the 'whole'.
- Reason and intellect proceed by dividing and fragmenting; therefore receptive mental silence, with an aspiration for directly perceiving the whole, the Self within, is indispensable.

The above blend of *ontology-epistemology* has always been amenable to systematic self-discipline, followed by experiential realization. A few examples of contemporary leaders cast in this mould will be given below. Long before the Christian era, in emperor Asoka (BC 304–232), the world had witnessed the example of a leader who had metamorphosed himself from Asoka-the-fierce (*Chandasoka*) to Asoka-the-benign (*Dharmasoka*). Vincent Smith has observed about him: 'he managed to reconcile the apparently inconsistent positions of monk and monarch', and that' … he was wonderfully successful in holding together for forty years an empire rarely exceeded in magnitude' (Smith 1988, pp. 24, 97). Asoka's grandfather, Chandragupta Maurya, too, symbolized the monk-monarch symbiosis, typical of Bharat's tradition. Asoka had built upon the foundations laid by Chandragupta. The latter's mentor was Chanakya, the former's Upagupta—both renunciant yogis. Such leaders in Indian history have been called *rajarshis* (i.e. royal sages or monk emperors). Plato's philosopher-king has some apparent similarity with them— only in theory, but hardly ever practised (Chakraborty, D., and Chakraborty, S.K. 2004, p. 94).

The following more or less descriptive definitions, embedded in the metaphysical framework just mentioned, should now be helpful—

Transcendence. Nature has already evolved by transcending to life above matter, to mind/reason above life. The next leap of transcendence implicit in the above evolutionary journey is towards Spirit above mind-reason.

The practical import of the transcendence principle in the social setting is its power to yield a more far-sighted (*door-drishti*), holistic view (*antar-drishti*) of complex ground-level happenings. It fosters an integral, long-term perspective which cannot be gained through seeing-by-succession on the ground only.

Consciousness. Consciousness is independent of the reactions of personality to the forces of environment. Consciousness is the *inherent reality*, the *fundamental essence* common to existence. When it is self-impelled to evolve slowly out of matter, it emerges as life, as animal, and as man. In man, it can transform beyond mind to Spirit. Evolution in form itself ceases (Aurobindo Sri 1999, pp. 5–15).

Spirituality. Spirituality means beginning to become aware of a Consciousness higher than that of the body-mind centered ego, and the ability to live more and more in it or under its guidance. It is this Consciousness—non-contingent, self-existent, pure of ego—which is Spirit or Self (Aurobindo Sri 1999, pp. 5–15). Uplifting leaders of humanity have always possessed this subjective power of cent per cent purity.

Transformation. Transformation, in the spiritual sense of Y-V psycho-philosophy, is the gradual progress to that state of Consciousness which is holistic, non-egoistic and hence flawless.

Ethics. It may be defined negatively. It is unethical when an entity, individual or collective, *intentionally* uses its power or authority to gain some advantage at the expense of another entity, of which the latter is unaware or defenceless (Chakraborty, S.K. and Chakraborty, D. 2006, p. 6). Minimizing the incidence of such unethicality should promote wide revival of ethicality. Transcendence of the empirical lower self, tied to the separative ego consciousness, could transform the perpetrating entity towards inviting/ awakening the awareness of the Self.

THE *RAJARSHI* LEADER—A CORPORATE EXAMPLE

The transforming leadership process is usually understood as flowing towards the followers. This naturally presupposes that it is the leader who originates and sustains such a transforming or metamorphosing flow. It is also implicit that transformation here is a positive notion—constructive, wholesome, elevating. The spirituality perspective necessarily embraces such elements. The source of the transforming influence, *the leader, therefore needs to 'transform' him/herself in the first place. Only a transformed leader can transmit transforming influence.* History bears ample testimony to this fact. Therefore, we concentrate on the transformation of the leader as a prior step. The examples given below will illustrate this principle.

There is a significant Indian proverb (from Kautilya—see chapter 10 for details) relevant to this issue: *yatha raja, tatha praja* (like leader, like followers). Although, there may be exceptions where the reverse (like followers, like leader) could be true, the more widespread, natural cause-and-effect relationship is understood in terms of leader-to-follower. This is as it should be. Although the keynote of reciprocal relationship has been continuously emphasized by Burns, yet he too mentions about the leader taking 'the major part', about the 'leader's main strength being the ability to operate close enough to the followers to draw them up to the leader's level of moral development' (Burns, op. cit., p. 426).

We may now offer some flavour of such a transformed leader by reproducing small portions from a published interview with R. K. Talwar. He was the most respected Chairman—Chief Executive successively of the State Bank of India (the country's largest and best commercial bank) and the Industrial Development Bank of India (the country's largest development banking institution) (Chakraborty, S.K. and Chakraborty, D. 2006, p. 243). Talwar's philosophy of work-life was based on the *Gita*. He had secret access to it from his mother when he was only thirteen. Ever since he had stayed with it, and it 'grew into him'. As an adult he had become a follower—

devotee of Sri Aurobindo and the Mother (Sri Aurobindo's spiritual protégé and partner).

'*Question.* How did the thoughts of Sri Aurobindo and the Mother influence your approach to work?

Answer. Let me narrate to you one incident…One day the president of the local Board of SBI came late for a meeting. Then for some unknown reason he began to talk ill of Sri Aurobindo and the Mother. That hurt me much. So I asked him, 'You are a big businessman. Why are you working so hard for your business?' He replied, 'So that my children will be happy'. My response was, 'Your aim is very low…My aim is: I am the Mother's appointee, let the Divine work through me'.

Question. When faced with problems which seem to baffle your reason or experience, what do you do?

Answer. 'The Mother … has explained the process by which one could receive Divine guidance in crisis situations. Her formula is:

Sincerity + Silence + No Preference = Divine Voice

Question. Any comment on the phenomenon called 'organizational politics'?

Answer. I am not a political animal … I am Mother's worker, it is her Bank. It is fortunate that the Mother runs this Bank. If there are claps or praise at any time, I close my eyes and remember the Mother'.'

The same book informs that three more CEOs, who were former juniors of Talwar and later headed other large banks/institutions, had also been interviewed. They all corroborated how Talwar had created a small enclosure in his office with a folding partition in one corner. Whenever he felt that a problem or a dilemma was proving to be beyond his experience, reason or logic, he would take a break and sit within that enclosure. All communication would cease for sometime. In that quiet space and time, Talwar would practise the formula mentioned above. Original clues, creative solutions and renewed convictions regarding nagging dilemmas or risky choices emerged, either during that very process of silent opening up to the higher and the whole, or within a few days thereafter.*

---

* Talwar's practice may also be viewed as one which tapped the dormant, 'right brain' by stilling the hectic 'left brain.'

Long after his departure from the scene he still continues to be an inspiring role model, and even today SBI is on top of the rung in the Indian banking industry. The lesson is: *let the leader be spiritualized first, the leadership process will then tend to be more spontaneously exalting in its impact on organizational members.* This is likely to be so because the leader's own existential matrix is no longer conventionally transactional (i.e. hunger for career, power, stock options, fame, etc.). In other words, the transformed leader radiates transformational influence because he/she functions 'essentially', not 'circumstantially'. Variable circumstances faced while leading are not avoided or ignored, but the essence stays in constant focus. This is the benefit that could accrue to the organizational situation from the leader's capacity for Spirit-centred transcendence when required.

Another part of the dialogue with Talwar quoted above, for example, contains references to the machinations of the very second person in the hierarchy headed by Talwar. He was a drag on the CEO's energy. With the large majority of other direct subordinates working for Talwar, the transformational influence was however positive. The same dialogue provides us with two such instances. He followed strictly the rule that no letter on his table should take more than 48 hours to reply. Talwar's subordinates responded to this self-imposed discipline by often handing over relevant papers to the doorman of his residence in the evenings (at times as late as 10 or 11 pm.). But he had not asked for this from them. It was spontaneous loyalty from their heart. On another occasion he was handling an intricate employee negotiation problem. The All-India Trade union leader of SBI one day came to talk to him on a contentious issue. The union leader soon turned aggressive and insolent. After a short pause Talwar told him coolly: 'Look, you are first an employee of SBI, then a trade union leader. So, behave yourself or go'. This had a dramatic positive impact on the whole process.

THE SELF OF THE SPIRITUALIZED LEADER

The above snapshots from Talwar serve to highlight a number of key aspects of a leader's self-transformation from the viewpoint of spiritual psychology. Talwar's leadership provides a genuine case of the *ontology* ('I am the Mother's appointee, Her worker'), and the *epistemology* (*silence + sincerity + no preference = Divine voice*) of transformation conceived here.

Margaret Wilson (the daughter of the American President, Woodrow Wilson) had written the following lines in a long letter to Sri Aurobindo in 1936 (Wilson 2002, p. 21).

'... I am convinced that I shall never again come under the illusion that the little self can be useful, except it be guided and activated by the higher self.'

She received an equally elaborate reply from Sri Aurobindo. The burden of this response was, as distilled by us for this Chapter (Aurobindo Sri 1987, p. 134).

(1) According to Y-V psychology, one method of understanding human personality is to visualize it at *two levels*: the 'lower self' and the 'higher self.

(2) The 'lower self' is constitutionally *deficit-driven*. These deficits are lurking or manifest, subtle or gross. Individual strivings prompted from this level, despite deceptive bright interludes, tend to degenerate into unethicality.

(3) The 'higher Self' is the inalienable, inherent core within every individual. But we remain severed from it due to the turbulent cross-currents of the lower-self.

(4) There is another technical phrase 'psychic being' which Sri Aurobindo employs synonymously for higher Self. It 'is the inmost being of all; a perception of truth which is inherent in the deepest substance of the consciousness, a sense of the good, true, beautiful...is its privilege' (Aurobindo 1989, p. 18).

Margaret Wilson had been able to correctly grasp and honestly admit the absence of Self-leadership in her. But, through some of Talwar's own words quoted earlier, and through other reliable sources (like other interviews incorporated in the book *Culture, Society and Leadership*), one may conclude that his higher-Self character was able to display sustained dignity and integrity. For instance, he did have a credit card or two gifted by others, but never used them. If he had to borrow sometimes, he would do so only against his own bank deposits. (*Culture, Society and Leadership*, op. cit., p. 246)

In so far as words can express, we may now hear from Sri Aurobindo himself a little more about the true nature of Self (Aurobindo Sri 1999, pp. 11–12).

(1) '...Self remains...pure and stainless, unaffected by the stains of life, by desire and ego, and ignorance. It is realized as the true being of the individual, but also more widely as the same being in all, and as the Self in the cosmos...'.

(2) 'The first realization of Self as something intensely silent and purely static is not the whole truth of it; there can also be a realization of Self...as the condition of world-activity and world existence.'

Thus, the journey from a 'self-transactional' leader to a 'Self-transformed' leader is a rather long and sacred haul. It may also not be immediately or entirely comprehensible at present. Yet, to be informed about its real nature can save us from premature confidence that a few short and hasty steps at the foot of the hill mean we are close to the summit.

The self-transactional leader is the ordinary 'deficit-driven self' tending to resort readily to greed, deception, manipulation etc. The Indian corporate world had witnessed during the 1990s a number of deplorable cases of top leadership which had been anything but transformational (e.g. ITC, TISCO, India Hotels, SAIL, UTI). There appears to be a deep contradiction between 'careeristic' leadership and 'transforming' leadership.

SPIRITUALITY FOR A TRANSFORMING LEADER
We turn to Sri Aurobindo again for authentic and adequate light on it (*An Introduction to True Spirituality*, op. cit., pp. 11–12):

(1) 'Spirituality has meant...the recognition of something greater than mind and life...a surge and rising of the soul in man out of the littleness and bondage of our lower parts towards a greater thing secret within him.'
(2) 'the divine perfection is always there above us; but for man to become divine in consciousness and act, and to live inwardly and outwardly the divine life is what is meant by spirituality—all lesser meanings given to it are inadequate fumblings...'.

The leader-in-transformation is informed through these benchmark statements that the lower self or lower parts are imperfect, whereas the higher Self is perfection itself. In spiritual discourse such perfection is called Divine. 'Be thou perfect as thy Father in Heaven is perfect' says the Bible too. This yearning for 'spiritual perfection' is poles apart from subservience to 'secular success'. Psychologically speaking, perfection is the capacity to preserve equanimity—through both success and failure. The Sanskrit word for perfection is *siddhi* or *sansiddhi*. Note that Aurobindo speaks of divine 'perfection', not divine 'success'.

The thinking, reasoning mental being is expected to guide, control and uplift our physical and vital being levels. But the persistent, painful reality is that the reasoning mind is itself being enslaved by the raw powers and instincts of the physical-vital levels. So, some conscientious thinkers have been feeling that the world is being led from chaos to crisis to catastrophe. It seems necessary to hold up this big picture as a backdrop while investigating uplifting change in leaders and organizations. While etching these contours of modern society, such *thinkers* have not felt obliged to express their views with reference to the huge accumulation of previous academic research and scholarship. Uninhibited extra-orbital insights from such thinkers, not researchers or scholars, are clearly more helpful.

Here is a sample of such big-picture cautions from the unfettered minds of Einstein (Einstein, 1950, p. 24), Russell (Russell, B., 1927, pp. 58–9), Tonybee (Toynbee, A.J., 1987, p. 219), Beer (Beer, S., 1994, p. 321) and Korten (Korten, D., 1998, p. 27) respectively:

(1) 'Everything is dominated by the cult of efficiency and of success, and not by the value of things and men in relation to the moral ends of human society'.
(2) 'Science is no substitute for virtue…If men were rational in their conduct… intelligence would be enough to make the world a paradise'.
(3) 'The present widespread disillusionment with politicians…is putting democracy in jeopardy.…Present-day man's social environment has become crushingly massive…this lowers his self-respect and, with it, his ethical standards.'
(4) 'The devastation wrought in the quality of life in the advanced industrial countries by the use of science and technology is plain to see. Do developing countries really wish to follow the same road?'
(5) 'Material monism has led us to the brink of self-destruction because it leads so naturally to the embrace of Hobbesian values that alienate us from any higher meaning or purpose'.

It is appropriate to add to the above citations an accurate forecast, made as early as in 1920 about the post-war crisis, by Tagore, India's Nobel Laureate sage-poet (Tagore Rabindranath, 1996, p. 613):

…with the help of science the possibility of profit has suddenly become immoderate. The whole of human society…has felt the gravitational pull of a giant planet of greed…It has carried to our society a distinct deviation from its moral orbit.

It is hoped all these sagacious, beyond-the-orbit, identical cautions from those who had or have transcended the domains of research and scholarship to those of pure thought and realization, may inspire *non-careeristic, spiritually-anchored* leadership to become holistically adorable.

Without the practice of *detachment*, however, such transcendence cannot be attained. But detachment here does not mean callousness. It implies commitment, but with a perspective uncluttered by egotism. Such a perspective and higher-Self wisdom flourish together. Spiritual perception represents understanding that is higher and wider than what mental thinking and reasoning can yield. The dominant left-brain leadership of the world during the last few centuries has been, on the whole, short-sighted as realized by the great minds above. The corrective move implies Spirit-centered, right-brain leadership informed by *transcendence* and *holism*.

The 'knowledge' of a Spirit-centred leader was characterized in these words by Sri Aurobindo, on the basis of life-long realization beyond intellectual speculation (Aurobindo, 1974, p. 6):

> It is sovereign stillness which is the calm of the yoga. The more complete the calm...the greater the force in action. In this calm right knowledge comes...in that voiceless stillness illumination comes upon the mind, error begins to fall away...clarity establishes itself in the higher stratum of the conciousness.... he rises above reason to that direct and illuminated knowledge which we call *vijnanam*.

Interestingly, Abdul Kalam has reported about Albert Einstein recalling Werner Heisenberg's words to him (Kalam, A.P.J., 2002, p. 5):

> 'You know, in the West we have built a large, beautiful ship. It has all the comforts in it, but one thing is missing: it has no compass and does not know where to go. Men like Tagore and Gandhi and their spiritual forebears had found the compass. Why can this compass not be put in the human ship so that both can realize their purpose?'

Recovery of this compass could thus be the true aim of tomorrow's transforming leader, drawing strength from spirituality.

Chakraborty has developed a five-step psycho-spiritual discipline, derived from the Y-V framework, to help go forward in this direction (Chakraborty, S.K., 1983, pp. 38–43). It is called the 'Mind Stilling Exercise' or 'Quality Mind Process'. [This is an approximate equivalent of the *Rajyoga* definition of Yoga as *chittavritti-nirodha* i.e. cessation of mental turbulence. (I.1)] It is a synthesis of some of the keynotes from the ontology-epistemology outlined earlier. Over the years it has been widely practised with managers/leaders in India, and occasionally abroad. The steps are as follows.

(1) Deep, slow, *mindful* breathing, in and out through alternate nostrils (12-15 cycles).

(2) Normal *mindful* breathing using both nostrils (5 min. or so).

These two steps help to stabilize the agitated nervous system, and to interiorize the discursive, centrifugal mind. It is a fundamental rule of yoga psychology that integral perception is positively correlated to consciously disciplined breathing. *Awareness interiorization* thus achieved is a great source of empowerment. Brief periods of *centripetalization* from the centrifugal workings of the mind recoup the power of integral effectiveness from within. It is also possible and necessary to use the attentive breathing process to *absorb* the fine particles, as it were, of human values and *purge* those of dis-values from within. Breathing thus becomes even more human and purposive.

(3) Becoming *aware of the space within the head* and suggesting to it gently and silently: 'let go, let go...' This step helps to unwind the congested, tight 'left brain', to make it relatively still and free from the mechanical, grinding, random thoughts. This is called '*thought stilling*' or '*brain-stilling*' (5–7 min).

This third step is crucial for 'right brain' revival, transcendence and holistic perception. Aldous Huxley had cautioned in 1946 that 'the habit of analytical thought is fatal to the intuitions of integral thinking' (Huxley, op. cit., p. 25).

(4) *Opening up upwards* above the head—by contemplating a lotus at dawn silently unfolding its petals and opening up to the pure golden rays of the rising sun (5–7 min).

This step attempts to put the ego-anchored awareness, imprisoned within the limited, conditioned body-life-mind cage, in touch with the infinite, unconditioned, universal and transcendent power, intelligence. Step 3 facilities this process (Aurobindo, 1991, p. 13). A kind of effortless but ardent receptivity is needed.

(5) *Concentrating the awareness* on the self-luminous, self-fulfilled higher-Self or Spirit in the centre of the psychological heart (*hriday guha* or cave of the heart). One may use a strong and steady golden flame as

a symbol of the Self to concentrate upon (5–7 min). Alternatively, one's benign *ishtam* or chosen deity may also be contemplated with quiet emotional ardour.*

This final step helps one to achieve a stable and holy inner anchor. One can cut loose from externals, and retire to it as and when the need for *re-centering* is felt. Steps 4 and 5 lend height and depth, respectively, to our flat consciousness. All the five steps together also strengthen the power of *introspection*. One can watch a sort of 'slow motion action replay' of the mind's wrong movements, and so check them.

EGO, ETHICS AND THE SPIRITUALIZED LEADER

Since Mahatma Gandhi has been mentioned as a transforming leader, it may be useful to listen to him a little. Way back in 1925, the concluding paragraph of the preface to his autobiography said this (Gandhi, M.K., 1972, p. xii):

'For it is an unbroken torture to me that I am still so far from
Him Who, as I fully know, governs every breath of my life,
And Whose offspring I am.'

This testament is a good example of what transcendence for a transforming leader could truly mean. Mahatma Gandhi yearns for transcending the ego-consciousness in order to experience the light and wisdom of the original source, i.e. God, Spirit, Divine, Self.

Burns mentions that it was in South Africa where Mahatma Gandhi was transformed into a leader. But no reference occurs about the central role of his spiritual struggles and aspirations. Curiously, attention has been drawn to his reading of Ruskin, Thoreau, Tolstoy, but not the *Gita*. The psycho-analytic framework has also been applied (rather mis-applied) to understand him (Burns, op. cit., pp. 90–2). However, a recent biography by an Indian authority (Rajmohan Gandhi, Gandhi's grandson) has christened the Mahatma's striving as one for *God-centered power*; the higher power which

---

* It could be beneficial to grasp the essence of step 5, this way also: Our executive, outer self is a tangle of 'variables' arising from the body, the vital energy, the mind etc. Yet, deep in our being there is a 'constant' too. This is like the constant in an equation comprising many variables. The constant is crucial to the whole equation. Awareness in contact with the inner 'constant' is Yoga.

pervades yet transcends everything (Gandhi, R., 1996, pp. 166–206). Elsewhere Gandhi himself had disclosed his childhood development in the following words (Gandhi, M.K., 1977, p. 3, 9):

(1) '...what I failed to get there (in school) I obtained from my nurse (who) suggested to me as a remedy for fear (of ghosts and spirits) the repetition of Ramanama ... So at a tender age I began repeating Ramanama to cure my fear' ...

(2) 'As a child I was taught to call upon Rama when I was seized with fear. ... I present it also to the reader whose vision is not blurred and whose faith is not damped by over-much learning.'

Such then were the true mainsprings of Mahatma Gandhi's transformed leadership process in early life. Outwardly, for his Indian followers, and masses in general, it was his spiritual depth and authenticity which had acted as the transforming force. Secular modes of interpretation applied to profiles such as those of Mahatma Gandhi (and Asoka, Talwar etc.) incur the capital error of trying to explain the higher through the lower.

It may also be noted that Burns has cited numerous political leaders as examples, of which only two are from Asia and among them all it is only Mahatma Gandhi who is spiritually grounded (Burns, op. cit., p. 78). His strikingly different evolution raises this issue: If spiritually transforming leadership theory is to be universal, can it exclude genuine spirituality from due consideration? Even if this can be done, should it be done? We may listen to the supra-scholastic Huxley once more (Huxley, op. cit., p. 25):

'A viable society is one in which those who have qualified themselves to see indicate the goals to be aimed at, while those whose business it is to rule respect the authority and listen to the advice of the seers. In theory at least, all this was well-understood in India, and until the Reformation, in Europe...'

This 'seer-ruler' (rajarshi) symbiosis still prevails in India in all professions—howsoever crudely maybe. This reminds one of the Vedantic parable - a lame friend on the shoulders of another who is blind, complementing one another.

Here is a telling example of the ethical and transformational influence of Mahatma Gandhi on his followers. This incident had occurred in the 1920s when he was also a labour leader. He had guided the workers of a textile mill to launch non-violent strike for some legitimate demands against a mill-owner who was well-known to him. But after two weeks the strikers began to lose moral strength and turned to violence, blacklegging, desertions etc. What happened then at the start of the third week is best heard in his own words (Gandhi MK, op. cit., p. 325).

> 'One morning—it was at a mill-hands' meeting—while I was still groping and unable to see my way clearly, the light came to me. Unbidden and all by themselves the words came to my lips: "Unless the strikers rally", I declared to the meeting, "and continue the strike till a settlement is reached, or till they leave the mills altogether, I will not touch any food."'
>
> 'The labourers were thunderstruck...(They) broke out, "Not you but we shall fast....Please forgive us for our lapses, we will now remain faithful to our pledge to the end."'

The strike was settled amicably and permanently at the end of the third week. The elevating power of a spiritually transformed leader is self-evident from above. Gandhi's spiritual charisma is entirely different from that of religious demagogues.

Swami Vivekananda (1863-1902), another realized master of Y-V psycho-philosophy, and the builder of an international sacro-secular organization, had made these startling remarks to an elite London audience in 1896 (Swami Vivekananda, 1958, pp. 62–3):

(1) 'Renunciation is the very basis upon which ethics stands. There never was an ethical code preached which had not renunciation for its basis.'
(2) 'The senses say "Myself first", ethics says "I must hold myself last." '
(3) '...the goal, the scope, the idea of all ethics is the destruction, and not the building up, of the individual.'

A dispassionate examination of the current spate of leadership unethicality in all spheres should prompt us to fathom the transformational message imbedded in Swami Vivekananda's words.*

---

*It is important for scholars and practitioners of leadership to know that the principle of 'servant leadership' was enunciated by Vivekananda way back in the 1890s (*Complete Works*, Vol. 6; pp. 284–5). There is much ignorance and varity in India and the West behind denying the 'devil' its due.

Yet this ego is a creation of Nature, to serve as an initial nucleus to form a distinct personality. But this is a provisional, intermediate individualization. Sticking to it, with coatings of reason, intellect etc., acts as a bar against exalting transformation. The bound and limited ego (or lower self) necessarily implies 'smallness of being', 'contraction of consciousness', 'limitation of knowledge', 'scission of oneness', 'disharmony and failure of sympathy' etc. (Aurobindo Sri, 1988, p. 342). It is for such reasons that in a letter written in 1894 Swami Vivekananda had declared: 'It is very difficult to take on the role of a leader. ...One must be a *servant of servants*, and must accommodate a thousand minds' (Swami Vivekananda, 1962, p. 284).

There is at present a huge corpus of 'compliance ethics' (codes, legislation etc.) and 'cognitive ethics' (intellectual theories). Yet, unethicality is on the rise. The clue to this paradox lies in not knowing or ignoring a third, higher level response. The third prong, termed here as 'consciousness ethics', should complement the prevailing two-pronged combat strategy against mounting unethicality. One of the key leaders in the Indian epic Mahabharata had confessed: 'I know what is right, yet I cannot act upto it; I also know what is wrong, yet I cannot desist from doing it'. This universal human predicament tells us that 'right knowing' does not automatically lead to 'right behaving'. The true answer for this breach has to be sought in 'Consciousness'. Sri Aurobindo had argued for this approach to ethics in the following words (Aurobindo Sri, 1995, p. 58):

'To do the right thing in the right way in each case and at each moment one must be in the right consciousness...it can never be done by following a fixed mental rule...'

True enough, as a Vedantic metaphor tells, the world is like a dog's tail, it can never be fully or permanently straightened. Yet, a three-pronged, rather than a two-pronged, strategy for ethics should work better. If we recall the views of the six great thinkers-realizers (Tagore *et al.*) cited earlier, it becomes clear that they all felt/feel that the 'cognitive-scientific-secular-rational' leadership approach has faltered on the moral and ecological planes. It may have been observed also that the above Y-V metaphysical framework for ethics does not hinge on any denominational, credal religion or its founder. So, 'consciousness ethics', anchored in a spiritual psychological theory and process as suggested here, is a surer bet. A modest degree of initial faith is needed to get started—as much in science for matter, as in spirituality for transformation.

What is this 'right consciousness'? It is a 'consciousness other than the ego'—as the definition of spirituality by Sri Aurobindo quoted earlier states. History has been repeatedly showing that egoistic reason becomes an accomplice of our vitalistic passions. All too often the leader (reason) becomes the led. Mahatma Gandhi says (Gandhi, M.K., 1962, p. 11):

'I know that ultimately one is guided not by the intellect, but by the heart. The heart accepts a conclusion for which the intellect subsequently finds reasoning.... Man often finds reason in support of whatever he wants to do.'

So, rational ethics from the thinking mental plane tends to fail again and again. Sri Aurobindo confirms this evaluation (Aurobindo Sri, 1982, p. 47):

'All attempts to moralize the race within the limits of his egoistic nature end in general failure....since reason has also to start from the senses which are consistent falsifiers of values, rational knowledge...is pursued by vast dimnesses and uncertainties.'

'Consciousness ethics' thus implies the leader's attempt to transcend his present proclivity towards reasoning of convenience. 'Spiritual consciousness' should help one to realize the Self in all and all in the Self. This 'right consciousness' is the antidote to the present consciousness of competitive divisiveness, which is the root of unethicality.

While explaining Aristotelean 'virtue ethics' for business, Solomon doubts the practical value of impressive tracts on cognitive ethics so full of intricate macro issues. He says: 'Accordingly, I want to defend business ethics as a more personally oriented ethics rather than as public policy' (Solomon, R., 1993, p. 111, 109). He is acceptable when he says that virtue is part of social practice 'which goes beyond the individual and binds him or her to a larger human network'. The Indian approach towards the 'transformed leader' has confirmed for long Solomon's primary focus on the personal dimension of ethics for the 'individual-in-society'. So long as the chronically divisive ego-consciousness remains the pivot, the 'bond' that Solomon rightly insists upon will not be forged.

CONCLUSION
Literature on transformational leadership has hitherto been concentrating on the individual, the group and the organization. This by itself is a major step forward from the limited focus in leadership studies on initiating

structure and consideration (Seltzer, J. and Bass, 1990, pp. 693–703). But this promising effort awaits a still higher leap towards sustainability beyond political and business organizations only. Thoughtful observers outside the commercial and political mainstreams are voicing great concern about growing psycho-social disintegration and irreversible ecological destruction (Hawken, P., 1993, p. 25; Quinn, D., 1993, pp. 143–5, 206–7).

Sri Aurobindo's transcendent spiritual insight had accurately foreseen and warned us about this gathering crisis sometime during 1916-1919—(Aurobindo Sri, 1970, p. 6)

'… in a commercial age with its ideal…of success, vitalistic satisfaction, productiveness and possession the soul of man may linger a while…but cannot permanently rest. If it persisted too long, Life would become clogged and perish of its own plethora or burst in its straining to a gross expansion. Like the too massive Titan it will collapse by its own mass, *mole ruet sua*.'

Leadership forces that tend to seduce humanity into a 24-hour, 7-day deficit-driven society, with no time to pause and draw a deep breath, to stand and stare, will nourish neither ethics nor happiness. The world beyond politics and business therefore awaits the arrival of more and more transformed leaders in every sphere who are able to grasp that, while economics may be the first activity of humanity, it is not its final aim. Pitrim Sorokin had thus diagnosed the human problem during the 1950s—(Sorokin, P., 1962, pp. 97, 198–9).

'Beginning roughly with the sixteenth century…the modern form of our culture emerged: the sensory, empirical, secular, and 'this worldly' culture. It may be called sensate. It is based upon, and is integrated around, this new principle-value: the true reality and value is sensory.'

He castigated this major premise of sensate culture as undesirable, and recommends its replacement by the more desirable major premise of altruism. After examining Hindu, Buddhist and other spiritual traditions, Sorokin was convinced about the efficacy of the supreme transforming principle: 'complete subordination of all values, norms, goals and egos to one absolute value, God, Nirvana, Brahman … this supreme singleness of value for transcending all relative values is exactly the right formula for integrating a multitude of antagonistic egos …' (Ibid., pp. 198–9)

Dag Hammarskjold had uttered these candid words—(Hammarskjold, D., 1966, p. 99)

'It is not sufficient to place yourself daily under God. What really matters is to be only under God. The slightest division of allegiance opens the door to day-dreaming, petty conversation, petty boasting, petty malice—all the petty satellites of death instinct.'

Thus, both Sorokin and Hammarsjkold point out the need to transcend the sensate, deficit-driven, conflict-ridden self for the sake of Self-transformation by leaders.

Once again Sri Aurobindo had articulated succinctly precisely the correct *subjective guideline* for the transformed leader of today and tomorrow, way back in 1910 (op. cit., p. 4), presaging Sorokin and Hammarskjold by several decades.

'The problems which have troubled mankind can only be solved by conquering the kingdom within, not by harnessing the forces of Nature to the service of comfort and luxury.'

The sacred moorings of power therefore need strengthening by transformed leaders for 'true' human needs (Chakraborty, S.K. and Pradip Bhattacharya, 2001, pp. 182–204). Leadership at present bends towards *consumerist business* or *divisive politics*. So, the 'hard' call of the transforming *rajarshi* (Y-V) model, in the 'soft' arena of leadership is: 'Leader, lead thyself'—*svarat samrat bhavati*.

The following Appendix briefly recounts three autobiographical narratives of spiritually-inspired leadership in the Indian corporate sector—one from the private sector, the other two from the public. They were interviewed during 2003–5. It is best to read them slowly, in quiet receptivity.

APPENDIX
Spirit-Centered Leadership-in-Action

(A) CEO OF A FIRM IN THE ENTERTAINMENT INDUSTRY

'My grandfather was a painter. In those days this vocation meant hand-to-mouth existence. So two of his sons were sent to Japan (one was my father), and another to Egypt—to fend for themselves. I did my B.Sc (Hons), followed by MBA from one of earlier IIM's. ... We are Jains. But my father's personal ideal and idol was Maryada Purushottam Sri Ram. Yet our home had no image. Under his direct tutelege I began to understand that Sri Ram was perhaps an appropriate leadership model for Satya Yuga, while Sri Krishna was so for Kali Yuga. Thereafter I got in touch with the thoughts of Ramana Maharshi and Christ. All seemed to push me towards spirituality.

'Turnaround cases are inherently more complex and demanding than normal on-going companies. So I began to study more and more of spiritual literature. It was becoming clear to me that I have an innermost Being which transcends the hectic turmoil of body-mind-thought. I was getting convinced about the need to access this Pure Consciousness which is happiness itself. I started meditating twice a day. At the same time, I became a little confused. Often I felt tempted to retire and devote full time to such pursuits. Somehow during the last three or four years I had mentally decided to attain *moksha* in this very life.

'At this stage came this new proposal to pilot another turn-around. I had then just got hold of the Gita. There I hit upon the right perspective for my immediate dilemma. This I did not get elsewhere. This book held out the full agenda of human life. So I accepted the fresh challenge, and resolved not to get stressed. The Gita has helped me to sustain my tempo for corporate life without losing sight of the goal of *moksha*.

'... the Gita helped me to realize that most of my life and work problems, including stress, were springing from personal ego. With the help of insights from the Gita I am now able to dis-identify more and more from ego-connected tensions arising from any cause. ... I was also able to realize from this book that one of the biggest causes of unethicality, as well as stress, is fear of failure. Not only this. If one is focussed all the time on success, the capacity for risk-taking also declines.

'... prayer or *prarthana* has been an unfailing prop in managing my personal effectiveness'.

(B) EXECUTIVE DIRECTOR OF AN OIL REFINING AND MARKETING COMPANY

'Today, the core of my existence is yoked to a kind of deep spiritual Being. All decisions, major or minor, emanate from this core. Sometimes it is a conscious process. But often it is natural. This core sums up my life and its purpose. Decisions are taken there for me. The individual "I" does not decide anything.

'My known spiritual journey began on June 20, 1996 when I attended a 3-day Workshop on "Management by Human Values" organized specifically for the top managers of our company. It was held at the Management Centre for Human Values at IIM-C. I became aware of my own spiritual and values dimensions the moment I filled up the questionnaire sent to us before attending the Workshop.

'I was more of a challenger and an investigator than a believer. I did manage to test the patience of the facilitator, and on four occasions got seriously counter-challenged in return. I did go through the experiential process in the Workshop. On occasions they touched me at a deeper level and I became more surprised and bewildered at the intensity of my own absorption in and response to these initial experiences.

'A couple of months later the Quality Mind Process became part of me. Soon its duration started reaching 30-40 minutes in the early mornings. I felt becoming more clear-headed, with immense energy at my command to fulfil challenging assignments, and ask for more. My temperament in the workplace became more gentle and responsive. ... We were a cosy and highly effective work-team.

'I had also recently visited the Sri Siddhi Vinayak Temple of Mumbai with a colleague. The visit to the Temple created a strong impression on my mind. My wife would accompany me almost every time, and the children too would join often. ... I submitted myself to the Grace and Service of my Lord Sri Siddhi Vinayak.

Meanwhile, my daily QMP continued. It's duration became one hour as I could wake up at 4.30 a.m.

'I got deeply interested in some additional books by Sri Aurobindo. I added them to the one given in the Workshop. Apart from *Living Within*, I read *Looking From Within* and *Growing Within*. I read the Bhagwad Gita many times—initially with some reservations and a large number of questions, but later with increasing understanding and deepening fascination. Each verse was meaningful, complete and a fundamental truth in itself.'

'My meditation continues through all my travels. So does my quest to reach, meet and unify with the Divine. I have in my heart accepted Swami Vivekananda as my guru, and have great reverence for Sri Ramakrishna and Sri Sarada Ma—his guru and guruma in turn.'

(C) GM—HRD OF A THERMAL POWER PLANT

'I see my life in three phases. In the first phase, as a student, things were more under my control. Then too some stress was felt; but that was due to hard work for better performance. But then, to help me to concentrate and to combat tension I used to repeat God's name and visit temples with like-minded friends. We used to sit there in silence for a while.

'In the second phase, at the start of my professional career, anxiety and stress sprang from the pressure of tasks assigned by superiors. This meant spending extra work-hours to master the job. Here *japam* proved very helpful. Reading of good quality fiction literature also was a healthy tension dissipater. I would also sometimes share my difficulties with a few elders outside the office. They would listen to me and suggest some tips. One good method I practised was invoking the *Gayatri mantra*.

'As I grew older and climbed up the organizational ladder, I entered into the third phase. I faced internal and external systems which are steeped in corruption, greed, jealousy etc. I have to live with them, yet ensure that I do not lose my own human values. The other major problem is that I am now neglecting my family—old father, young children, wife and others.'

'So, now I have drawn up a self-regulating charter like: Not to initiate anything unethical from my side, regular prayers in the morning (20 mins) and before sleeping (5-7 mins) etc. I also practise written *japam* of Shri Ram Naam in a specially preserved pad. My family members have been cooperating positively in such efforts.

'However, the turning point was attending the the first in-house 'Human Values Worshop' in 1999. I then saw vividly that "silence in solitude" is essential for introspection. This is the key to conquer stress.

'After attending the advanced modules, since I now occupy a leadership role, I was convinced that *svarat samrat bhavati* is the one way to lead well and without stress. I also now subscribe to the *nishkam karma* philosophy of the Gita. I try to imprint this upon my brain at the end of prayers. I now realize better that when there is success, one should be ready to take failures/ brickbats in stride too. Listening to *bhakti sangeet* at home also leaves positive residues in the sub-conscious. A combination of such methods, coupled with the sincere belief that God shall extend support for correct actions, makes for a more secure feeling and peaceful sleep.

'Moreover, I nowadays prefer reading spiritual literature rather than fiction. I bring my family too into discussions. They compare my actual conduct against the sacred guidelines. This helps us to evolve together bit by bit, with the Grace of God'.

*   *   *

The following conclusions might be highlighted from the above three narratives, and from the references to Talwar and Gandhi earlier in this chapter:

- As mentioned at the end of chapter 1, the spiritual approach in organizations presupposes the prevalence of an unbroken, living tradition in the wider social matrix. This is borne out unmistakably by all the five instances above. In the absence of such an over-arching ambience, superficial or intellectual attempts to incorporate spirituality in secular organizations will tend to be counterfeit. It will be wiser for such cultures to proceed from the roots, with humility to learn from those who have all the precious details and authentic experiences.
- The Bhagwad Gita is one common anchor for all the leaders. This gives the lie to the allegation by some renowned intellectuals, Indian and Western, that the Gita incites violence. Violence might be a strong emotion ruling the minds of such critics themselves! For, people see what they are pre-disposed or want to see in someone or something. Demolition or denunciation is their a priori intention. Yet, millions indeed are the common folk in India who, even today, are devoted to the struggle of life on the basis of timeless spiritual principles the Gita embodies.
- Y-V, or Hindu psycho-philosophy has been rendered practical through concrete processes like deep breathing, silent japam, written japam, prayer and meditation. This ensemble is clearly demonstrated by the self-imposed discipline in the daily routine of all the individuals cited above. Faith and sincerity are their hall-marks. Positive proof follows their ardent faith.
- Prevention or reduction of stress, equality of mind in success or failure, clear-thinking, strength to take difficult decisions, ego-reduction, heightened ethicality, better credibility with team members, trust in God or Higher Consciousness/Intelligence—these are the common positive

fruits reaped by all of them. But they flow as derivatives of the more primary motives for spirituality e.g., attaining *moksha* for the CEO, becoming an agent or instrument in the hands of the Divine or the Mother for Talwar etc.

- All the five leaders above border on being 'yogis'. In their own ways each one has been striving to be 'in yoga' with the spiritual consciousness—a sort of plugging into a spiritual charger socket. Among them they illustrate the application of *yogah karmasu kaushalam* (yoga is the skill of works), *tasmad yogi bhavah* (be thou a yogi), *tasmaad sarveshu kaleshu mamanusmarah yuddha cha* (remember me always and fight)— the perennial verities of the Gita. Laboratory research on yoga has no relevance here.

The Spiritual Law of Ethical Work

Nishkam Karma

PRELIMINARY

The 1980s have often been called as the 'greedy decade'. This imported phenomenon had exploded in India in the 1990s, triggered by the stock exchange-banking system mega scam. Several highly rated Chairmen, CEOs, for example, those of ITC, SAIL, TISCO, India Hotels, UTI, were seen in bad light during this period in India. Besides them, Chief Justices, Vice Chancellors, Senior bureaucrats, Chairmen of State Public Service Commissions, Ministers and several other important public figures have also been involved in unethical practices (Chakraborty, S.K. and Chakraborty, D., 2006). Such events have shaken public confidence. These unethical actions have occurred among the highest functionaries in our society who possessed more than sufficient wealth, power and prestige. They were neither deprived, nor poor. Why should then such mega unethicalities spring up from such quarters?—this is the key question which keeps haunting the man on the street. It is important to note also that all these instances were pre-meditated and carefully executed. They were all *direct* and *voluntary* unethicality cases, not imposed ones.

Faced with similar upheavals, imposed changes, instability, and uncertainty, several countries have been found searching for fundamental clues in their own *deep-structure* ethos. For example, Japan has been searching for *bushido* (Fukuda J., 1994, H. Kao, D. Sinha, S. Wilpert, pp. 76–9) and *amae* (Christopher, R.G., 1983, p. 70), Thailand for *baramee* (Komin, S., op. cit., p. 279), China for *guanxi* (Borsuan, C., op. cit., p. 237), Taiwan for *chin-shin* (Shu-Cheng, C., op. cit., p. 252), Korea for *hyo* (Kim, D., 2002, pp. 99–100) and Malaysia for *rukun-negara* (Baharom, H.Z., op. cit., p. 119). Such widespread efforts to dig deep into their own cultural sub-stratum by the respective countries in times of moral bewilderment and decline carries an important lesson for India too. In India often benign indifference or even cocky irreverence towards such indigenous insights seems to affect large sections of policy-makers. Such literate ignorance ultimately undermines the prime source of energy leverage for national upliftment. It is considered here both necessary and possible to discover some perennial, saving principle in a longstanding, sustainable culture like the Indian. This chapter is therefore addressed to practising managers and professionals in different walks of life, in order to provide them all with a firm common ground. Polemics and scholastic forays have therefore been kept to the minimum. The focus is on the essence of a rather uncommon perspective in contemporary work-life. Although this perspective may have been alluded to in some conferences or symposia in recent times, it has not yet been adequately handled either in its application or practice.

The chapter title states that the principle to be explored is that of *nishkam karma* (NK). This maybe rendered into English as 'detached involvement' (DI). The inspiration to deal with the NK principle has arisen out of significant recent testimonies from some respected CEOs of large and well-regarded organizations. Thus, in response to a question in 1997, 'Which early boyhood learning proved to be your mainstay throughout your illustrious career?', R.K. Talwar (former Chairman, SBI and IDBI) had replied (Chakraborty, S.K., 1999, p. 36):

> 'I began my schooling in Karachi, and shortly thereafter, we moved to Lahore in 1939. There I found my mother reading a Hindi Gita daily. I also took to it— without her knowledge. For sometime, I could understand very little of it. But gradually the Gita grew into me—though I was around 13 or 14 only at that time. As I grew older, my mechanical reading habit became enriched with meaning. I later joined the Imperial Bank of India in Calcutta in 1948-49 as a Junior Officer. And eversince, I have been working on the foundation of verse II.47 of the Gita.'

It maybe recalled that by then the Stock Exchange scam, ITC scandal and the TISCO imbroglio had already rocked the country.

K.N. Shenoy (former Executive Chairman of ABB (Ind) Ltd., when asked around the same period, what kind of reading had helped him to shape his outlook, answered (Ibid., p. 9):

> 'I cannot claim that I have read much of sacred literature. My wife has professional training in Yoga though. This is of some help. I read the Gita. I can

connect its messages with my work-life, e.g., do your duty and don't worry about its fruit. Such principles are practical.'

It is widely accepted that both Talwar and Shenoy were unflinchingly ethical throughout their career.

More recently in 2005, Dilip Mehta, CEO of SAREGAMA, in response to a question on how he was managing a very difficult turnaround situation, replied (Chakraborty, S.K. and Chakraborty, D., op. cit., pp. 190–3):

'... at a more fundamental level the Gita made me realize that most of my life and work-problems, including stress, were springing from personal ego. With the help of insights from the Gita I am becoming more able to dis-identify from ego-connected problems with respect to anything, for example, food, competition, etc. My present company operates in the entertainment industry. It has two very special problems: rampant piracy and prima donna top artists. As for the latter, I quickly realized that unless I mastered my ego much better than any of them, I could not be effective in carrying the group forward. The Gita has taught me this principle.'

Such examples of excellent as well as ethical CEOs, drawing their inspiration from the NK principle, have provided the impetus for this chapter.

DEFINITIONS AND EXPLANATIONS
The five key elements of this Chapter essay may now be defined with brief explanations:

(1) (UN)ETHICALITY—
It is unethicality when an entity (individual or collective) acts *intentionally* to gain some advantage or inflict some loss over another entity (individual or collective) who is either unaware of such intention or is defenceless against it.

Since the field of ethics is broad and subtle, it has appeared more convenient to define unethicality first, so that ethicality can then be deduced from it. This definition emphasizes that *conscious intentionality* is the keynote of unethical practices. Of course, consequences of such unethicality on the afflicted entity are built into the definition. This definition is applicable to individual, organizational and even broader entities. Sometimes such intended unethicalities may stop short of causing harm to the other party because the latter has been able to defend against it, or the mischief has backfired. Even if no adverse consequence has thus actually occurred for the intended victim, the action remains unethical in principle because of the *malafide intention* of the doer. This is still unethicality in terms of the above definition, though it may not be so in terms of law.

In the *Mahabharata* war all the leading characters were fully conscious of the consequences of a full-scale war. Therefore, Krishna had sacrificed all his ego and begged for merely five villages for the Pandavas. But he was insulted in the open court by Duryodhana, and all efforts for reconciliation failed. Some so-called pacifists would say the Pandavas should have swallowed all this, even after prolonged denial of their legitimate rights. But this would amount to imbecile surrender to unethical forces. Would any pacifist personally accept this in his/her own case? Therefore, the war was the only reluctant last option to combat the unethicalities perpetrated by the Kauravas. To re-establish moral order in society the righteous war (*dharmayuddha*) thus became inevitable. It entailed consequences which were apparently bloody and destructive. They were known in advance. But these were derived, subsidiary or secondary outcomes, springing from the intention to protect a *larger cause* for the society as a whole. An apt comparison would be the role of Winston Churchill and the Allied powers against Hitler during World War II. What would the pacifists say to this? Ahimsa, non-violence, *satyagraha*?

The 'intention-consequence' inter-relationship imbedded in the NK principle may be clarified further—

i) The motive or intention of an agent at the start of a decision or action should be pure of egoistic, selfish desires. The work is to be done as *kartyavam karma*—duty for sake of duty in the given circumstances, according to one's calling.

ii) But while implementation goes on, the consequences, for the agent and others, could be pain or pleasure, loss or gain, victory or loss, success or failure, blame or praise etc. i.e. 'bad' or 'good' in general terms.

iii) Such dualistic consequences arise because of several emergent reasons during execution. They cannot all be anticipated or controlled by the agent. (*Bhagawadgita* XVII. 13–14)

iv) NK however steers the *initial* intention towards the good or right or correct. This in turn, promotes and supports evenness of mind (*samatwa*) in the midst of such fluctuating, dualistic consequences (*Bhagawadgita*, II. 48)

v) *Samatwa* strengthens the agent's stamina to resist making compromises, often by resorting to rationalizations. A principled stand is possible, especially against likely adverse consequences to the agent. By the same token, in some unfortunate cases principled pursuit of NK may entail striking even against venerable persons.

vi) The Teacher's instructed the Disciple in the *Bhagawadgita* to overcome depression and confusion due to imagined dualistic consequences of a reluctant war. The Disciple's duty in the given context was to act with the 'intention' of *lokasamgraha*—the well-being of all peoples, of society. (III.20 and III.25) This was the 'ethical' or 'good intention' highlighted by the Teacher. This inner motive alone was under the Disciple's own control (Aurobindo, Sri, 1977).

Scholars are sometimes found to wrestle with western theoretical constructs like 'de-ontology', 'consequentialism' while attempting to interpret the ethics of the *Gita*. This is faulty. The *Gita* stands on the higher plane of spiritual quest and attainment. The works of Aristotle, Kant and Mill, however engrossing at the intellectual level, are bereft of the spiritual mainspring. They offer sophisticated speculations and abstract assumptions. No guidance for upward evolution to the level of the Spirit or Self, through experiential insights, is available in them.

(2) DECISION MAKING—

Decision making involves *choice* from a set of options or variables with a *purpose*, be it individual or organizational.

The question of being ethical or unethical does not necessarily appear in every decision. However, when it is a question of another party being affected adversely by the decision, then such a decision needs to be judged in terms of 'should' or 'should not'. Thus, decision-making to be ethical under relevant circumstances needs to satisfy certain universal and local *normative* standards.

(3) WORK PERFORMANCE—

It means *accomplishment* of certain tasks with given *resources* within a *time limit*. This involves selection and pursuit of various means and methods to achieve the chosen or accepted task.

In other words, decision-making is required continuously. This, in turn, poses questions of ethicality or unethicality most of the time.

(4) NISHKAM KARMA(NK)/DETACHED INVOLVEMENT(DI)—

It means performing work, accepted on the basis of agreed *remuneration*, *with little calculation* or concern, especially in comparison with others, for *additional* personal recognition/gain/reward, during or on completion of the work.

The principal points in the above definition are—

i) Work is being done for remuneration, not otherwise. This much has to be accepted for people who take up employment or business for earning a livelihood.

ii) There is no end to dissatisfactions arising from comparisons with peers within the same organization or outside. Hence, the NK theory advises control of mental agitation on this score. Such control can contribute both to durable ethicality and effective performance.

iii) Verse II.47 in the *Bhagavad Gita* enunciates the principle of NK thus (Ibid., p. 47):

Thou hast a right to action, but only to action, never to its fruits; let not the fruits of thy works be thy motive, neither let there be in thee any attachment to inactivity.

Thus, every action by anyone will produce some results or consequences. This is a cause-and-effect relationship. The consequences, despite sincere endeavour, cannot be wholly foreseen, or controlled by an individual entity. This is because reality is more complex than human intelligence can comprehend (Ibid., p. 246). Be that as it may, outcomes from action fall into two broad categories—

• *Results* relating to the organization (or for any other entity)
• *Fruits or rewards* for the performer of action(s)

The NK principle never negates or berates *results for the organization*. Its chief message is in respect of hunger for *fruits for the individual performer* of the work. Pruzan explains this matter lucidly,

'This should not be confused with indifference to the work itself; rather the work is to be performed with detachment. Nor should this be confused with fatalism. We must do what we find to be important to do to the best of ability. But such action is selfless in that it is performed with indifference to the outcomes, be they, success or failure, praise or blame.' (Pruzan, P., 2001, p. 180)

An alternative expression therefore could also be 'desireless action'.

(5) SAKAM KARMA (SK) OR ATTACHED INVOLVEMENT (AI)—

It means performing work, accepted on the basis of *agreed remuneration*, *with anxious comparative calculations* vis-a-vis others, for *additional* personal recognition/gain/reward during or on completion of the work.

Going back to the definition of unethicality suggested earlier, it is clear that SK as just defined would be the major cause for violation of ethical norms. Obsession with gaining fruits, whether personal or corporate or national, will erode the decision-maker's sense of proportion and prudence. This, in turn, will prompt adoption of illegal or unethical means. However, practice of the NK-orientation will restrain and reduce such negative propensities—whether individual or corporate or national. The essence of verse II.47 is long-term practice of gradual *detachment from hankering* for personal fruits (recognition/gain/reward) from work, accompanied by increasing *involvement* in the accepted task itself. The bulk of the mounting unethicality and ineffective work-performance in various institutions today may be traced to the unquestioned acceptance and espousal of SK as the only practicable basis of work-life.

It is also useful to distinguish here between what is 'desired' (*preya*) and what is 'desirable' (*shreya*). Given the common human nature, there is always the possibility that what is 'desired' need not be 'desirable'. SK characteristically emphasizes more on what is 'desired'. NK on the otherhand provides impetus for the 'desirable'. It is this subjective struggle in man which gradually enhances his ethical capability.

There is an alternative phrase to SK: *kamya karma* (KK). Srinivasachari, a scholar in ethics and the *Gita*, explains that KK has only market/commercial value, and makes man a slave of passions or sensual propulsions (Srinivasachari, P.N., 1986, p. 74). In other words, SK (KK) makes man the slave of the sensually provocative environment. He draws further attention to the inherent unethicality of SK (KK). 'KK is the offspring of pathological love seated in the propulsions of sense and is, therefore, influenced by inclination.' (Ibid., p. 59) In the light of these theoretical insights into SK we may appreciate Gandhiji's view about what work-life, grounded wholly in this motive, could reduce itself to—

- '...he who is ever distracted (for results), he says goodbye to all scruples, everything is right in his estimation and he therefore resorts to means fair and foul to attain his end.'(Gandhi, M., 1990, p. 14)

- 'We should do no work with attachment…If we are attached to our goal of winning…we shall not hesitate to adopt bad means.'(Gandhi, M., 1994, Vol. 32, p. 125)

The multiplying incidents of large-scale unethicality in corporate, public and academic life mentioned in the beginning can be understood clearly in the light of Srinivasachari's theoretical explanation and Gandhiji's practical elaboration.

Moreover, both the theoretician and the practitioner arrive at the same conclusion, specifically regarding the ethicality of Arjuna's battle in the *Mahabharata*. Srinivasachari says the following—

'It is really a case of *niskama karma* when a true *kshatriya* fights for a just cause, not because it excites his instinct or is expedient, but because it ought to be done as duty.' (Srinivasachari, P.N., op. cit., p. 73)

Similarly, Gandhiji has the following comments to offer on Chapter 2 of the *Gita*—

- 'If you refuse to fight this righteous war, the consequences will be the very reverse of what you expect and you will become an object of ridicule.' (Gandhi, M., 2001, p. 225)
- 'To fight is the duty you have to discharge at present. Gain or loss, defeat or victory, is not in your power.' (Ibid., p. 226)
- 'The success of an act lies in performing it, and not in its result, whatever it is. Therefore be calm and do your duty clear of consequences.'(Ibid., p. 226)

The word 'result' is used here in the sense of 'personal fruit'. In other words, the correct interpretation of NK, as against SK, is that of integrity, honesty and selfless motive behind the decision or action. 'Organizational results' are admitted. Therefore, fighting a righteous war involving unavoidable killing of elders (*gurus*), who have given tacit approval to the intentional unethicalities inflicted by the Kauravas on the Pandavas, is ethical on behalf of the society. It is this spirit of NK, which contributed to the strong ethical base of Talwar, Shenoy and Mehta.

(6) Effectiveness or Excellence—
Effectiveness or excellence is defined here as follows:

Excellence or Effectiveness = Ethical Motives + Efficiency

Efficiency as usual stands for output-input ratio. NK, by contributing to ethics, raises efficiency to effectiveness.

Thus, a student may have set a goal for securing A+ grade in his summer project report. But he attempts to achieve it by shortcut means like copying substantial portions from the report submitted by a student in an earlier batch. He may thus be efficient, but he is not excellent or effective.

Careful reading of the *Gita* reveals its clear emphasis on 'perfection', not 'success'. The Sanskrit term for perfection is *siddhi* or *sansiddhi* (verses III.4, VIII.15, XVI.23). Success however is *safalta*. All sacred or spiritual literature gives priority to the striving for *subjective perfection*. *Objective success*, in common parlance, may or may not follow. The sagas of the self-less freedom fighters who gave their lives for Mother India are good examples of this distinction.

(7) SYSTEM—
A system is an arrangement of *inter-related* entities/parts/ procedures/ components for their effective *combined* functioning towards achieving a goal, implying relevant regulatory guidelines. Thus, having a system in place helps to meet certain desirable goals within the framework of given internal and external compliance rules.

In an ethically-oriented organization such requirements include ethical norms also. This is clear from the formulation of detailed ethical codes by several organizations in recent years. For example, the system of placing purchase orders to competing suppliers is usually formulated quite elaborately. The system maybe adequate, yet people in the purchase department could make secret deals with some suppliers for personal gain. Thus, 'system adequacy' is not implemented due to lack of 'system adherence'. System adequacy is more a function of skills and techniques. It is more about 'form'. *System adherence is more a function of values and ethics. It is more about 'spirit'.*

The next section, with the help of the above definitions and explanations, will explore a few real-life situations involving ethicality and unethicality.

ILLUSTRATIONS FROM THE PROFESSIONAL WORLD
Here is a series of nine vignettes (not detailed case studies) from industry and other professions, interpreted briefly with the help of the following principles already outlined above:

(a) detached involvement rather than attached involvement (NK and SK);
(b) consequences of the respective approaches on Ethical Decision Making (EDM) and Effective Work Performance (EWP);
(c) emphasis on 'system adherence' as much as 'system adequacy'

The capsule illustrations below are expected to demonstrate that practice of NK/DI helps in taking ethical decisions, along with improved work performance. Also, the common apprehension that this principle cannot be put into practice may be mitigated.

VIGNETTE 1

XYZ, a profit-making PSU, decided to expand its power generation capacity by about 500 mw. This meant huge investment in setting up the infrastructure. One of the first requirements was erection of a towering 300m. chimney. Of all the raw materials needed, steel according to tight specifications was most vital.

A tender was issued by XYZ. Price quotations were received duly. Among the quotations received there was the one placed by an ailing PSU, ABC. Some people believed that XYZ had accepted its quotation as a gesture of goodwill to alleviate the financial crisis of ABC.

It transpired later that the quality of steel supplied by ABC was sub-standard. This was unexpected. But by that time forty percent of the construction work was complete. Vigilance officials became alert. One of the experienced officials suspected that ABC was only putting its own stamp on the steel delivered which was actually manufactured by a third party.

Investigations opened a Pandora's Box. The initial suspicion of the officials was vindicated. Since it was beyond the ability of ABC to supply the quantity of steel ordered, it was sub-contracted. But ABC could not pay the sub-contractors since its coffers were empty. Therefore, while quoting to XYZ it had cleverly added five thousand rupees extra per tonne. This resulted in an additional drainage of rupees one crore for XYZ, but helped ABC to pay the creditors. It was found to be true that after the steel plates rolled out from those plants, ABC did put its mark on them. There was prima facie evidence that some top officials from XYZ were also involved in the game.

If a company faces fund crunch, or is beset with infrastructural problems, then sub-contracting is legal. However, before sub-contracting, ABC should have verified the sub-contractors' capability to meet the requirements of XYZ. This is a normal precautionary measure. But this was not done. 'System adherence' was compromised by the top officials of ABC, probably in connivance with some of the seniors of XYZ. Self-regarding SK is the primary explanation for such unethicalities. We may in this context recall the quotation from Gandhiji cited earlier: '...he who is ever distracted (for results), says goodbye to all scruples.'

VIGNETTE 2

Having received advice to bid for Electronic Voting Machines required by the Election Commission (EC), some prototypes were designed, constructed, and submitted for evaluation by both ABCL and MNCL. MNCL's bid was lower in comparison with ABCL's. EC's office was also somehow well-disposed towards MNCL. The order seemed most likely to go to it. In the joint meeting of the EC and the two competing companies it was agreed that it would be alright with ABCL if the order went to MNCL since the price quoted by the latter was lower. At this meeting the quality differences between the two prototypes were not known because field testing had yet to be done. The EC thought this would be a mere formality. Since 100 units of ABCL's prototype were, however, already manufactured, and there was no other buyer, they were proposed to be gifted to the EC. There were no hidden motives in this.

However, the machine manufactured by MNCL subsequently failed to satisfy the field trials. ABCL's machine, though more expensive, scored over it on account of better quality. So, unexpectedly ABCL got the order from the EC.

The above incident is an inspiring instance of 'system adherence'. If ABCL had wanted, it could have lobbied with the GOI. But it did not do so on principle, and stuck to what it deemed to be honourable, ethical. This also indicates that ABCL was operating on the principle of NK. Instead of aiming at immediate success, ABCL did the work with perfection and ultimately got the reward without hankering for it. Thus, both EDM and EWP were accomplished simultaneously. This dispels the common notion that NK and ethicality do not yield material payoffs.

VIGNETTE 3

Gopal* was internal auditor at the middle level in a large PSU. For some flimsy reasons the MD had stalled his promotion for one year. Many people in the organization were sad about this incident. Next year the MD was

---

* All names here and below are pseudonyms.

accused for showing alleged favouritism to his son-in-law, a marketing director in another organization, by placing a high-value purchase order to the latter. The first stage investigation was handed over to Gopal. After meticulous inquiry he found the MD to be above board. He was, however, provoked by another senior executive to settle his score with the MD, and not to exonerate him. Gopal rejected this suggestion. He refused to be swayed by the denial of 'fruit' of promotion in the previous year. Consequently, the angered senior executive spoiled Gopal's annual report for the following year also. This was done out of grudge because the senior executive had a personal tussle with the MD. He had wanted Gopal to act on his behalf and fix the MD. Thus, Gopal missed promotion for the second time too. This prompted him to write a one line letter to the Chairman about the unfair treatment meted out to him. The Chairman merely acknowledged the letter but took no action. Gopal dropped the matter there and handled the situation by having recourse to the NK principle of 'perfection' rather than 'success'. He had imbibed this value towards work from his father. His work continued to be as ethical and excellent as before.

VIGNETTE 4

The regional Chief Accountant (CA) of a private company had triple professional qualifications in the accounting field. At one stage the newly appointed technocrat MD of the company, based on a consultant's report for developing a trust-based organization, had relaxed certain vouching procedures of the internal audit system. Meanwhile, the CA had been vigorously investing in shares during the stock market boom of the early 1990s. Suddenly, however, the stock market collapsed. The CA was chased by his friends and relatives who had given him loans for stock market deals. Finding no means to satisfy them, the CA used his professional skills to tamper with the weakened system and fleeced the company to the tune of rupees twenty lakhs. After internal audit verified this to be true, the matter was referred to the CBI. He was 'suspended' from the organization. Thus, driven by greed-centric SK (KK), a highly skilled professional attempted to mitigate losses due to his personal recklessness by flouting to the system. He betrayed the organization's goal of creating a trust-based company.

VIGNETTE 5

Mathur had just been appointed at the beginning of a financial year as the regional Marketing Manager of a private sector pharmaceutical company. Over the last ten years this region had not been doing well. So, its field sales force were not getting extra bonus unlike their counterparts in other regions. In order to motivate them Mathur promised that he would see to it that they got such incentives at the end of the current year. But half-way during the year, at the review meeting in the corporate head quarters, along with other regional managers and the MD, it became apparent that this year also the company's performance norms would not be achievable in Mathur's region. He did not then discuss the matter frankly with the MD. Instead, back in his own region he called the sales force and assured them they would definitely get the bonus, provided they carried out exactly what he would ask them to do. Then he implemented a plan comprising several fraudulent practices to boost sales figures. After sometime the plan leaked out and ultimately Mathur was asked to resign under embarrassing circumstances. Although he was apparently doing all this for the sales force, not himself, yet there was a hidden underlying 'fruit' he was craving for. He wanted to be a hero in the eyes of his subordinates. Once again a more subtle type of SK led to system violation, although a proper system was in place.

VIGNETTE 6

Das did his engineering from an IIT and post-graduation in management from an IIM. Having graduated in 1977, he worked in different organizations before establishing his own company, Network Ltd., in 1992. The focus of the company has been on software development, and also on offering web-based business solutions. It is useful to know how Das operates his business in a volatile industry. The following are some practical guidelines he follows for wholesome business practices (quoted mostly from his letter to the authors)—

(a) 'Things happen continuously in business. Many situations occur vastly at variance from expectations. In such situations instead of getting anxious about why it happened or why it did not, it is more meaningful to ask oneself: 'What next?' This helps to deal with uncertainties without anger, disappointment, frustration, etc.

(b) 'The second principle is to do the right thing, taking the right action at all times and under all situations, and not focusing on the result. After all we all know that the *fruits* accruing out of one's actions are not in one's hand. This should not be equated with fatalism because it does not act as an impediment towards goal-setting and high performance.'

(c) 'Strength of mind is indispensable. It pays to make the mind understand that what is not in one's control, there is no use worrying about it. An uncluttered mind helps an individual to appreciate a situation in totality.'

This example is somewhat different from those given earlier. On the one hand, examples (1) and (2) mainly reflect organizational efforts, and example (3) focuses on individual effort in ethical decision making along the principle of NK. Examples (4) and (5) on the other hand illustrate the unethical consequences of SK. Das (6) corroborates the validity behind the application of the NK principle in simple terms, specifically in point (b) above. He echoes the *five-factors* (the body or *adhisthan*, the doer or the *karta*, the various instruments or *karanam*, many kinds of efforts or *vividha chesta*, and super-personal causality or *daivam*) which govern the final outcome or result of human action (see XVIII.14 of the *Gita*). He tells from experience that the practice of NK at personal level equips one to deal better with anger, frustration, disappointment, etc. A clear and steady mind then provides the basis for *moral stamina* against unethical decisions. In point (b) he also refutes the supposition that NK cannot inspire goal-oriented work.

VIGNETTE 7
The following incident was narrated to one of the authors by Prof. Rajan, the coordinator of a Centre in a prestigious technical University of India. During a particular semester Dr. Rampal, the head of a particular department, was to take evening classes in the Centre. However, it soon came to light that he, on one pretext or the other, failed to hold classes on a number of occasions. Yet, the next day he made it sure that the attendance register contained his signature. It was not difficult for Rajan to realize that Rampal was utilizing his position to extract undue benefit at the cost of the institution. But he felt helpless to intervene as he feared severe retaliation because of the rapport Rampal enjoyed with influential persons of the governing body.

This incident illustrates that even highly-qualified academics, who are expected to be role models for the rest of the society, can indulge in petty unethicalities. SK drags one's behaviour down to a level involving crude system violation. While this may bring some 'fruits' of a few extra thousand rupees, it destroys also the more honourable 'fruit' of respectability amongst the people around. It shows how SK accentuates craving for what is not fair or legitimate. Rampal's attitude to work performance is in contrast to

Das's. The latter had been exercising self-restraint and introspection before taking any decision. In other words, what was expected of a teacher was practised by an entrepreneur. Whatever be the degree of 'system adequacy', people with a strong SK bent frequently find new ways to *bypass 'system adherence'*. Thus, thrives unethicality.

VIGNETTE 8

A Mumbai-based gynaecologist, Dr. Manjrekar, had built up a roaring practice. During a career spanning twenty five years he had performed around 30,000 pregnancy terminations. He was a specialist in late-stage abortions. However, Manjrekar's philosophy of life underwent a sea-change after attending a discourse in 1993 on *Srimad Bhagavatam*. Inspired by the discourse, he read the *Gita* also and realized 'that the solution to poverty and disease lies in spiritual education and not in abortion'. After that he stopped performing abortions. But it meant huge drop in income. This incident points to the fact that *whatever is legal may not necessarily be ethical*. In other words, ethical decision-making might transcend legal boundaries. That apart, Manjrekar's courage to go against the tide could also be attributed to his reliance on NK. Otherwise, it may not have been possible for him to refrain from monetary greed. His new higher consciousness made him realize that abortion, though legal, will *accelerate social unethicalities*. It will tend to make promiscuity acceptable, and thereby deal a moral blow to the social fabric. It was 'existential reward', not monetary reward, that Manjrekar gained.

This illustration shows how an individual's consciousness was transformed from SK to NK, and became associated with a higher spiritual aim. We know of a few other gynaecologists who also adopt a stance akin to that of Dr. Manjrekar.

VIGNETTE 9

A former Chairman of a reputed government company was put under house arrest on account of involvement in a mega scam that had sent the stock market reeling. In his heydays he was looked upon as a role model by many. During custody a young CBI official was deputed to look after him. This official had recently disclosed to us that one day, after the interrogations were over, the Chairman broke down and confided in the young official thus: 'My impatient ambition to grow big and fast has been instrumental for all the mess I am now in'. His decision about life-goal to be as famous and wealthy within as little a time as possible had triggered a whole series of subsidiary and derivative decisions which were unethical in different degrees.

This event portrays the pathetic consequences of SK. He had neither dearth of money nor of power and position. Going by the common theories of work- motivation, he certainly had enough of social esteem and apparently self-esteem too, and was also self-actualised. Yet, he was so much attached to the *secular goals* of name, fame, power, etc. that he could not desist from unethical actions. This was much like Duryodhana who had confessed to Sri Krishna: '*Janami adharmam na cha me nivritti, janami dharmam na cha me pravritti*'. (I know what is wrong, yet I cannot desist from it; I know also what is right, yet I cannot perform it).

From all the above definitions and illustrations the following learning points emerge:

(a) EDM implies *courage of conviction* to stay on right lines, and cultivate the discipline to overcome temptations e.g. the behaviours of ABCL, Gopal, Das etc. They spring from NK.
(b) What is legal need not always be ethical e.g. the stance of Manjrekar on abortion. *Ethicality goes above legality.*
(c) 'System adequacy' is not all. It is confined to matters of skills and techniques only. 'System adherence' requires a different kind of learning and the culture of human values e.g. probable involvement of the top officials of the power plant of XYZ in collusion with ABC while purchasing steel, the role of the CA milking the organization etc. The most adequate system, if not adhered to, will fail. Similarly, a not-so-adequate system, if adhered to, is often found to be more disciplined and reliable. Therefore, sustained education for values-based 'system adherence' is at least as important as emphasis on skills-based 'system adequacy'.
(d) SK commonly leads to *short term gain* and *long term pain*, for example, the Chairman of the PSU, Mathur and CA. This phenomenon has been captured wisely and forcefully in the *Gita* (XVIII.37-38) (Aurobindo, Sri, 1977, p. 254).

SVADHARMA–NISHKAM KARMA, ETHICS AND YOGA
The endeavour to arouse and keep alive a *holistic cosmic awareness* within social life has been an abiding impulse among the founding fathers of Bharat's culture. These sages and realizers lived in humble and joyful harmony with

Nature in forest *ashrams* and *tapovans*. No feeling of superiority over Nature, nor any urge to subjugate it ruled their minds. They could realize that there must be a Supreme Master Worker performing His many-sided work through countless agents in Nature, e.g., the Sun, the tree, the flower, the air, the water, the earth and so on.

The common principle on which all the works of the *rishis* rests is their *direct vision*. They thus discerned that there is an inherent *law of being* for each work-agent. They called this the principle of *svadharma*. Elaboration of categories like *sadharan dharma*, *jati dharma*, *kula dharma* etc., and their relative circumstantial prioritizations, are not relevant for this book. The *Bhagwad Gita* too (verses II.31 and III.35) steers clear of such details. Thus, the Sun gives light and heat; the tree gives fruit, flower or shade; the flower gives beauty and fragrance—all following their respective intrinsic laws of being. They do work for the sake of work, duty for the sake of duty. Their performance is not dependent on reward, recognition, praise, increment, etc. Hence, their *svadharma* ensures *spontaneous application of NK*. Their motivation does not fluctuate according to whether they are 'recognized' or 'rewarded'. It is because Nature as a whole functions on such NK principle that the human world has a foundation which is predictable, consistent and reliable. Unfortunately, this is taken for granted by deluded humanity.

Therefore, when the *rishis* focused on the *homo sapiens*, they discerned that, unlike other work-agents of Nature, the humans possessed the *faculty of choice*. If the human beings were to exercise this choice in work life along NK, then their work would also be in harmony with Nature's rhythm and spirit of work. The keynote of the Master Worker is working *without* calculating or bargaining for returns. This is the fundamental *svadharma* of the whole of Nature at work. If human beings could consciously follow this principle, they would develop the *potential* to draw wisdom and power from the transcendental or cosmic plane itself. This would also reduce or prevent discordance between human action and Nature's work.

However, human beings grow up unconsciously on the basis of the SK mentality right from birth. Therefore, their worklife usually becomes obstinately *problematic*, entailing both inefficiency and unethicality. Examples of Gandhiji, Vivekananda, Manjrekar, Talwar, Gopal etc. mentioned earlier, illustrate the *potential* being realized by them to a great extent. By trying to apply NK, they were in close alignment with the *svadharma* of Nature herself. On the other hand, Mathur, CA, former Chairman of a reputed Government company etc. demonstrate the problems created by man's deviation from the NK *svadharma* of Nature as a whole. In other words, *it is necessary for human beings to cultivate NK for harmonizing with all other agents of work* in Nature. The widespread human tendency towards SK through the exercise of choice is a challenge which needs overcoming through sustained education and culture of NK. This is the true solution to growing unethicality in all fields.

Pertinently, it maybe noted that Arjuna was counselled to face the challenge of the *Mahabharata* war because of his *svadharma* as a *kshatriya* prince. It was to be done for the protection of righteousness, for social well-being, not for egoistic self-aggrandizement (i.e. SK) (Srinivasachari, P.N., op. cit., p. 64). Another simple illustration could be helpful. For a teacher, writing a book falls within his *svadharma*. If such work is done out of a sense of duty because of his calling, then this would be close to NK. But if he does not stop at that, and goes on speculating or calculating about different kinds of mileage he would like to get out of it, this would be very close to SK. This mentality entails greed for fame, hankering for promotion, eagerness for good reviews, competitive rivalry with other authors etc. These tendencies will cause dissipation of psychological energy, and often prompt manipulative or unethical behaviour e.g. plagiarism.

Karma Yoga and *Anasakti Yoga* are also fairly common expressions cognate with *Nishkam Karma*. The word *yoga* means realization of union by the human with the Divine, or the union of the individual consciousness with the Universal Consciousness. The idea here is the same as *alignment* with the cosmic rhythm, or *empowerment* from the cosmic plane as mentioned above. *Yoga* theory holds that *Sakam Karma*, with ego as the pivot, will act as a wall against this kind of union, or *yoga*. NK dissolves or replaces the small ego in the performer, and facilitates the yoking of individual consciousness with the original Universal Consciousness. Hence, *Karmayoga*.

Sekhar correctly points out the need for equanimity through *yoga* (Sekhar, R.C., 2002, p. 39). At the same time, it is also relevant to note that the practice of *samatwa,* or equanimity as a *process* is the cause, and eventual *yoga* is the consequence[*] (Gita II.48). This *yoga* is a psychological state when the individual mind or consciousness becomes poised for union with the Universal Mind or Consciousness. As this state becomes more and more stable, both ethical rectitude and performance effectiveness become spontaneous. (i.e. *yogah karmasu kaushlam*, Gita II.50—yoga is the skill in works, and not skill in works in yoga—the common but wrong rendering).

---

[*] See diagram on p. 206 illustrating *samatwa* for *yoga*

NK AND SK: DIFFERENCES AND CORROBORATIONS

It will be useful now to crystallize the major differences between NK and SK in a tabular form below.

Nishkam Karma (DI)	Sakam Karma (AI)
(a) Psychological energy conservation	Psychological burnout
(b) Perfection is the aim	Success is the aim
(c) Socio-economically appropriate	Socio-economically questionable
(d) Work-commitment	Reward-commitment
(e) Enhances ethicality	Undermines ethicality
(f) Mind enrichment	Job enrichment
(g) Liberating	Binding

The above contrasts maybe explained briefly—

(a) NK helps conservation of psychological energy. It focuses on systematic effort for gradually detaching from selfish or competitive calculations for personal gains, with increased involvement in the work itself. In SK, even if such work is meant ostensibly for the organization or any other larger entity, it usually conceals a strong personal ego-drive. But through NK the mind becomes more and more free from speculations, worries, anxieties, tensions etc. Greater energy is available for the work itself. SK, on the other hand, implies primary attachment to personal reward/gain, and incidental involvement with the work/job for that purpose. This tendency foments rivalries with colleagues or clashes with superiors, resulting in loss of energy and reduced work-effectiveness. Hence, it is helpful to appreciate that NK is an *intrinsic* safeguard against stress and burnout. On the contrary, SK tends *inevitably* to aggravate these obstacles against equanimity, effectiveness and ethics. NK enables one to maintain greater equilibrium amidst the play of opposites or *dwandwas* e.g. praise and blame, success and failure. This is called *samatwa* - a critical energy conserver. SK, however, generates *dissipative mental fever*.

(b) NK impels to do work with perfection (*siddhi* or *sansiddhi*). Such an ideal is often considered impractical in work-life. But this is not true. For example, in cricket, a perfectly executed stroke may fail to fetch even a single run due to good fielding, or the ball may hit the stumps at the non-striker's end. The scoreboard does not move. But perfect strokeplay increases the probability of high scores in the long-run. This apart, a discerning spectator will also appreciate such batting. On the other hand, an atrocious stroke may hit the boundary. There is measurable success. However, such batting may get him out in the very next ball. A connoisseur of cricket will not praise such wild strokes. Besides, perfection is also the psychological state of *samatwa* where the doer aims at protecting his/her inner steadiness and poise in the midst of externally induced emotional turbulences.

(c) Recent data tell us that 29 crores of Indians live below the poverty line (i.e. Rs. 327/person/month in rural India and Rs. 454/person/month in urban India). Against this national scenario we may recall that in August 2006 the Central Cabinet had approved a hefty monthly remuneration of Rs. 65,000 per month, plus enormous sums of various perks for the MPs (*The Hindustan Times*, 18.8.2006). We also have the recent example (April 2005) of a state CM (where 53 per cent of the population is below the poverty line) gifting a car worth Rs. 42 lakhs to the Governor, apparently to buy peace. Not only that, the CM along with the MLAs supporting him will also get new cars (each worth Rs. 5 lakhs) replacing the existing ones. In this overall context it is clear that the NK principle of work, specially for people in leadership positions, is certainly more moral and equitable than the SK approach. It needs hardly any emphasis that NK never implies that normal and due earnings for meeting one's personal and family responsibilities shall be denied. There is a widespread perception that, whereas leaders of various categories were inspiringly NK-oriented during the pre-independence period, leaders in independent India have been indecently SK-driven.

(d) 'Commitment to work' as a principle implies work for work's sake. Consequently, there is less disappointment or depression if recognition and rewards (like promotions, perquisites etc.) do not flow according to expectations. But 'commitment to rewards' etc. tends to make work merely an instrument for such fruits The latter are the real goals. Thus, a workaholic is usually a *sakam karmi*, not *nishkam karmi*. The common workaholic is usually spurred by the craving for such fruits as reward, recognition, money etc. But this may be better than being a *tamasic* shirker.

(e) Since NK tries not to be contingent on personal rewards, it gives natural support to ethicality in work. By contrast, SK being essentially geared to the accrual of rewards or fruits from work, one readily succumbs to extrinsic temptations. This, in turn, provokes unethicality. The means adopted tend to become foul and corrupt.

(f) Management literature has been advocating job-enrichment as an 'intrinsic' motivator. Examined closely, it is still external to the mind. Motivation here is made dependent on outer design and composition of the work package. So, it is also close to SK in prnciple, although in a relatively milder dose. In any case, in practice very few jobs can be enriched to the liking of every employee. Yet there is a huge bulk of jobs which have to be done in all organizations. So, motivation/commitment/dedication in all these cases will need a temperament which is more independent of external factors. Thus, NK says, for example, the job of a data-entry operator or bank cashier can hardly be enriched, yet they have to be done with care and precision. Such care and precision will follow from 'mind-enrichment' rather than 'job-enrichment'. The principle is: it is the *mind which imparts enrichment* to a job, not the other way round. With an enriched mind even menial jobs or ordinary chores can become uplifting e.g, sweeping the floor, or washing the clothes etc.

(g) Perennial philosophy and true psychology, whether Vedantic, or Buddhist, or Biblical, have advised that seeking motivation by satisfying ever-increasing desires and wants tightens the chains of bondage. Yet such a pursuit is the real nature of SK. Hence, perceptive observers realize that humanity is becoming more and more bound, not free, by following the gospel of SK. Buddha had uttered a deep truth: a desire conquered yields more satisfaction than a desire satisfied. Therefore, the NK approach to work is more consonant with the goals of *freedom and meaning in life*.

We have attempted above to differentiate NK and SK more precisely after the previous sections had introduced some of the major aspects of the theory. However, we are aware that such thinking and orientation are unfamiliar, except for casual references. Hence, the reader is offered below some more personal testimonies from professionals and modern seers to corroborate the implications of the preceding presentation. These personalities have not been interested in the NK approach as intellectual critics, or as vacuous sceptics. Instead, they had plunged into it with firm *shraddha* and made its practice a life-long engagement. The testimonies of some personalities have already been cited in a preceding section. A few more will be presented now.

Swami Vivekananda is quoted below for a few lucid insights to the implications of the two approaches to work (all emphasis added)—

i) 'Men run after a few dollars and do not think anything of cheating a fellow-being to get these dollars; but if they would restrain themselves, in a few years they would develop such *characters* as would bring them millions of dollars—if they wanted them. Then their *will* would govern the universe. But we are such fools!' (Vivekananda, Swami, 1990, p. 19).

ii) 'The public speaker wants a little applause or a little hissing and hooting. If you keep him in a corner without it, you kill him, for he requires it. This is working through *slavery*' (ibid., p. 22).

iii) 'Next comes the work of the servant, who requires some pay; I give this and you give me that ... There is a motive somewhere. If it is not *money*, it is *power*. If it is not power, it is *gain*' (ibid.).

Vivekananda's observations about the attitude to work under the impulse of SK are embarrasssingly candid. There is continuous display of such ignominies of SK in society, business, politics, academics, entertainment etc. He mentions the word 'will' (point i). But writings on personality development usually ignore the importance of will-power. Consequently, there are huge gaps between theory and practice. For the journey from SK to NK, application of will-power is essential.

Next, some observations on NK and SK by a few well-known leaders from Indian industry are being presented briefly—

(a) L.N. Jhunjhunwala, Chairman Emeritus, Bhilwara Industries, had recalled an incident related to stress in managing business:

'I recall when I once told him (Swami Budhananda of R.K. Mission, Delhi) about my unbearable stress in managing my business affairs, he said: 'Look Jhunjhunwala, you have to decide clearly whether you are going to run the business, or the business is going to run you,' This powerful statement left an indelible stamp on my mind' (Chakraborty, S.K., 1999, p. 64).

The pithy yet profound comment by the Swami, which Jhunjhunwala took close to his heart, was a lesson in NK. It is true that worries and anxieties become unbearable when personal or corporate goals are highly egoistic. The meaning of 'business running you' is this. Vivekananda's allusion to 'slavery' and 'servant' also means this.

(b) S.M. Dutta, former Chairman, Hindustan Lever Limited, made this remark on 'corporate respect'—

'I feel that earning corporate respect should be the result of combining competition with business ethics. Whenever we lose sight of the need for maintaining this blend, corporates tend to lose respect, though they may win success' (ibid., p. 59).

Thus, Dutta corroborates the distinction drawn above between success and perfection, which is essentially SK versus NK.

(c) On being asked to describe his philosophy of business, Suresh Krishna, Chairman, Sundaram Fasteners Limited, replied—

'I would not play the game of business by trying to conform to the unstable standards of a confused society. I would rather play it by my own permanent standards of integrity and feel good about that. I favour the reputation that is born of ethics plus conservatism' (ibid., p. 45).

Krishna seems to echo the same opinion as Dutta's. He believes that the *conservative temperament helps to maintain integrity* because it mellows aggressive ambition for quick success. This puts a brake on the use of unethical means. His principle seems to be: bear short term pain for the sake of long term gain. This helps in EDM, and brings sobriety to the way an organization is run. He tames SK by the power of NK. His reference to *unstable standards of a confused society* is significant.

(d) Interpreting the death of an Indian business tycoon operating in Singapore, this is what Humayun Dhanrajgir, former Managing Director, Lupin Laboratories, had to say:

'It proves what unlimited desires and greed can ultimately lead to. ... But initial success went into his head and he lost his sense of proportion, his sense of right and wrong waned.... What untold sufferings would he not have inflicted upon himself through his own devious ways!' (ibid., p. 4).

Dhanrajgir's mention of *unlimited desires and greed* reinforces the danger inherent in the one-way approach to work through SK only. He candidly admits that *obsession with success makes one blind to the means adopted*. A man thus possessed loses his sense of prudence and propriety, which impels unethical decisions. High performance is also apparent and short-lived.

Thus, the views expressed by the four CEOs above and three CEOs earlier do not support current mainstream reservations regarding NK. They have all successfully steered their organizations to high levels of economic excellence, and towards laudable reputation. Attempts to adhere to the fundamental principle of NK for effective work performance may not therefore be regarded as utopian. They all indict runaway SK. The practice of NK is a matter of 'conviction' and 'willpower'.

For further inspiration, the words of three personalities outside the orbit of business are now appropriate. The late Bede Griffiths, a British savant, settled in India, made the following observation—

> 'Even work which appears to be good and really is good—for instance the work of a person who cares for the sick…will be *corrupted* if the ego goes into work.' (Griffiths, B., 1983, p. 93)

Thus, even service, if it is ego-driven, loses its intrinsic merit. The true motive becomes not the service of the needy, but service of one's own ego. This is SK.

Rabindranath Tagore had once written—

> 'In the *Gita* we are advised to work *disinterestedly*.…The man who aims at his own *aggrandizement* underrates everything else…This discipline (NK) we have to go through to prepare ourselves for *our social duties*' (Tagore, R., 1996, p. 288).

Tagore also alludes to the idea of 'social duties' like Griffiths does. To discharge these duties effectively he too advocates the principle of NK. The reason: it requires one to look beyond selfish goals and egoistic achievements. Both of them define 'social duties' not from the conventional perspective of 'corporate social responsibility'. The first phrase includes all types of work undertaken by different professionals e.g. a doctor, a manager, a politician, an academic. They all have their respective duties towards society through whatever type of work they do.*

Sri Aurobindo had been emphatic in declaring the following—

> 'Such desireless action can have no decisiveness, no effectiveness, no efficient motive, no large or vigorous creative power? Not so; action done (with NK) is

---

* There are two phrases with opposite meanings: *kamya karma* and *kartavyam karma* The former is nothing but SK. The latter synchronizes with NK. The delight of *kartavyam karma* is lucid and serene. The pleasure of *kamya karma* is complex and dissipative.

not only the *highest*, but the *wisest*, the most potent and *efficient* even for the affairs of the world' (Aurobindo, S., 1977, p. 37).

Aurobindo allays a common apprehension that NK leads to indecisiveness or sloppiness in work. He declares that, by practising it, work can be done more effectively even in the secular sphere.

This inspiration for practising NK from Sri Aurobindo has been fully echoed by Srinivasachari: '*Karma Yoga* has always the three-fold advantage of *naturalness*, *ease* and *efficacy*' (Srinivasachari P.N., op. cit., p. 63). This becomes possible because a *nishkam karmi's* mind is not clouded or burdened with apprehension about immediate success or failure. He can thus work with unwavering confidence and spontaneous assurance.

The world of business may now be revisited. In a letter to Vivekananda (1898) the father of India's industrialization, J.N. Tata had written the following,

> ' I recall these ideas (of the Swami)) in connection with my scheme of a Research Institute of Science for India ... It seems to me that no better use can be made of the *ascetic spirit* than the establishment of monasteries or residential halls for men *dominated by this spirit* ... (who) devote their lives to the cultivation of sciences—natural and humanistic'(Chakraborty, S.K., op. cit., p. 210).

Tata had been able to seize the essence of the principle of NK. He had realized that the *ascetic spirit* (i.e. NK), which curbs the *acquisitive instinct* (i.e. SK), would channelize all energies for the development of sciences (both sacred and secular). He took many concrete steps in putting this philosophy of NK into practice. In fact, JN Tata had requested the Swami to flag off this project by writing a 'fiery pamphlet' about it. We believe that it is the cultivation of the NK mentality which is a sure basis for self-regulation from within. The *Kural* affirms this tenet by referring to the problem of desire which is the core of SK (Kallapiran, T.R., 1995, p. 74):

> 'To be afraid of 'desire' is Righteousness;
> Desire is a snare which leads man to disaster.'

This verse categorically links SK with unethicality.

CONCLUSION
Simple living nourishes deep living, and deep living ensures ethical working. This is a basic message enshrined in all wisdom literature. The modern

zeitgeist has, however, been functioning in the opposite direction: complex living leading to shallow living, and shallow living inducing unethical working. Discussions on NK and SK in this chapter could be set against this panorama. Any fundamental response to accelerating unethicality will depend on which way the leaders of society exercise the choice: NK or SK? There are a few other important theories bearing on NK e.g. the *Guna* theory, the theory of Self, and *pravritti marga* vis-a-vis *nivritti marga*. These themes have not been addressed here. They need separate elaborate treatment. Very briefly, *sattwa guna* (as against *rajo* or *tamo guna*),* the self-contained higher Self (vis-à-vis the deficit-driven lower self), and inward contentment i.e. *nivritti* (against endless external cravings i.e. *pravritti)* would provide the necessary supporting pillars for progressive stabilization of the NK approach in life and work.

Before the chapter ends a few words about the Appendix to follow. The theory, principle and practice of NK have stood the test of time across several millennia right upto the present day. Therefore, its validity and importance do not stand or fall by the support of any kind of quantified information. This apart, the theory of NK does not figure in any curriculum. So, the extent of awareness, not to mention its understanding, is minimal. Therefore, there is widespread misinterpretation about it. Hence, the primary aim here is to generate a greater degree of awareness before it is put into wider practice. It is only after a reasonable period of efforts to apply it by a much wider cross-section of professionals that some statistical studies may be useful. In any case, enough real-life examples have been given above where NK has been practised with strong commitment without waiting for corroboration by statistical figures. Nonetheless, two simple questionnaires were developed based on the authors' field-experience. No claim is made about their technical sophistication. Similarly, the summaries of responses are only indicative of the *general predisposition* or *mental-readiness* for NK prevailing today within a modest sample of Indian respondents. The authors had no role in the choice of respondents, or the organizations to which they belonged. The organizations had either themselves approached the authors, or had sent nominees to the general Workshops open for all, or for

---

* Very briefly, the Universal energy of Nature has three concomitant and inseparable modes or powers equilibrium, kinesis and inertia. The corresponding psychological energies are: *sattwa* as illumined and harmonious understanding, *rajas* as desire-and stress-ful activity, and *tamas* as darkened sloth. *Sattwa* supports spirituality; *rajas* and *tamas* detract from it.

conducting in-house values-workshop. The questionnaires and respective summaries of responses received are presented in the Appendix.

In the light of the above observations and the data, a few specific thoughts may be crystallized below—

(a) Indian professionals tend to be mentally receptive to the principle of NK—almost by instinct as it were.

(b) Systematic exposition of this principle, with examples from various professions, should make it more widely and expressly upheld. Otherwise, although sometimes intellectually understood, NK is commonly treated as too philosophical and impractical.

(c) The suspicion that this principle cannot be practised in industry, in the face of competition, has not been justified by the positive NK examples above.

(d) NK can constitute one of the long-term foundations for sustainable development. The dominance of SK today is rapidly undermining sustainability—both materially and ethically.

(e) The focus has to be on one's own self, instead of readily blaming the system or society. Acknowledging this common human weaknesses in secular pursuits should be the true beginning for EDM and EWP.

(f) It maybe reiterated that NK is a steadfast mental mode during work. It helps to keep the person above conventional and temporary successes and failures. Thus, all the real-life examples of NK given above show that they have practised it more as a matter of conviction than calculation. Moreover, not being overawed by the fear of failure by conventional measures, they have been able to maintain higher standards of ethical decision-making and work-performance.

(g) The expressions *anasakti yoga* or *karmayoga* are also used interchangeably with *nishkam karma*. *Yoga* here means the union of the individual personal intelligence or consciousness with the Supramental, Cosmic Intelligence or Consciousness. The latter is the Universal fountainhead, the former an individual outlet. Spirituality in management, as an end, requires this critical learning. NK is a necessary facilitator for such *yoga*.

APPENDIX*

The following figures come from respondents from the 'defence services' (ranks of Major and above) and 'others' (managers comprising public and private sector enterprises). The questionnaire was distributed in course of cross-company and in-company management development programmes conducted by the authors during the period 1999-2001. In almost all cases authors were present when questionnaires were distributed personally and collected on the spot (293 nos.). Responses so collected are termed as 'Instant Response Data'. For defence personnel, however, replies were sent by mail from the College of Defence Management at Secundrabad (2001-2).

Thus, a total of four hundred and twenty six (N=426) responses were collected between October, 1999 to March, 2002. The questionnaire consisted of twenty-six items against which respondents were expected to tick either NK or SK. The definitions of the two phrases, NK and SK, as cited above, were provided to the respondents. Even though the authors were personally present in several cases, they did not entertain any queries about the questionnaire. Respondents were allowed to exercise their own judgment. After collecting the responses, the questionnaire items were segregated into five clusters of allied questions which indicated a particular contextual aspect of work-performance.

Table 1 presents the summarized figures of the five clusters.

TABLE 1: INSTANT RESPONSE DATA

Cluster	Total (N=426)		Defence Services (N=133)		Others (N=293)	
	NK(%)	SK(%)	NK(%)	SK(%)	NK(%)	SK(%)
(a) Scope –Universal or Local	75	25	73	27	75	25
(b) Effectiveness in workplace	68	32	67	33	70	30
(c) Secular character of work	39	61	58	42	42	58
(d) Sacred character of work	77	23	77	23	77	23
(e) Leadership	84	16	82	18	88	12
Average of all clusters	**69**	**31**	**71**	**29**	**70**	**30**

* The matter in this appendix has been abridged from *Leadership and Motivation* by these authors.(New Delhi: Rupa, 2004, pp. 248-65).

Of the five clusters, only cluster (c) on 'secular character of work' shows a marked departure from responses to the other clusters. As against the responses to other clusters, which are around 75 per cent in favour of NK, cluster (c) shows only 39 per cent. Some of the components of this cluster are target consciousness, productivity, ambition, competitive spirit etc. A probable explanation for the reversal of trend in this cluster is that the conventional mental conditioning of most people tends to be such that they believe secular objectives can be achieved only through SK.

There is also substantial difference in response pattern between the managerial and the defence personnel. The principal reason for such difference could be the nature of work. In the defence services the personnel are in principle educated and trained for *a self-sacrificing outlook* in defending the integrity of their country. But, in industry the virtue of self-sacrifice does not receive much attention. It is almost wholly self-oriented and career-centric.

The pattern of response for the other four clusters shows only minor differences. Thus, very small differences occur between the responses of the two sample sub-groups in respect of clusters A and D. For both of them responses favouring NK is almost 75 per cent each. Thus, the high level of *mental readiness* of professionals regarding the relevance of NK in workplace is encouraging. Cluster B responses in respect of NK appear to be relatively the most subdued among the four clusters. Still, a 68 per cent favourable NK response for N=426 is appreciable.

Cluster-E on 'Leadership' shows the highest favourable response for NK i.e. 84 per cent. The responses in favour of the two sub-groups on 'Leadership' is 82 per cent and 88 per cent respectively. Although the difference between these two sub-groups is not much, yet it is a bit intriguing. One would have expected the 'defence services' to show greater affinity towards NK, compared to 'others'. Here it is the reverse.

However, as already said, one need not labour to read too much into the figures presented above. The intention is to get some overall feel of the instinctive mental readiness among Indian professionals towards NK. This should be a *culturally-congruent indicator*.

Next, the opinions of those respondents who had attended specific in-company Workshops on Values during 1990-92, and were given some time (2 to 4 months) to *internalize the attitude*, are presented. This set of information has been described here as 'Lagged Response Data (Table 2).' The questionnaire used for this purpose is also given. Figures from this set allow us to compare the pattern of responses between two different groups. Respondents in the previous sample (N=426) got only the bare definition of the principle before responding. The sample members below, however, had received *enough conceptual exposition* as well as reasonable time to assimilate the NK principle, along with several other inputs on values and ethics.

TABLE 2: LAGGED RESPONSE DATA

Companies	Very Good %	Good %	No Change %	Bad %	Respondents (Total: 536)
(1) Godrej and Boyce	20	57	23	00	61
(2) Indian Oil Corporation (IOC)	16	48	28	00	64
(3) Bharat Electronics (BEL)	9	54.50	36.50	00	11
(4) Others (combined) (RBI, TELCO, BHEL Bhilwara Group, IPCL etc.)	20	48.80	31.20	1	400

The above response patterns from some well-known organizations show that NK is on the whole deemed to be conducive to EWP. Half of the respondents from each organization feel that the idea of 'work for work's sake', or 'duty for duty's sake' is 'good' for organizational health. A little more than two-third of the respondents for all the subsets in Table 2 have agreed that the practice of NK has had 'very good/good' effects. It is noteworthy that only one out of N=536 respondents felt NK to be 'bad' for EWP. This fundamental trend of responses may act as an impetus for detailed empirical studies. However, such studies could be more appropriately done through anecdotal and qualitative investigations. Quantified statistical analysis, although attractive for the 'left brain', will not add to or detract anything from the intrinsic worth of NK. Of course, meanwhile its actual practice should spread more widely through systematic management education programmes as mentioned earlier.

QUESTIONNAIRE 1 (for Table 1)
Questionnaire on Two Approaches to Work-Motivation

	Cluster	(Circle any one)
1. Valid as a universal principle	A	NK or SK?
2. Efficiency in work-performance	B	SK or NK?
3. Freedom from tension and anxiety	D	NK or SK?
4. High target consciousness in work	C	SK or NK?
5. Ethics in the work-place	B	NK or SK?
6. Effectiveness in work-performance	B	SK or NK?
7. Healthy work-relationships with others	B	NK or SK?
8. Practical feasibility	B	SK or NK?
9. Harmony within the team	B	NK or SK?
10. Decline in productivity	C	SK or NK?
11. Promotion of quality consciousness	D	NK or SK?
12. In tune with work done by Nature e.g. a tree, a flower, a bee, the sun, etc.	A	SK or NK?
13. Loss of ambition to succeed	C	NK or SK?
14. Gaining perfection in work	D	SK or NK?
15. Meaningfulness in work	D	NK or SK?
16. Covers every kind of work situation	A	SK or NK?
17. Relevant for sadhus (monks)	A	NK or SK?
18. Relevant for householders	A	SK or NK?
19. Worship of God through work	D	NK or SK?
20. Worship of ego through work	C	SK or NK?
21. Need for systematic education and training	E	NK or SK?
22. Contribution to inspiring leadership	E	SK or NK?
23. Competitive spirit needed for excellent performance	C	NK or SK?
24. Greater relevance for a materially poor country like India	E	SK or NK?
25. Regular praise for work-performance is important	C	NK or SK?
26. Spiritual satisfaction in work	D	SK or NK?

Name (in capital letters):

Designation:

Organisation:

QUESTIONNAIRE 2 (for Table 2)
Managerial Effectiveness and Values Systems Questionnaire

S. No.	Abridged	V. Good	Good	No Change	Bad
1.	Personal health				
2.	Domestic life				
3.	Boss relationship				
4.	Colleague relationship				
5.	Subordinate relationship				
6.	Ethical sensitivity				
7.	Coping with frustration, etc.				
8.	Introspection ability				
9.	Work for work's sake				
10.	Creative thinking				
11.	Encouragement from boss regarding ideas of values-system courses				

Crumbling Values and Ethics
What Scientists See and Say?

There are some indications, even if hesitant, that education in values is necessary to pre-empt the collapse of an individual's psychological stamina, and the rupture of the social fabric due to an unsustainably fast pace of life forced upon mankind. So, we are pressed to ask: What is human values education? As mentioned in the earlier pages, such education must fuse the *sacred* with the *secular* pursuits of life. It also implies the acceptance of the priority of the former over the latter. In other words, education for spiritual unfoldment should proceed one step *ahead* of fostering scientific temperament.

Thus, the Radhakrishnan Commission on Education had advised the nation, way back in 1949 (S.K. Chakraborty, 2006, p. 30):

- 'If we exclude spiritual training from our institutions we would be untrue to our whole civilization.'
- 'All educational institutions should start work with a few minutes of silent meditation.'

However, post-1950 secular India chose to dismiss such counsels.

In India, efforts to understand and bridge this gap between spirituality and science got due attention from a number of contemporary Indian 'spiritual scientists' like Tagore (Tagore, R., 2002, pp. 43–82, 119–62), Vivekananda (Vivekananda, Swami, 1962, pp. 1, 33, 62–82), Gandhiji (Gandhi, M., 2001, Vol. III, pp. 3–30), Aurobindo (Aurobindo, Sri, 1985, pp. 70–3, 87–93, 145–6), Coomaraswamy (Coomaraswamy, A., 1989, pp. 4–8), Radhakrishnan (Radhakrishnan, S., 1967, pp. 9–12, 15–25, 39–41) and their ilk. Their thoughts on this subject (1890-1960) could fill up several pages of this chapter. But the educated Indian mind generally being what it

is, we have, for the sake of objective appraisal of the real issues, drawn
upon some renowned scientists (mostly from the West). Their searching
introspection, which usually escapes general discussions in the field, has
been briefly captured below.

SCIENCE—WHAT IS IN IT FOR US?

Indebtedness of humanity to science and technology also called 'sci-tech',
(Chakraborty, S.K., 2003, pp. 186–91) can hardly be ignored. It has made
our external lives physically comfortable and attractive. As Roger Penrose
has put it (Penrose, R., 1995, p. 9):

> '...technology...has given us our modern society, with its comforts, its
> considerable freedom from...disease and need, and with its vast opportunities
> for intellectual and aesthetic expansion, and for mind-broadening global
> communication.'

Technology, which applies scientific knowledge for utilitarian purposes, has
for example increased our average life-span through the invention of life-
saving drugs. Today in a country like India, a CTV or a refrigerator is no
longer considered a luxury. An average urban household without either of
these will feel relatively crippled.

A revolution of sorts is taking place in the field of wireless telephony
too. The rapidity with which communication media are evolving is startling.

With the advent of PCs, huge volumes of data can be mined and processed
within seconds. This has multiplied the rate of data generation, often
enabling speedy decision-making.

Today sci-tech has made cloning a reality. Days are probably not far when
human beings will be cloned as well. Nanotechnology promises to
revolutionize the way we live by selling its marvels. All these advancements,
and many more, have seriously challenged the supremacy of Nature over
man.

However, on the other side of the coin some of the alarming facts of
modern existence also cannot be ignored. For instance—

(a) Before September 11, 2001 a devotee could enter the premises of the
Kali Temple at Dakshineswar (near Kolkata) without hindrance through
the main archway. However, after the catastrophe that took place on
that day, the situation has changed once and for all. At the entrance a
visitor is now made to stand in queue. He is frisked by armed security

personnel. Inside the temple premises too, surveillance cameras and security guards keep a close watch on all visitors. All the entry points to the Kashi Vishwanath temple at Varanasi look like gateways into an armed fort—far more elaborate than at Dakshineshwar. Thus, at an existential level we are more panicky and fearful than ever before. Natural simplicity and trust now stand replaced with technological complexity, coupled with mounting threat and fear.

(b) A few MNCs develop and distribute genetically-modified seeds. Once the farmers buy such seeds, which promise higher yield and better pest resistant capabilities, they cannot preserve the seeds of those crops for utilization in the next season. They have to go to those very MNCs once again for the procurement of seeds because they are patented. If any farmer violates this condition, even inadvertently, he has to compensate the concerned MNC, or else is dragged to the court. The MNCs justify their stance by claiming that since they had invested millions to develop those seeds, it is legitimate for them to recover the expenditure by applying such conditions. Thus, the alliance between technology and business seems to be hyper-creative in throwing all human values to the winds.

(c) Another illustration of the misuse of science by man is provided by nuclear technology. When scientists first achieved nuclear fission in a lab, it was hailed as a development that would help meet all the energy needs of the world in the foreseable future. Today, nuclear energy constitutes a tiny fraction of all the power generated in the world. But there are enough nuclear weapons to destroy this planet several times over. This negates the claim of sci-tech to be holistically beneficial.

(d) Among the pernicious instances of dis-values (DV), fuelled by sci-tech, is what a woman author, DL Spar, has felt compelled to call 'the baby business'. 'Advances in reproductive medicine have indeed created a market for babies'—she writes (Spar, D.L., 2006, pp. XI–XIII).

SCI-TECH CRITIQUED
As mentioned earlier, etymological root of the term 'sci' is 'to split'. Thus, science belongs to that field of study where knowledge is acquired through *analysis* of sensually observable events and measurable entities. By implication, science is not concerned with anything sensually unobservable or non-measurable. Thus, values and morality, which belong to the domain of feelings and character, are ignored in the pursuit of sci-tech. This folly has not escaped some of the best scientists, particularly physicists. Among

them two categories of views are available. One belongs to the category of intellectual writings on or about science in relation to religion or God. We cite below two examples of this category, from Hawking and Davies in that order:

(a) 'If we discover a complete theory, it should in time be understandable in broad principle by everyone, not just a few scientists. Then we shall all...take part in the discussion of the question of why it is that we and universe exist. If we find the answer to that, it would be the ultimate triumph of human reason—for then we would know the mind of God.' (Hawking, S., 2005, p. 142)

(b) 'So far in this philosophical excursion I have been largely concerned with logical reasoning. ... the arguments are only a signpost for the existence of a necessary being. This being remains shadowy and abstract.' (Davies, P., 1992, p. 193)

The paramount question is this: is it possible to know the mind or nature of God when, in the first place, the vast majority of human beings possess little command over the obstinate contaminations and deficiencies of their own mind? Many leading figures of sci-tech are no exception. More importantly, is it going to make human life more moral and peaceful even if the mind of God were to be one day successfully unravelled. Besides, can a one-litre bottle hold ten litres; can the river hold the sea? Another ignorance is imbedded in the second question: logical reasoning leads the author to the suggestion that God is shadowy and abstract. In that case this Being cannot have a moral or ethical dimension. But it is a settled fact of spiritual experience that God is much more intensely concrete than sensual, material realities. Because human beings can enter into deep communion with such God-consciousness, ethics, values and morals have a secure basis. Hence, left-brain intellectualism alone, however brilliant but without perception and realization, cannot contribute to holistic human education.

However, there is a more significant category of thoughts from both (a) physical scientists of the highest standing, and also (b) a few social scientists who possess a penetrating grasp of socio-psychological dynamics. Such thoughts will now be gleaned at some length.

(A) PHYSICAL SCIENTISTS
(i) *Albert Einstein* (Nobel Laureate, Physics):
We may begin by listening to a few thoughts of Einstein (1953).

- '...a positive aspiration and effort for an ethico-moral configuration of our common life is of over riding importance. Here no science can help us. I believe, indeed, that overemphasis on the purely intellectual attitude, often directed solely to the practical and factual, in our education, has led directly to the impairment of ethical values' (Einstein, A., 2003, p. 53).
- 'Fulfillment on the moral and aesthetic side is a goal which lies closer to the preoccupations of art than it does to those of science' (ibid, p. 53).

Einstein, who has been hailed as the greatest scientist of the 20th century, clearly states that the 'ethico-moral configuration' of our lives is the most important aspect of education. But he adds further that science, in its overvaluation of facts and numbers, undervalues the significance of values (i.e. human values). Therefore, he advocates the study of arts (drawing, music, painting etc.) to make-up for the general neglect of learning about and for values and ethicality.

(ii) *Werner Heisenberg* (Nobel Laureate, Physics):
Heisenberg admitted (in 1985) that technical advances have created new ethical problems, and therefore asserts that 'all too rational arguments' from science can do little to resolve these problems (quoted by Ken Wilber, *Quantum* Questions, 1985, p. 43). He displays clarity of thought and humility about the limitation of scientific rationality for the deeper issues of life. Science does not possess a holistic perspective on life because of its inevitably fragmented approach by insisting upon measurement. Normative aspects get sidelined.

(iii) *David Bohm* (Nobel Laureate, Theoretical Physics):
Bohm (in 1987) had further clarified the issue of fragmented approach in science—

- '... there has been an overall fragmentation in our general attitude to reality. This leads us to focus always on particular problems, even when they are significantly related to a broader context.' (Bohm, D., 1987, p. 12)
- '... in an age in which science is taken to be the key to increasing progress and the betterment of life, this fragmentary approach can never resolve the deeper problems which now face our world.' (Ibid., p. 15)

The gist of what Bohm suggests is that the whole cannot be understood by understanding the parts (fragments). Aggregation cannot restore the vision of the whole. He also believes that although the rate of material progress is measured in terms of scientific advancement, yet one has to admit that the deeper non-material issues still remain unsolved by it. And the latter are by no means immaterial.

(iv) *Erwin Schroedinger* (Nobel Laureate, Physics):
Schroedinger, too, reiterated a similar view as held by his compatriots Einstein and Heisenberg—

- 'The scientific picture of the real world around me is very deficient. It gives a lot of factual information, puts all our experience in a magnificently consistent order, but it ... knows nothing of beautiful and ugly, good or bad, God and eternity.' (*Quantum Questions*, op. cit., p. 180)

He admits that a world view defined only in terms of facts and figures, and their brilliant analyses is deficient. In the midst of hard data there is no place for the cultivation of *normative ideals*, the soft core of human existence.

(v) *Max Planck* (Nobel Laureate, Physics):
Planck, who is the father of Quantum Physics, expresses the following views—

- 'Even the choicest mathematical speculations melt into thin air, unless substantiated by definite facts of experience.' (Quoted in *Reason, Science and Shastras* edited by N.R. Sengupta, 2003, p. 38)
- '... a careful study of the views and ideas of our great philosophers might prove extremely valuable. A feeling of doubt persists whether the new theory of the structure of the physical world, with all its radical innovations, is really on the right path.' (Ibid., p. 38)

There is enough similarity between the observations of Schroedinger and Planck. Planck feels that scientific postulates are not beyond doubt, unless validated by the *experiences* of life which are subject to the interplay of values.

(vi) *John Eccles* (Nobel Laureate, Neuro-Science):
Here are some confessions shared in 1977 by a non-physicist—

- 'In short, the public was led to believe that science could and would...solve all the problems of mankind...The marvels of scientific technology provided assurance for this faith in the promised scientific utopia...We scientists should have been more modest in our claims.' (Eccles, J., 1977, Vol. I, p. 14)

Eccles has been forthright to indicate the need to tone down the overconfidence of science in solving the problems of mankind with the aid of technology alone. Instead, he laments that 'man has lost his way in this age'. He also feels that science has gone too far in breaking down man's belief in his spiritual greatness.

(vii) *Maurice Wilkins* (Nobel Laureate, Bio-science):
Wilkins had aired similar sentiments in 1985.

* 'The whole question of moral, spiritual and other dimensions is pushed out of science normally. So it is something to do with the nature of science that leads people towards destruction.' (Quoted in *Interviews With Nobel Laureates and Other Eminent Scholars*, 1986, p. 37)

Wilkins re-emphasizes that the *subjective aspects* of an individual's life, and that of his community, do not figure in course of scientific investigation. So, primarily the objective goal of material acquisition is pursued. In order to fulfill various short-term egoistic desires he often ends up by inventing devices which could lead to destruction in the long-term.

(viii) *J. Weizenbaum* (former Professor, Department of Computer Sciences at MIT):
Weizenbaum, who had made major contributions to the field of Artificial Intelligence, made the following observations in 1985—

* 'Big science today has characteristics very much like that of any other big business—huge administrative apparatus, enormously expensive overheads and so on. And that has caused a lack of self-examination in science' (ibid., p. 83).
* 'I am sad to say that if at all we look for an aspect of human nature that comes most into play in modern science, it is greed—the need to be funded, the need for promotions, and so on' (ibid., p. 83).

The reflections of Weizenbaum hit the core. He has been bold enough to admit that the biggest casualty of a business-like approach to science has been *self-examination*. He feels that it is the business-like mentality of return on investment in sci-tech that gets priority over *introspection* related to values and ethics. Therefore, the duty of assessing the consequences of sci-tech innovations is avoided, for example the injudicious, even harmful, use of cell phones and internet by their possessors.

(ix) *Alexis Carrel* (Nobel Laureate, Medical Science):
Carrel, a distinguished French surgeon, had remarked in 1935 that—

- 'It is quite evident that the accomplishments of all the sciences having man as an object remain insufficient and that our knowledge of ourselves is still most rudimentary' (Carrel, A., 1961, p. 19).

Carrel humbly concedes that so long as the study of mind (the seat of values) is not brought within the ambit of medical sciences, knowledge about humans will remain inadequate.

Summing up the forthright and transparent observations of some of the leading physical and other scientists of the 20th century, the following points of *principle* emerge:

(a) The speed of technological innovations has left the scientific community with little time for self-examination. This is because often *selfish interests* provide fuel for sci-tech investigations.

(b) Many leading scientists feel that science needs to be modest in claiming to solve human problems. It is a matter of common knowledge that alongside tremendous advances in the field of sci-tech, deterioration of moral standards in every walk of life is worrisome. In other words, there appears to be a *negative co-relation* between scientific and ethical progress. In fact, sci-tech is often a part of the problem itself.

(c) The contribution of sci-tech towards improvement of, or being even neutral to, the quality of *inner life* will be zero. A *conscious attempt* has to be made at the individual level to assimilate the secrets of existential ideals. For example, what is the deeper meaning of daily living? Does life make sense? Does the cosmic drama have a purpose? Science grapples with rational meanings in certain limited material aspects; on vast existential meanings it is mute. As Willis Harman, former President of Institute of Noetic Sciences, observes:

'Modern industrial society appears to be extraordinarily confused about values. With ever-increasing technological 'know-how', it seems to be most unsure of what is ultimately worth doing' (Quoted in *Physics and Beyond*,1986, p. 36).

(d) Business and commercial extensions of sci-tech have been systematically thriving on human *greed.*

It is fitting to mention here that all the misgivings and cautions about sci-tech aired by the scientists above had been voiced (in the 1920's) in exquisite mystic-spiritual language by the sage-poet-philosopher, Rabindranath Tagore—

- 'Science deals with (the) element of sameness ... Science does this by eliminating from its field of research the *personality* of creation and fixing its attention only upon the *medium* of creation' (Tagore, R., 2002, p. 58).
- 'An inquisitive mouse may gnaw through the wooden frame of a piano, may cut all the strings to pieces, and yet travel farther and farther away from the music. This is the pursuit of the finite for its own sake' (ibid., p. 61).

(B) Social Scientists

Part (A) has focused on physical scientists who had the humility to evaluate the 'hard' aspects of sci-tech in relation to the 'soft' aspects of human life. (B) concentrates on a few social scientists who scrutinize the social aspects of sci-tech and their impact on values.

(i) *Bertrand Russell* (Nobel Laureate, Mathematics-Philosophy)—
With a long career as an activist for world peace, Russell had made these observations in 1927:

- 'I am compelled to fear that science will be used to promote the power of dominant groups, rather than make man happy' (Russell, B., 1927, p. 5).
- 'I shall confine myself almost wholly to the effect of science in enabling us to gratify our passions more freely...' (ibid., p. 7).

Although the sharp words of Russell transmit a tone of pessimism, yet current facts prove him to be correct. Thus, countries which are technologically most advanced also have the biggest arsenal of weapons for mass destruction. This engenders a spiralling sense of fear and insecurity in the world. This apart, technological wonders like mobiles, internet, credit cards etc. are exploiting human propensity for excitement and greed. Newspapers and magazines are replete with such reports and messages. The cumulative effect of all this has been steady decrement in the corpus of human happiness and peace. Technology may be values-neutral. But the human agent using it is certainly not.

(ii) *Aldous Huxley* (Philosophy and Literature):
Huxley, who believed in changing the individual through mystical enlightenment, had shared the following thoughts in 1946—

- 'Physical noise, mental noise and noise of desire—we hold history's record for all of them. And no wonder, for all the resources of our almost miraculous technology have been thrown into the current assault against silence' (Huxley, A., 1994, p. 260).
- '...the end of human life is contemplation,...a society is good to the extent that it renders contemplation possible for its members;...(in) our own time, it goes without saying, that the end of human life is action; that contemplation is the means to that end; that a society is good to the extent that the actions of its members make for progress in technology...'(ibid., p. 355).

There is remarkable coincidence between the views of Weizenbaum and Huxley. Although they represent two different streams of science, yet they feel in common that one of the biggest casualties of sci-tech in our times has been 'lack of silence', and absence of 'self-examination'. An unavoidable outcome of this is that methodical contemplation is often regarded as vegetative wastage of time. As a result, 'doers' are no longer 'seers', nor even 'thinkers'. According to Quinn's Gorilla-the-Guru, the world is thus left at the mercy of man-the-taker 'who introduced disorder into the world.' (Daniel Quinn, *Ishmael*, Bantam, New York, 1993, p. 145)

(iii) *Radha Kamal Mukherjee* (Sociologist, former Vice Chancellor, University of Lucknow):
Mukherjee, who has been one of the early leading sociologists of our country, had echoed a similar view in 1964—

- 'The more the tempo of life and work is quickened and organic periodicities nullified by the industrial system, the more are there mental tension, irritation and anxiety and the poorer become the qualities of human ideas and feelings... he is seriously hindered in contemplation and imagination...(for) completing himself' (Mukerjee, R.K., 1964, p. V).

He adds a qualitative dimension to the problem of mental noise. He feels that due to mental agitation associated with tension and anxiety, cultivation of human values gets a back seat. Ability to centripetalize and contemplate is a pre-requisite for such qualities to sprout and take root. The 24-hour society syndrome of today, and its problems, had been correctly anticipated by Mukerjee more than four decades ago.

(iv) *Pitrim Sorokin* (Sociologist, Harvard University):
Sorokin, probably the most widely translated sociologist, had cautioned us about the following in 1958—

- 'Science and technology have created not only beneficial inventions but also the most destructive devices for mass murder and for the extermination of cultural values. The fruits of science and technology have invariably been misused' (Sorokin, P., 1962, p. 43).
- 'The widely accepted opinion that science, technology and education invariably exert only moral, pacific and socially ennobling effects is a sheer myth. The highly dangerous, anti-social effect of misapplied science and technology is now evident to everyone' (ibid., p. 46).

Of all the commentators reflecting on sci-tech and values, Sorokin appears most forthright. Although he agrees that science and technology have created beneficial inventions, yet he minces no words in admitting that the fruits of such inventions have been mostly misapplied, including the demolition of cultural values.* He also challenges the 'myth' that progress in the field of sci-tech will automatically make us good human beings. This argument echoes the phrase 'scientific utopia' used by Eccles.

(v) *Arnold Toynbee* (Historian, London University):
Toynbee, a contemporary of Sorokin, was one of the most celebrated historians of the 20th century. Some of his thoughts (1976) on sci-tech and its consequences are as follows:

- 'The enormous subsequent advance of science has been superfluous for the purpose of survival, and it may actually end in the self-destruction of mankind' (Toynbee, A. 1987, p. 35).
- 'Modern scientific-technological civilization has given virtually free rein to human greed—it is in fact a product of liberated material greed...' (ibid., p. 38).

---

* The grim reality of today: Invention is the Mother of Necessity! 'We have invented such-and-much. You must jolly well buy them! We will see to it that you need it!'

The term 'superfluous' used by Toynbee is significant. It challenges the opium of 'endless progress' peddled by the commercialized guardians of the world. He also feels that mankind can still live decently without many of these inventions. He warns about the environmental backlash due to 'material greed' getting the better of moral restraint. Blind sci-tech does not know where and when to stop.

(vi) *Huston Smith* (Professor of Philosophy, University of Syracuse):
Smith, a major contemporary American scholar of philosophy and society, had made these penetrating comments in 1976—

- 'Science can deal with values descriptively but not prescriptively. It can tell us what men *do* prize, but not what they *should* prize' (Smith, H., 1976, p. 15).
- 'Science itself is meaningful from beginning to end, but on certain kinds of meanings, ones that are existential and global—it is silent' (ibid., p. 15).

Smith argues that science cannot occupy the position of a judge. Judgement is the sole prerogative of values (feelings). This underlines the importance of cultivation of human values (HVs) through integrated values education. Having acknowledged the worth of science in its own sphere, he draws specific attention (like Einstein, Bohm, Schroedinger, Carrel, etc.) to its limitations in the sphere of existential issues.

All the social scientists quoted above echo identical reservations about sci-tech, and its consequential effects on human values. There is thus a complete convergence between their assessments and those of the physical scientists quoted in part (A). In terms of principles, both sets of authorities have been able to go *beyond the orbit* of facile, conventional addiction to sci-tech. The consequent honest and objective appraisal of the fragmentary or non-holistic after-effects of numerous sci-tech mis-hits is salutary. They have displayed intuitive, integral perception of a wide spectrum of life's circumstances (both internal and external). They have refused to confine their sights to the immediate glitter of inventions. Recovery of such a wise outlook on a wider scale is possible only by adopting an authentic and painstaking approach towards human values education. In this regard another issue needs to be sorted out.

A QUESTION OF PRIORITY
In some quarters nowadays a blend of scientific pursuits with some kind of spiritual discipline is suggested. But all this appears to be either a reluctant

concession or vaguely platitudinous. The Indian Constitution, however, emphasizes exclusively on the duty to cultivate the 'scientific temper'. Those who support a blend of the two tempers, also do not appear to be clear or frank about the desirable direction of movement from one class of temper towards another. However, it is submitted here that dodging will not do. The issue of priority has to be faced squarely and sorted out carefully if spirituality in management is not to become yet another hoax. For this purpose the opinions of those very scientists and thinkers, who have already been referred to in earlier sections, may be sought again.

(i) J. Weizenbaum
'I only hope that our present predicaments will lend us the desperation and inspiration to look at the first and last source of knowledge—*ancient knowledge*' (*Interviews With Nobel Laureates and Other Eminent Scholars*, op. cit., p. 88).

(ii) A. Einstein
'... (the) spring of moral action is that which is left to *religion* ... (it) forms an important part of education' (Einstein, A., op. cit., p. 54).

(iii) A. Toynbee
'In order to save mankind from the consequences of technology inspired by greed, I believe that we need worldwide cooperation among the adherents of all *religions and philosophies*. I hope that Hindus, Buddhists and Shintoists will take the initiative in this' (Toynbee, A., op. cit., p. 85).

(iv) A. Huxley
'We cannot act rightly and effectively unless we are in the habit of laying ourselves open to *leadings of the divine Nature* of things. We must draw in the goods of eternity in order to be able to give out the goods of time' (Huxley, A., op. cit., p. 41).

(v) Roger Sperry (Nobel Laureate, physiology and medicine)
'Instead of renouncing or ignoring consciousness, the new interpretation gives full recognition to the *primacy of inner conscious awareness* as a causal reality' (Quoted in *Physics and Beyond*, 1986, p. 26).

(vi) Huston Smith
'The wave of the future will be a *return to the past*' (Smith, H., op. cit. p. 145).

(vii) *Pitirim Sorokin*

'The values of *Karma*, *Bhakti*, and *Jnana* ... represent the highest peaks of creativity, all ennobling man morally, enlightening him mentally, and elevating him aesthetically' (Sorokin, P., op. cit., p. 67).

(viii) *Bede Griffiths:* (A former Oxford University scholar of Comparative Literature, later lived in India as a Benedictine monk for more than three decades.)

In his view modern sci-tech has by its marvels turned away the focus of man from higher Self towards Nature and his ego. The remedy is to conduct a return journey from the ego to the *Self which is Eternal* (Griffiths, B., 1976, p. 58).

(ix) *Werner Heisenberg*

Heisenberg had coined a phrase 'spiritual pattern' a community which, he argued, promises to uncover the whole and the wider network of interrelations. And he felt that it was in such a community that questions about values are first decided (*Quantum Questions*, op. cit., p. 41).

There is remarkable consistency insofar as the statements of Weizenbaum, Huxley, Smith and Sorokin are concerned. All of them are unanimous that to avert the probable destruction of mankind and environment due to over-application or misapplication of sci-tech, scientists and technologists need to educate themselves about the *ancient eternal wisdom*. This may prompt them to ask some of the fundamental questions about existence: what is the mission of our life? What is the true source of happiness? What is the meaning of progress?

It is relevant to observe here that Chakraborty has used the phrase '*sacro-secular symbiosis*' [3S] (Chakraborty, S.K., 1991, pp. 176–7) in viewing life. This carries the implication of giving *priority* to the sacred for proper guidance of the secular. It does not speak vaguely about some nebulous blend between the scientific and the spiritual tempers. This 3S formulation matches quite well with the thoughts of the scientists and thinkers quoted above. The remark of Sperry on the issue of prioritization is quite categorical. It may be recalled that Einstein too had advocated the study and appreciation of art. Art being creative, enriches itself through the synthesis of different ideas and thoughts. It should not avoid exploring issues related to values, morality and spirituality, however much uncomfortable they may appear. Here Rabindranath Tagore is worth listening to: (*Personality*, New Delhi, Rupa, 2002, p. 15)

'There is the world of science from which the elements of personality have been removed. We must not touch it with our feelings. But there is also the vast world which is personal to us. We must not merely know it...but we must feel it...'

Art is born then.

On the question of the immense power wielded by sci-tech on the educational process, Wiezenbaum has it right:

'Scientists as a group are not elected by anyone. And they don't, in any political sense, report back to a constituency. For so much power to be with a group which essentially represents itself is, on the face of it, very dangerous and raises some serious moral problems.' (*Interviews With Nobel Laureates and Other Eminent Scholars*, op. cit., p. 80)

One of the ways to counteract such consequences would be to once again draw inspiration from *ancient verities*. For example, recently the socialist Chinese government had recommended the country to draw nourishment for values like trust, nobility, dignity, patriotism etc. from Confucianism and Buddhism. This would contribute better towards a brighter economic and political future also ('China Visit: Return To Traditional Values' in *The Statesman*, 5 December 1996). Otherwise, secular power alone, magnified by sci-tech, will accelerate fragmented and incoherent changes. And all such short-sighted actions shall cumulatively militate against individual happiness and world peace.

The *shastras* (sacred texts of Bharatvarsha) had revealed long ago the catch implicit in what passes for 'scientific temper' in popular discourse. They had employed the telling metaphor, 'magic-Magician', to point out the fundamental limitation of physical or material sciences. It borders on the mesmeric impact of the incredible magic show of Nature, which casts so much of a spell on the audience that everyone forgets the Magician. Denial of God or the Supreme, the un-created Creator of all that Nature is amounts to rejecting the Magician while revelling in his magical feats. More simply, it is to look at this book, handle it, but deny there are authors behind it. The spiritual artists of ancient Bharatvarsha had, however, spent millennia for knowing the Magician, inside–out. They dared to discover and realize the uncaused causal basis of all that is *vyakta* and *avyakta* (manifest and unmanifest), *khanda* and *akhanda* (part and whole), *chintya* and *achintya* (thinkable and non-thinkable), *vyavaharik* and *paramarthik* (temporal and eternal). And the long-term, total view of Bharat's unpoliticised history corroborates the proverb: the proof of the pudding lies in its eating. The leading edge of Western ethos was given by the Greece—'measurement'. Modern science has been pursuing it to the hilt. The result is a groaining globe. The leading edge of Bharatiya ethos has been, on the other hand, the 'immeasurable', the 'non-measurable'. Its planetary consequences have been *low greed-low need*, and hence, thoroughly sustainable. Which then is the *saving science*: secular science of the measurable, or the spiritual art of the immeasurable/non-measurable? The question of priority cannot be dodged.

BACK TO THE HOME GROUND

The foregoing discussions clearly show that many scientist-savants have been capable of profound understanding and introspection. They share a remarkable degree of consistency. They have not been shy to accept that the *jugalbandi* of science and technology alone shall fail to foster human values for a happy and secure world. Therefore, they have unequivocally supported the conscious culture of *moral principles rooted in religion*. Only such sacred education can insure us against ego-aggrandizing economic and ecological crimes. In practice this can be achieved through:

• personal discipline to imbibe human values;
• guidance from a teacher or mentor (in person, or through biographies/ autobiographies) who has personally progressed in guiding his own scientific temper and character through spiritual discipline.

That scientific temper does not clash with spiritual pursuit can be illustrated through a few testaments from the life of Acharya Prafulla Chandra Ray. As a world-class scientist of early years, he can be an inspiring role model for integrated education. PC Ray is known as the father of the Indian Chemical and Phramaceutical Industry. He was a D.Sc. from the University of Edinburgh, the inventor of mercuric oxide, a professor of Chemistry at the Presidency College, Kolkata, and an entrepreneur who had established the Bengal Chemical and Pharmaceutical Works in 1892.* The company is still doing reasonably well. It is interesting to know how he could direct his scientific bent of mind towards socially responsible scientific experiments:

---

* Chapter 10 devotes more space to him.

'In response to a growing surge of nationalism from within, he decided to utilize the thousand and one raw products which Nature in her bounty had bestowed on the land. His mind was ruffled over the problem of how to provide sustenance to ill-fed young men of the middle class.' (Chakraborty, S.K. and D. Chakraborty, 2006, p. 4)

We thus see how compassion and patriotism, which are human values, coupled with his scientific temperament, had led to socially beneficial outcomes. Surely, the manufacturing of chemicals for personal use and industrial purposes through renewable resources would not have been termed superfluous by Toynbee. More inspiring has been PC Ray's approach to work. A few excerpts from his autobiography are quoted—

- 'All through my varied activities I felt the force of the saying:
    Tvaya Hrishikesha Hridisthitena
    Yatha niyuktohosmi tatha karomi–
  O! Lord, be Thou seated in my heart, and guide me in Thy appointed work.
  I commit myself to Thee, O Lord! Make me Thy agent' (Ibid., p. 6).
- 'The writer lacks the essentials of a successful industrialist or businessman, as he has always realized the force of the saying,
    Artha anartha bhavaya nityam –
  Love of money is the root of all evil' (ibid., p. 6).

Commemorating his 70th birthday (1932), the-then Secretary of the Indian Science Congress, Donnan, had described Ray as the St. Francis of Indian science. He said that Ray epitomized the two greatest virtues of leaders in Indian history since the Buddha—*modesty* and *devotion*. (Ibid., p. 6)

This reminds us of Eccles' comment that the scientists need to be modest in their claims. Such a mentality, as the working philosophy of PC Ray demonstrates, is most likely to be achieved through some spiritual discipline. It is only then that integrated values education will begin to make sense and become practical. Obviously the 'secular' sci-tech efforts of Ray were not serving the goal of the much -dreaded 'sensate society' of Sorokin. It is pertinent here to recall the repeated cautions against sense-driven life and society uttered in the *Bhagavad Gita*, verses II 58-68.

The thoughts of another contemporary world-class scientist, Abdul Kalam, may be added here.

'When one possesses such noble thoughts, patriotism is but natural. That's why we say, if spiritual knowledge is given from the beginning, love and pride for one's country, society and dharma is a natural result. However, spiritual values should form the foundation of life.' (Kalam, A.P.J. Abdul, 2002, p. 78)

Thus, Kalam too reiterates that our *principal* endeavour in life should be to stay anchored to a spiritual foundation, and that such a foundation should be built at the beginning of one's life.

Kalam's emphasis on instilling 'spiritual values' at the very beginning of life naturally reminds us of the *brahmacharya* phase in the four-stage *ashrama* scheme of ancient education in Bharatvarsha. This period of nearly twenty-five years was meant to implant the highest values and emotions first, followed by the learning of appropriate skills to earn one's keep in the *grihastha ashrama* (i.e. *para vidya* and *apara vidya* respectively). Thus, the principle of the *sacred preceding the secular*, advocated by Kalam (and so many others quoted above) has been very much a part and parcel of the holistic educational framework of India's ancient culture. Incidentally, this has been strongly corroborated by Weizenbaum who declares that the ancient Hindu, Chinese, Greek and other sources had amply addressed values-centered issues of life much before modern science. (*Interviews With Nobel Laureates and Other Eminent Scholars*, op. cit., p. 87)

Ultimately the problem of values education boils down to this:

• We cannot eat the cake and have it too.
• We cannot keep on running with the hare and hunting with the hound.

These proverbs highlight the need to confront the paramount difficulty about spirituality. The imbibing of human and spiritual values requires appropriate intervals of silence, quietness and peace in daily life to undertake the inward journey; but the centrifugal mode of living being promoted today by commercialized sci-tech innovations is hostile to these qualities.

OF TEMPERS AND INQUIRIES: SCIENTIFIC AND SPIRITUAL

The 8th duty prescribed by the Indian Constitution for every citizen is: 'To develop the scientific temper and spirit of inquiry'. The previous paragraphs have shown that the hyper-scientific temper can often commit grave blunders beyond the bounds of laboratory and its physical experiments. The simple truth eludes it that the brain is only an instrument for recording measurable effects from non-measurable causes. Leadership and managership with subjective human beings can derive little light from such 'objective blindness'.

As for the 'spirit of inquiry', experience suggests that here the implicit secular message seems to be: 'Question all the sustainable, enduring cultural values, beliefs, practices etc. of Bharatvarsha, and revile or reject them as regressive. Simultaneously, embrace unquestioningly all the unsustainable or incongruent values, etc. which keep storming in from affluent, aggressive quarters, as progressive'. It is pertinent therefore to recall, especially in this book, what the 'spiritual spirit of inquiry' has meant in Bharatvarsha.

Narendranath Dutta, as a college student in the early 1880's and not yet Swami Vivekananda, had knocked at the doors of every great and learned stalwart of Calcutta with just two sharp 'inquiries': 'Sir, have you seen God? If yes, can you show God to me?' Consumed by sacred hunger, this haunted soul had probed every possible corner, only with disappointment in store. Then at last the near-illiterate Sri Ramakrishna shot these straight answers at Naren, 'Yes, I have seen God. If you want, I can show to you too.' These emphatic answers to the two 'inquiries' were proved to the hilt instantly, and also over five relentless years of merciless scrutiny. The rest is history.

Aurobindo Ghosh had spent fourteen years of education (from the age of seven to twenty one) in England—Manchester, London and Cambridge. He too was far away from Sri Aurobindo when he returned to India in 1893. He hardly knew much Bengali or Sanskrit then. In a long letter (August 1905) from Baroda to his wife Mrinalini he wrote about his 'three madnesses'. He pleaded with her to be a true Hindu sahadharmini (co-spiritualist) in his pursuit of these madnesses. The second of these is germane for the present. He wrote to this effect: 'If God exists, I must become one with Him'. Indeed, this 'inquiry' was consummated in the dark and suffocating 100 square feet cell of Alipore jail (1909) through his yogic darshan (vision) of Vasudeva. (His two other madnesses were: to give back to society seven-eighth of his earnings and resources, retaining only one eighth for his needs, to avoid the sin of theft; and to love India as his Mother, not treating her as merely a geographical landmass.) Here too the rest is history.

CONCLUSION

The central theme of this chapter has been the current state of growing unethicality in managership, leadership and society. Three main sets of extra-orbital thoughts have been gleaned:

- *Those of Einstein-Schroedinger and their likes;*
- *Those of PC Ray-Abdul Kalam;*
- *Those of Vivekananda-Aurobindo.*

The first pair is ready to accept that mere intellectual culture is insufficient to support ethics; the super-sensual or trans-rational has to be accepted. The second pair is more forthright and spontaneous in the invocation of Providence or God for the holy temper. The third pair is the acme of complete ethics by Realisation of Spirit or God within, behind and above.

Several Indians often lament that India has produced awfully few Nobel scientists. But this is not really a matter of shame. For, so far close to a thousand such scientists would have adorned the world-stage. What has been the cumulative aggregate impact of all their acclaimed achievements? Two world wars, ecological devastation, entropy, ethical collapse, psychological impoverishment, hi-tech terrorism etc. A-moral scientific knowledge has been consistently hijacked by technology and business for nether ends. Bharatvarsha's scientists of Spirit knew very well 'what to seek' and 'where to stop'. Fortunately, Nobel or other awards did not dangle before our *rishis* and *tapsawis* to deflect them from the realization of ultimate Truths. The insane world of today sorely needs them. The real shame of it all is that secular India disowns, even ridicules, these award-shunning saviours of the earth.

Human Stress
Secular and Spiritual Approaches

Stress is an engrossing subject. A panoramic view of the human condition shows that psychological stress has been spreading and rising along with the vigorous promotion of ego-driven, technology-dependent, greed-fuelled secular life-ethos. But one often misses this main line of thinking amidst a plethora of diverse issues the subject deals with. Therefore, to demystify the subject at least four aspects need to be sorted out at the outset. First, human beings are higher on the ladder of evolution compared to the animal and other sub-human species. Therefore, they are also intrinsically more prone to stress than the latter. This is a price paid for a more sophisticated mental apparatus humans are endowed with. Second, secular literature on stress often does not acknowledge that a major source of stress lies in various psychological contaminations within an individual. These pollutions are essentially the dis-value emotions (*shadaripus*) like anger, greed, vanity, competitiveness, jealousy etc. and physiological disturbances like loss of sleep, lack of appetite, irritability etc. They are often the visible symptoms of these emotional pollutants. Third, it should be understood that the subject (emotions) is the *cause*, and object (physiological discomforts) is the *effect*. Fourth, it is useful to grasp the difference between *stress* and *challenge*, and whether there is anything really like 'positive stress'. These four aspects constitute the core of this chapter.

TWO MAJOR FRAMES OF REFERENCE
As a prelude, it is worthwhile to compare the approaches to stress adopted by two different schools of thought i.e. mainstream or secular, and Yoga-Vedanta or spiritual. The sample reference for secular literature is Pestonjee's book (Pestonjee, D.M., 1999), and for the spiritual or Y-V literature Akhilananda's book (Akhilananda, Swami, 1950).

Mainstream literature (which is primarily Western) generally outlines the following as the causes of stress within organizations (Pestonjee, D.M., op. cit., pp. 29–30):

i) 'Role ambiguity' resulting from lack of clarity about the role.
ii) 'Role expectation' conflict due to different expectations by different significant persons.
iii) 'Role overload' because there is a feeling of too many expectations from the significant roles.
iv) 'Role erosion' which signifies that some functions which should properly belong to his/her role are transferred to/or performed by some other role.

It is true that these organizational variables cause stress to almost all people at the visible level. But these role-related reasons are almost wholly beyond the control of most individual organizational members. Moreover, it is also a fact that the capacity to handle such stress differs substantially from person to person. It has been regularly observed that this variation can be adequately explained by the differential *emotional resilience intrinsic* to each individual.

Mainstream literature seems to be silent about this issue. For example, Pestonjee's book does not include emotive factors like competition, greed, jealousy, philosophy of life, spirituality etc. in the Index, except a single reference to anger. However, Akhilananda's book is replete with the above states of mind in the Index. This aspect will be addressed in detail after a while.

There is yet another fundamental difference in the way the subject of stress is approached by these two schools of thought. The mainstream approach tries to investigate and analyse a problem as subtle as stress through questionnaire surveys, measurement scales, inventories, indices, quotients and other similar tools. This is demonstrated in the Index of Pestonjee's book which contains ninety five such entries. The Y-V approach, on the other hand, is fundamentally experiential and intuitive. The former tends to be heavily quantitative, whereas the latter is totally qualitative. However, since quantification is academically impressive and weighty, this methodology has produced a large body of literature in the West and India. It maybe emphasized that questionnaires etc. can hardly capture the immense complexity and variation in the emotional world of respondents.

When it comes to the coping strategies developed by the two streams of study, then again significant differences are perceptible. Mainstream researchers have adopted a two-pronged strategy to tackle stress. One is at the individual level and the other at the organizational level. A few examples follow (ibid., p. 99):

Individual Strategies
(a) If there is a conflict between the self-concept and role then an attempt for self-integration should be made by analysing the various aspects of role causing the distance and acquiring the skills to bridge the gap.
(b) If the cause of stress is conflict between role and expectations then the solution lies in clearly partitioning the role, or role elimination, or role negotiation.
(c) Cases of role overload maybe sorted out through prioritization.

It is pertinent to observe that none of the individual strategies recommend any *process or values for self-culture*. Besides, they only provide some clues about 'what' might be done organizationally in stressful situations, but not about 'who' will do, or 'how' it is to be done. The approach is external to the individual, not *internal*.

Organizational Strategies
(a) Undertake stress audit
(b) Check-up with in-company doctor
(c) Spread the message of importance of work, leisure, proper diet, exercise and mental peace.
(d) Stress Management Training Programme
(e) Employee Assistance Programme
(f) Stress Reduction /Intervention Programme

The utility of medical check-up and allied steps like proper diet is beyond question. But they tend to be temporary palliatives, without addressing the deep-rooted, *existential difficulties*. More crucially, different programmes suggested for stress management usually lack adequate depth. If such measures comprise some games and tools, or lie-and-speak formulae, then although they may be instantly popular with managers, their enduring efficacy remains doubtful.

On the other hand, the Y-V approach suggests a stepwise sequence of concrete methods for each individual to achieve *inner anchoring* and emotional integration. They are as follows (Akhilananda, Swami, op. cit., pp. 171–6):

(a) To create a steady mental atmosphere through study of the teachings of religious realizers.
(b) To develop a higher philosophy of life beyond one's career only.
(c) To direct the emotions towards the Super Personal or Divine so that there is an elevating hub in the centre of life's wheel.
(d) To practise control over disruptive emotions or dis-values (anger, rivalry, greed etc.) at their incipient stage, so that stress is prevented.
(e) To consciously cultivate higher qualities or human values (compassion, gratitude, contentment, forbearance etc.) to quieten the mind. This will enable the integration of emotions at a higher level.

Significantly, in the above processes there is no reference to any survey, or index, or even questionnaire. The role of an organization is also not given importance for stress reduction. On the contrary, the focus is squarely on individual efforts. *Existential guidelines* to be followed to either prevent stress, or to stem the corrosive nature of stress constitute its core. Moreover, the artificial barrier between work–place and family-life has not been recognized. After all, the workplace is one act in a bigger drama. It cannot therefore remain immune from the impact of societal and family problems. The reverse is equally true. Thus, the Y-V approach aims at the *subjective fundamentals* which is holistic in the long run.

BACK TO BASICS
A more elaborate exposition of how the spiritual Y-V literature has provided perennial insights for the prevention or remedy of stress is now in order. For, in the end the Y-V approach boils down to showing the practical path towards unconditioned *ananda* (Nikhilananda, Swami, 1983, pp. 88–9; Bharati, Jnanananda, 1985, p. 115). It starts on the premise that every human being is an *energy processor*. For instance, in the workplace an individual may confront two broad conditions:

(a) There may be situations where *challenging* tasks or roles inspire and energise a person. In other words, the individual's energy gets *stimulated*. He feels as though he is in *command* of the situation.
(b) There could also be situations where a person is unable to cope with the pressure of work, or a difficult boss etc., and feels helpless. This

results in *dissipation* of energy. He becomes *stressful*. A feeling of *losing grip* over a given situation tends to overpower him.

Therefore, this book regards stress as entirely negative because it is an *energy dissipator*. This runs contrary to the mainstream argument that some amount of stress is good for increasing effectiveness and professional competence (Pestonjee, D.M., op. cit., p. 20). *The Oxford Thesaurus of English* (Waite, M., 1995, pp. 917–18) lists the following synonyms for stress:

strain	pressure
nervous tension	worry
anxiety	nervousness
trouble	difficulty
trauma	pain
grief	suffering

Thus, the aggregate of all the items listed above paints an entirely negative picture of stress. That apart, there is yet another critical question: How to determine that 'some amount of stress' which is good, and who is to determine it? Being purely subjective in nature, no tools or techniques can probably measure that 'some amount of stress'. Infact, the truth is that a person who is stressful realizes it only when the symptoms manifest after some damage has already been done. Also, the threshold level for 'some amount of stress' always varies from person to person.

Refocussing on point (b), it is evident that an individual dissipates energy when he is confronted with stressful situations of two different categories:

Group A	*Group B*
Transfer order	Competitive rivalry or jealousy
Loss of job	Greed
Heavy work pressure	Vindictiveness
Obsolescence of skills	High ego
Denial of promotion etc.	Unethical practices etc.

The situations in group A indicate causes or conditions which are dependent on external variables not within one's control. In other words, this group comprises *non-controllable* variables. On the other hand, group B represents emotional states which are internally generated. They can be managed through personal efforts. This group constitutes *controllable* variables.

The two lists of factors above have one aspect in common—both of them cause stress resulting in dissipation of energy. Group A variables can rarely be prevented, but one's *psychological stamina* may be increased to cope with them. Careful scanning of the list of variables under group B, however, shows that these causes of stress are rooted in *dis-values* or negative emotions. Therefore, if dis-values can be reduced and *human values* (positive emotions like gratitude, honesty, patience, calmness, contentment etc.) can be nourished, the psychological stamina for stress prevention or coping should increase. Vulnerabilty to the vagaries of non-controllable variables can be lessened from within.

It is noteworthy that some of the dis-values correlated to stress have something to do with the culture of consumerism also. A positive co-relation between consumerism and stress can be inferred. Our mind, a little introspection reveals, is usually outgoing and therefore agitated. Multiplicity of choices adds to cravings. This never allows the mind to settle down and let the individual enjoy what is already possessed. However, the idea is certainly not to deprive one of the basic amenities for comfortable living. But comparison and showmanship with others only provokes jealousy, greed and competition, which are stressful mental states. A comparison-addicted showman is really a *slave*. His exteriorized (*bahirmukhi*) mind is heavily cluttered, excitable. Therefore, *exciting times are usually followed by depressing times*.

Again, from the existential viewpoint, *pleasure* and *pain* are but two sides of the same coin. They are inextricably linked. An individual can never be a winner always. This is the very design of existence. Hence, it is practical to train the mind to accept reverses in life with grace and humility. If this reality of life is not understood, then failures will be resented, treated as undeserved. This unrealistic attitude itself will cause stress. In the *Gita* two important psychological concepts for understanding and coping with stress have been emphasised (Aurobindo, Sri, 1977, p. 18). These twin concepts should be learned and practised by all:

• First, it acknowledges the truth that pain and pleasure are inseparable companions which pull a person in two *opposite* directions. This is called *dwandwa* in the *Gita*. The extent to which such stretch can be withstood depends on the emotional resilience or threshold level of each person. One person of feeble resilience, failing to cope with this stretch, may breakdown. Another of stronger resilience can bear it with fortitude.
• Second, the *Gita* offers the concept of *samatwa*. It means cultivating even-mindedness in the face of *dwandwas*. In its absence, a person may

swing towards extremes by the ups and downs of life. He will then be unable to maintain mental equilibrium or restore inner poise. This will impair his holistic excellence.

Some research studies in the West indicate that deeply spiritual or religious persons seem to manage severe stress well. They also reveal that women performing the role of men exhibit the same stress-related symptoms, e.g., heart attack, high blood pressure, insomnia, etc. (Morse, D.R. and Furst, M.L., Stress 1979, p. 35) The truth conveyed by such findings is this— exclusive emphasis on the 'rational-left brain-material' basis of life robs human beings of an alternative subjective platform. Religion or spirituality provides this alternative. Similarly, women, though characteristically more 'intuitive-caring-right brain', lose these qualities by taking up the secular roles of men. Hence, they also become stressful.

Considering together all the ideas above, a two-pronged strategy for stress management can be proposed:

- *To prevent degeneration of* challenge *to* stress.
- *To promote regeneration from* stress *to* challenge.

These two dimensions of stress-challenge management may be appreciated well with the following examples.

(a) History offers two most telling examples—that of Alexander and Asoka. He dreamt of conquering the whole world, hence willing to accept any challenge that came his way. He did come upto the north-west of India, but at the cost of the lives of thousands of soldiers. He died on his way back at Babylon. Thus, what was initially a challenge degenerated into stress later. There was nothing or no one to guide him to recoup from that state.

Emperor Asoka offers the contrary case. He also had challenged the Kalinga Empire, and won a bloody war. He too suffered extreme stress. Fortunately, under the guidance of a monk, he overcame stress and became committed to the new challenge of running a peaceful and stable kingdom. Alexander did not receive such advice. His conquered territories did not get consolidated into an empire. He died in a stressful state. *Spiritual counselling had, on the other hand, saved the day for Asoka.*

(b) The two-pronged theory of *dwandwa* and *samatwa* forms the psychological background of the battle of Kurukshetra. The two warring armies were led by the members of the same royal family, the *Pandavas* and *Kauravas*. When the war was about to commence Arjuna, the leader of the Pandavas, broke down. He faced a dilemma. On the one hand, as a warrior (*kshatriya*) it was his duty (*dharma*) to fight a *dharmayuddha* (righteous battle) when the situation so demanded. On the other hand, the persons against whom he had to fight were his seniors and kinsfolk. He was thus torn between the opposites or *dwandwa* of duty and sentiment. He collapsed from *challenge* to *stress*. It was then that Sri Krishna, his mentor, counselled him on *dwandwa* and *samatwa*. Thus, Arjuna was lifted up to *challenge* from *stress*. (Aurobindo, Sri, op. cit., p. 24)

(c) Now follows an example from industry: U.S. Prasad, Chief Manager–Human Resource (CM-HR), of a large power generation company, currently faces stressful dilemmas in the performance of his duty. He was earlier working for four years in another plant of the same company. Things were going steadily there. But after transfer to the present plant everything seems to have been thrown out of gear. He admits of his moral values being in jeopardy in the present work-profile. The situation becomes particularly stressful if, for instance, an accident occurs due to a workman's own negligence inside the plant. In such a case the CM-HR has to invariably get involved.

A medico-legal case of this type demands that it be filed with the police. The Executive to whom the workman reports is now in a fix. There is an unwritten convention in industry that for such accidents inside a plant a workman is never at fault. So, the blame is directed towards the concerned Executive for no fault of his either. Therefore, the CM-HR has first to cover up the case by bribing the contractor if the worker is under contract, or the union if his name is on the company payroll. This is done to prevent them from filing a case against the company. It also saves the career prospects of the Executive. In addition, there is also pressure on the CM-HR from the Executive Association to ensure that no harm is caused to one of its members.

However, despite all efforts, information leaks out to the police. It is then that the Superintendent of Police swings into action demanding his pound of flesh. His requests could range from the company footing his bills during his stay in a five star hotel, or providing for his travelling expenses when holidaying, or even sending a new refrigerator to his home etc. If the CM-HR refuses to oblige him, he is blackmailed: The case will then be re-opened. All these expenses are booked under the head 'Entertainment and Liaison' which does not have a specified budget.

Psychologically, Prasad finds the going tough. On the one hand, he has to safeguard the Executive because he is not to blame. This is possible only through appeasement of some influential persons. His conscience pricks.

On the other hand, he has to see that the aggrieved party also gets its due. He questions his moral authority to teach his children the values of honesty and integrity. In order to tide over such trying situations he practises regular silencing of mind. He also writes daily, in an exercise book, one page of simple *Ramnaam*. This is done with great devotion after the morning bath. Such concrete steps enable him to rejuvenate his battered nerves. He argues within himself by saying that *when there is an effect, there must also have been a cause* which he may not be able to recollect. He finds peace of mind when he reads sacred literature and performs regular *japam*. He tells himself that he is not doing any of these things for himself. By God's grace nobody accuses him personally of being in collusion with the mischief-makers.

These examples show that restoration of *samatwa*, or balance,* can be achieved by reverting or sticking to human values, and through elementary breathing exercises or *pranayam*. The resulting purity of emotions or *antarshuddhi*, and interiorization or *antarmukhita* will both forewarn an individual about challenge degenerating to stress. Asoka, Arjuna and the CM-HR – all of them show how through faithful practice of *intrinsic* psycho-spiritual methods they had achieved (or achieve) freedom from stress, or got back to challenge, or coped with continual stress. Various mainstream approaches hinging primarily on the 'role' (see above) do not provide any answer to such complex situations. Role elimination, role negotiation etc. are hardly feasible in the majority of instances.

CONTROLLABLE STRESSORS—SOME DETAILS

Some of the major internal (controllable) causes of stress will now be examined in more detail. The list starts with *selfishness*. The consequences of selfishness can be appropriately understood through unselfishness. Mothers in traditional Indian homes exemplify this. They devote their time to the well-being of the family members like no one else does. They play the role of fortifying a fortress from within by holding together individuals of different temperaments. This calls for astute application of management art. In the happiness or success of the family members they find joy and fulfillment of their dreams. Peace, on the whole, is better maintained. Families do not break up on flimsy, egoistic pretexts. However, this mindset fostered by our tradition is fast eroding in the name of progress! Running after their personal goals and career ambitions, new generation mothers and wives are themselves

---

* For a diagramatic representation of *samatwa* see p. 206.

now facing heightened stress. Children are being neglected, aged parents are considered liabilities, and social life is becoming hollow and superficial. Not only this. The tensions and anxieties of the working couples spill over into the home and make family life more unbearable. Earlier the wife or mother of a family acted as anchors and shock absorbers under such circumstances. Bruised minds used to get some balm. But this is no longer so. As a result, stress is snowballing into increased rates of divorce, suicide, depression etc.

A correlate of selfishness is *high egotism*. Over-estimation of one's qualifications or beauty, wealth or power, capabilities or pedigree usually causes over-sensitivity to even the smallest departure from one's pre-conceived or rigid ideas or expectations. The 'you are special' syndrome as a motivational message to individuals is destroying the spirit of accommodation and adjustment. The resultant social fractures are aggravating stress for all. This affliction quickly throws the person off-balance in various human interfaces. Stress overtakes such an individual much sooner than in the case of another who is more humble, modest and adjustable. It is also commonly found that persons with high ego tend to be filled up with the emotional dis-values of *vindictiveness* and *suspiciousness*. This combination accentuates inner vulnerability to stress.

Two of Patanjali's Yoga aphorisms provide a sound basis for reducing or avoiding stress due to the above causes (Vivekananda, Swami, 1976, p. 148):

I.33   'Friendship, mercy, gladness, and indifference, being thought of in regard to subjects, happy, unhappy, good and evil respectively, pacify the *chitta* (heart or mind).'

II.33 'To obstruct thoughts which are inimical to Yoga, contrary thoughts should be brought.'

Thus, through the discipline of *pratipaksha bhavana*, or raising of contrary positive emotions, the grip of the negative emotions, can be gradually weakened, even eliminated.

Jealousy or envy is yet another dis-value which invites stress. The role of envy is like that of a corrosive chemical. It eats into the psychological vitals of a person with far-reaching consequences. For example, the success of a colleague often creates negative feelings among peers. Consequently, the latter cannot pursue their own duties with full devotion. They may indulge in speaking ill about the winner, and conspire against him. When such actions assume an acute form, stress sets in. Energy dissipation accelerates.

Competitive consumerism is yet another factor which accentuates stress. For this nothing else but the cult of 'more is less' is responsible. It is thriving on the dictum mentioned in the *Hitopodesha*, 'I need your greed to fulfill my greed.' Although such a view will not go down well with those engaged in financing, manufacturing and marketing of consumer goods, yet they can hardly deny its truth. Therefore, in order to mitigate stress some psychologists are now counseling their patients to go for 'curtail therapy', instead of 'retail therapy'. Modern consumerism is the culmination of a wrong philosophy that continuous aggregation of finites leads to happiness. Y-V theory insists that (Lal, P., 2002, 7.XXIII.1. p. 271)—

$$\Sigma \text{ FINITES} \neq \text{HAPPINESS}$$

But the contrary false gospel has been translated into the craze for big bazaars and shopping malls. It is expected that a stressed-out person will become balanced by indulging in a buying spree. Recent findings however show that acts of impulse purchase only fan more greed, with the accompaniment of guilty conscience due to extravagant spending. This adverse impact aggravates further when such extravagance is prompted by competitive buying of more expensive and latest models of consumer goods with reference to one's neighbours and friends. The tragic story of King Yayati in the *Mahabharata* may be recalled.

Competitive careerism causes stress because achievement in life, in comparison with colleagues, is measured in terms of money, position and power. As a sequel, individuals are pitted against one another. There is all-round suffering and misery. The following vignette, based on a real-life account narrated to one of the authors, aptly highlights this characteristic cause of stress.

VIGNETTE*

Yang was a middle-level executive in an American multinational bank with several branches in the southern province of China. Like any other Chinese professional he was extremely ambitious and wanted to join the Board of the bank before he turned forty. On the other hand, his wife, Chi, was a coy housewife and diligently managed the household chores like any other traditional Chinese woman does.

---

* Based on a true account narrated by a visiting Chinese scholar in India.

Yang was so obsessed with his job that he hardly paid any attention to his wife and daughter, Chu, until he came to know one day that Chi was afflicted with cancer. It was in a pretty advanced stage. The dream castle that he had visualized came down crashing. Yang was seated near Chi's death-bed when she said, 'Look, I have not asked of you anything all my life, nor made any claim of love upon you. So, if you would agree, before I bid adieu to you, I have only one plea to make. If you promise to honour it, I will speak it to you.' Yang had already started repenting at his folly for the great delay in bringing her for medical attention. So, he was more than eager to honour her request. Chi then held his arms close to her chest and pleaded in very soft gentle words, 'After I am gone, you will visit me, talk to me....' She wanted to say something more but became unconscious and passed away moments later.

Yang felt smitten by pangs of conscience. He asked himself as to how he could meet a dead person? A perplexed and crestfallen Yang met his friends and explained to them his predicament. None could help him. But perchance someone advised him to visit a para-psychology institution in Virginia, USA. However, he returned empty-handed. Amidst confusion he visited a Bhikshu in a Buddhist monastery. After listening to Yang he suggested Yang to visit a wise soul in Varanasi.

Yang thus embarked on his journey and ultimately came to the village near Varanasi where the wise soul was supposed to be living. Upon inquiry, the villagers informed him that the hut occupied by the noble soul was lying vacant for quite sometime. He had gone to the Himalayas. No one knew when he would be returning. Yang broke down – so near yet so far!

He sat down beside the hut with the holy Ganga silently flowing in front of him. No habitation was visible. There were only a few mango trees to give him company. Soon the western horizon turned crimson-red and finally the sun plunged beneath the horizon. In the midst of this silent drama Yang seemed to see the figure of a serene Bodhisattwa. The Bodhisattwa appeared to be gazing at him. He raised his palm in the *abhaymudra* and blessed him with a smile. This vision, and the emotions it stirred, calmed down his tormented mind. He never got such peace of mind before. Yang felt the silently flowing Ganga washing away the sins of millions, yet herself remaining ever-pure. He now realized that Chi, too, had through all her life been absorbing all the storms and stresses in their family with silent forbearance. The Ganga and Chi became one.

Chi seemed to ask him to nurture Chu as if she was Chi herself – through the murmuring waves of the Ganga.

The above episode confirms once again the genuine and basic efficacy of the *spirituo-religious* approach to the problems of stress. Such an approach is available for human beings alone. It also substantiates a profound fact about the culture of *Bharatvarsha*: Her very atmosphere is charged with peace and tranquillity. But this is being recklessly demolished. Yang did not need any formal counseling or other techniques. His stress was eliminated by his ardent surrender to the peaceful vibrations of the Ganga. As to one chief cause of stress, Yang's case validates the thesis that *career-centric secularity* and stress are compatible bedfellows.

Unethical practices also aggravate stress. The torment arises from either going against *socially conditioned norms*, or from actions which are considered to be *universally unethical*. The former may result, for instance, from having an extra-marital affair with an office colleague which is not sanctioned by the Indian culture. Although one might vociferously argue that such a tradition is archaic, yet deep within, the person cannot bear it because of culturally-rooted *samskars*. However, the same practice may be considered normal in some other cultures. This type of impropriety may not lead to stress there. However, the stressful fallout of practices universally regarded as unethical (like evasion of tax, murder, copying in the examination hall etc.) is self-evident. These points may not apply to those who have somehow become immune to conscience-pricking due to such unethicalities. Unfortunately, their number seems to be increasing. Then again, there are some who put up a brave face to show as though nothing has happened. But the sub-conscious mind is far from being at peace with itself. So, conscious culture of ethicality can be an *insurance policy* against stress.

STRESS, HAPPINESS, ANXIETY, ANGER AND INTEGRATION

The Mother of Sri Aurobindo Ashram, Pondicherry, had once commented that the aim of human life is to discover the *Divine* within and express it without. The natural *consequence* of this priority is *happiness*. However, making the consequence the aim, and the aim subservient to the consequence is a major source of stress in life. It is wrong, according to her, to define the aim of life as gaining happiness, however popular a hold this might have on peoples' minds. For, like pleasure and pain, happiness and misery are also inseparable. So, the real answer to such *dwandwic* stress is to strive for a transcendent, spiritual, Divine aim as one's goal of life and living.

Anxiety, which is a common symptom of stress, may be considered next. There are three levels of consciousness:

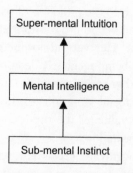

Animals possess *submental instinct*. Their range of perception is limited. Within that range their instinct is more accurate and certain compared to that of ordinary human beings. For example, ants can instinctively feel the impending rains in advance and make a beeline into our homes for safety. Similarly, dogs are used by the police to track criminals. Accompanying such precision is the capacity of animals to live mostly in the *present*. Hence, animals do not brood over the sufferings they may have undergone. Due to limited perception they also do not get stressed out apprehending future uncertainties or mishaps.

Supramental intuition grows out of the development of spiritual capacity. One's consciousness is lifted to a *level higher than mental reasoning*. Such a person can forsee the culmination of individual or group efforts, and also surrender spontaneously to the Providential will. This capability can keep the mind free from speculative worries.

In between these two levels of consciousness lies *mental intelligence*. Human beings belong mostly to this state. Their instincts are not as sure as those of the animals because of a stronger dose of mental reason. On the other hand, due to lack of spiritual discipline, the trans-mental intuitive power too remains dormant. Naturally, such a person fails to anticipate many of the present happenings, what to say of the future. Such an indeterminate dangling–in–the–middle state of consciousness (*trishanku*) renders the human being almost irresistibly anxious and miserable.

Thus, the root of human anxiety is his/her half-way consciousness which manifests in the form of stress. The Mother suggests the true remedy for anxiety as follows (Dalal, A.S., 1989, p. 44):

'This torment can come to end only with a *total surrender* to a higher consciousness than his own to which he can totally entrust himself, handover his worries and leave the care of guiding his life and organizing everything.'

This implies breaking out of the intellectual or reasoning process, and shifting to a plane of faith and conviction in the trans-rational. *Prayer* in silence to the Divine is a universal process for achieving this.

A relevant *Pauranic* story will be appropriate. Once Garuda, the bird-chariot of Lord Vishnu, had gone to meet Lord Shiva in the Kailasha mountain. A little bird was perched on the palace wall. Suddenly Yama (Lord of Death), while entering Shiva's abode, cast a hard glance on the little bird. Garuda, meanwhile waiting at a distance, saw this incident. He got worried about the bird because of Yama's glance at it. His anxiety was—whether to save the bird from death, or to leave it to the operation of the karmic law? His mind was in great torment, unable to choose the correct course. At last he told himself: 'My power of judgement is failing me. So let me remember and invoke the Providence who is all-wise, and then do what my heart impels me to do.' Thus re-organizing his anxious mind, he flew with the bird at lightening speed and put it on a tree in the dandakaranya forest. But lo! A snake crawled up the tree and devoured the bird.

Sri Aurobindo has also suggested another simple practical method—*stepping back*. This requires the discipline of gradually cultivating concentration on something which is a *luminous* and *perfect constant* within a zone of stillness in the heart.* This process is facilitated by visualizing and identifying with, say, a perfectly stress-free human form like the deeply meditating Buddha or Shiva or Vivekananda. (There are many alternatives in regard to this chosen deity, called *Ishtam*, in Indian psychology). One who does not favour this method, may contemplate upon a serene, vast and peaceful natural scenery. The troubled mental consciousness can be dipped and soaked, as it were, in the profound peace of such imagination.

In all such meditation/concentration practices the mind begins to absorb the stress-free poise of the object or theme contemplated through the *law of association*. Two vivid real-life pictures are reproduced below. They could be used for recollection and meditation during stressful times.

---

* see step 5 of QMP in Chapter 3.

(a) About Sri Aurobindo, reported by the Mother (Mother, 1990, pp. 39–40)—

'Not only can attacks of men be warded off, but beasts also and even the elements can be affected. I can give you a little example. You remember the night of the great cyclone, when there was a tremendous noise and splash of rain all about the place, I thought I would go to Sri Aurobindo's room and help him shut the windows. I just opened his door and found him sitting quietly at the desk writing. There was such solid peace in the room that nobody would have dreamed that a cyclone was raging outside. All the windows were wide open, yet not a drop of rain was coming inside.'

(b) About Swami Vivekananda, reported by Marie Louis Burke (Burke, M.L., 1973, pp. 501–02)—

'They took the Turk street cable car to Market Street .... And then to a larger Market Street car. This transfer point, incidentally, was a noisy, bustling spot in San Francisco, where Swamiji must have often stood, waiting for a street car on his way to the East Bay. In a lecture some weeks later he gave what one can take to be a picture of himself at that precise point. Speaking of the attainment of yoga, he said, "This is the question: with every sense and every organ active, have you that tremendous peace in which nothing can disturb you? Standing on the Market Street, waiting for the car with all the rush going on intensely around you, are you in meditation, calm and peaceful? If you are, you are a yogi, otherwise not."'

Anger is yet another common symptom of stressful conditions. Modern psychology suggests the method of *accept* and *express* to tackle it. It is reasoned that by letting go of the inner heat and steam the stressful state is mitigated. But Sri Aurobindo, in accordance with Indian psychology, recommends the opposite formula: *deny* and *reject*. Here the theory is that the source or cause of anger is always *external* to the person. Its vibration enters into the consciousness without our awareness. This makes us own it up as if the anger were springing from within our own selves. Therefore, Sri Aurobindo's advice is (Dalal, A.S., op. cit., p. 59):

'What you must always have and feel as yours is this will: the power to refuse assent, to refuse admission to a wrong movement.'

If this is not done, every time anger is owned and expressed, it gradually tends to solidify into an automatic, permanent habit.

Swami Vivekananda, addressing on a similar issue, had emphasized the same principle (Vivekananda, Swami, 1976, p. 178):

'A man says something very harsh to me, and I begin to feel that I am getting heated, and he goes on till I am perfectly angry and forget myself, identify myself with anger. When he first began to abuse me, I thought, "I am going to be angry". Anger was one thing, and I was another: but when I became angry I was anger.'

The expression *integrated personality* is often employed to imply the same characteristics as expected to prevail in a *holistic*, self-possessed personality. Human personality can be considered as a composite of four subtle variables: *reason, will, emotion* and *conscience*. In order to integrate the personality, effort is needed to habituate these four factors to work in harmony, instead of running at cross-purposes. This ideal can be amplified as below:

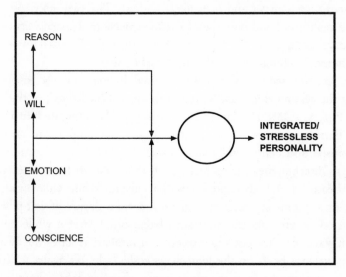

Calm self-analysis (especially after *pranayam* or QMP in Chapter 3) can indicate to an individual whether the above four aspects of the mind are operating in consonance with one another, or working at cross-purposes. If it is the latter, then it is a case of disintegrated or fragmented personality. Application of will power, along with prayer, is needed to restore coherence.

Verse IX.27 of the Gita recommends another process for achieving holistic integration:

Yatkaroshi yadadnashi yajjuhoshi dadasi yat,
Yat tapasyasi kaunteya tatkurushwa madarpanam.
(Whatever you do, whatever you eat, whatever you offer in sacrifice, whatever austerity you practice, O Kaunteya, do it as an offering to me.)

This formulation provides us with a process of unbroken mental discipline by which all our actions, enjoyments, charities, penances etc. can converge on the Supreme or God. Over a period of time such practice helps the scattered human mind to unify around a *central organizing principle, a hub of life.* However, integrated personality will *not* develop if the central organizing principle happens to be secular things like money, power, fame etc.

For those who are a little more spiritually inclined, the *Taittiriya Upanishad* offers the concentric *five-sheath* (*pancha kosha*) model of human personality. The three *outer* layers comprise the material, vital and mental sheaths (*annamaya, pranamaya* and *manomaya koshas*). The two *innermost* sheaths are the realization and bliss sheaths (*vijnanamaya* and *anandamaya koshas*).

Stress is confined to the three outer sheaths only. The two inner sheaths are inherently, characteristically *unaffected by stress.*

The *pancha kosha* (or five-sheath) spiritual discipline may be best practised during the second step, 'gentle, mindful, normal breathing', of the Quality Mind Process (QMP in chapter 3). It could also be integrated into the fifth step. During step two one's entire being becomes more composed, harmonised and centripetal (*antarmukhi*). In this state of awareness it is easier to discriminate, successively, each inner sheath from its contiguous outer sheath. Thus, body-related sensations like an itching palm, or an aching tooth, or a griping stomach etc., given a certain degree of will power, can be treated as affecting the *annamaya kosha* only. After a while perhaps a sudden wave of vehement anger or envy or retaliation seizes the awareness. This movement bears on the *pranamaya kosha* only. Yet again, a little later one may get caught in a spinning tangle of speculations about a crucial pending decision. The poise of steady awareness is gone. This state pertians to the *manomaya kosha.*

However, all the while, in the background, a steady and gentle awareness of the two innermost *koshas* (*vijnanamaya* and *anandamaya*), free from agitation or stress, continues to prevail. Progressive detachment or dis-

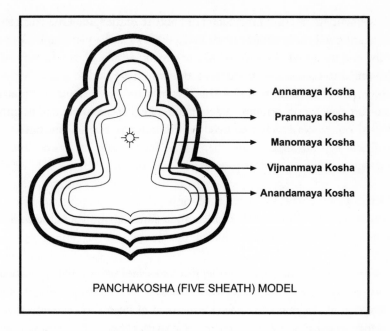

PANCHAKOSHA (FIVE SHEATH) MODEL

identification, by vigilant observation of the alternating or jumbled up workings upon the three outer *koshas*, helps one's awareness to gradually settle on the ever-peaceful and luminous fourth and fifth *koshas*. By resolute practice the duration of this association with or immersion in the self-existent inner reservoir of positive tranquillity, *ananda*, should increase.

The real issues however are:

- How desperately does one aspire to discover and treasure this core of *ananda* deep in oneself?
- How strong is the conviction and resolve to practise this process–at once preventive and curative?

Professional, secularist stress therapists are unlikely to grasp the profound merit of the above Vedantic theory and Yoga process. For example, sometime in late 2004 we had been invited to conduct a 3-day Workshop on 'Effectiveness in Academic Roles: Insights from Indian Psycho-Philosophy'. The Faculty Members of a vintage Engineering University were the audience. One session of ninety minutes, combining presentation and discussion, was devoted to the triune *guna* theory (*sattwa-rajas-tamas*). The intimate relevance of these psychological forces for decision-making and stress management are discussed in chapters 14 and 18 of the Gita. One participant had maintained stony silence, with knitted brows and a piercing look at us. At the end we asked, if he would like to say something. Curtly he replied, 'I have failed to connect with anything that you have said so long'. We were stunned. Later we were told that this person was a professional psychiatrist, hired part time for on-campus student counselling! Incidentally, earlier during 1962-67 our whole family had lived on this campus. Such a counsellor was absolutely beyond imagination then. This, incidentally, is a peep into the backstage of modern secular progress in New India!

STRESS PREVENTION—LET'S BE SERIOUS
Towards the end of his book Akhilananda sums up the thoughts outlined above like this (Akhilananda, Swami, op. cit., p. 176):

> 'When the integration of personality is accomplished through the application of the six-steps—desire for integration, acceptance of a higher philosophy of life, direction of the emotions to God, expression of inner divinity, cultivation of higher tendencies, and the practice of concentration – the person becomes established in the idea (of *samatwa*).'

It will be noted from the *Time, Fortune* and *Tillich* quotes in the Appendix to this chapter that the undertone in all of them points unmistakably in the direction of the extract given above

Mainstream, secular research literature, however, largely keeps such fundamental and saving principles at bay. Thus, although Pestonjee's book adds a few paragraphs on spirituality at the end, they are hesitant and casual. For instance, the last page mentions one research study which supports the usefulness of non-attachment in reducing or preventing stress. However, the more precise Sanskrit technical phrase, *nishkam karma*, is avoided. By contrast, authors in other Asian countries do not feel shy to employ indigenous terminologies whenever they are poorly translatable in English or other foreign languages. Similarly, spirituality is called 'Factor X' because different people understand it variously! (Pestonjee, D.M., op. cit., pp. 252–70, 286) A strange new kind of untouchability! Yet, the great scientists (Chapter 5) are not confused or reticent about this ultimate response to stress. Being employed in organizations is secondary to one being a human being in the first place. The beginning, and end, of stress management has to be this larger frame. And spirituality is the 'core competence' of the *homo sapiens*.

In verse II.66 the Bhagwad Gita has clearly warned thus: *ashantasya kutah sukham* (how can the unpeaceful be happy?). *Ashanti* or unpeacefulness here is existential in nature. Material poverty has little to do with it, nor has technological backwardness. Limitless greed for money, merciless bombardment of our senses with advertisements, fruitless speed of life leading to nowhere, senseless rights-based conflict–creation within homes and schools—all these allied forces are fomenting 'headlong outward movement' as says Sri Aurobindo. The growing business of stress management by stress counselors, ill-equipped as they usually are with deeper spiritual insights into the causes of stress, can scarcely help. Often they only mislead or exploit persons in a hurry. Rather than relying on conventional or secular professional advice, it is wiser by far to seek help from great mystic-poets like Rabindranath Tagore. Let us listen to him intently (Tagore, Rabindranath; trans. by S.K. Chakraborty and P. Bhattacharya, 1999, p. 130):

'From time to time, even in the very midst of furious pace of work, try to feel your inner being as detached. This you have to sense at every moment, repeatedly... There it is calm, silent, and pure. No, by no means shall we allow any external agitation to enter there...go and see there the lamp is burning in hushed stillness, the lament of sorrow does not reach there; there the roar of anger is calm.'

Once someone had asked Sri Aurobindo about 'how to remain quiet even while performing all works?'. Sri Aurobindo had answered (Inner Peace, op. cit., p. 8):

'By having a separate consciousness, calm and silent within, separate from the mental, vital or physical activity'.

This is a terse paraphrase of what Tagore has already communicated in his touching, soulful words. And the keynote of both is the 'bliss sheath'—the inmost *kosha*—of the *Taittiriya Upanishad*. Gradual intensification of meditation around this 'bliss sheath', by steadily withdrawing one's consciousness successively from the outer sheaths, is the true art. Further, trying to dissolve stress by a direct combat with the mechanical grind and churn of the physical-vital-mental layers is a common but fruitless method. The real art is to create, by devoted self-discipline, a distinct, separate and alternate niche for the troubled consciousness to rest. And this sanctuary is the 'bliss-sheath' inherent in our being. All this can very well be integrated with the final step of the QMP in Chapter 3. Positive results may not be very long to come.

As days pass, attainment of the above existential state is, however, becoming more difficult even to understand, far less to attain. Yet no other true remedy for stress is available. The two imageries of the 'still flame' and 'waveless ocean' lend concreteness to the meditation-contemplation process. This is the controllable, spiritual route to manage stress from *within*. We also found it fruitful in our 2-day Workshops on the subject of stress etc. (Chapter 1, Appendix) to begin by showing the participants two large photographs: one of Swami Vivekananda in his well-known *samadhi* posture in ochre robe and turban, with eyes closed; the other of the saintly Tagore, with white flowing beard, gazing far out into the Infinite. Thus, one is fully absorbed in the *anandamaya kosha* in the 'cave of the heart', the other completely lost in the limitless 'immeasurable'. One has dived *deep below* the tangle of finites, the other has soared *far above* the mess of finites. These two pictures offered vivid representations of what it means, concretely, to be free from stress. Conceptual discussions were then appreciated by the audience with more genuine feeling than otherwise.

CONCLUSION

Readers may recognize, on the basis of what has been explained above (and also in Chapter 3), that the specific subjective disciplines associated with spiritual human development comprise a 'healthy' blueprint. This is because it is the *rishis* and *munis*, ascetics and God-seekers, of Bharat's ancient *tapovans* and *ashrams* who had mapped out this vast psychological landscape. These locales were veritable hamlets of integral peace and serenity – *shanta rasaspadam ashramam idam* as Kalidasa had exulted in *Abhijnan Shakuntalam*. And, they were themselves epitomes of mental health. Mainstream modern (i.e, Western-Freudian) psychology was, however, born of 'clinical experience with patients', in a modern city, during the second half of the 19th century. Several Western critics have, in recent years, been passing strictures on psychoanalysis and therapy (Masson, J., 1993, pp. 298–9; Torrey, E.F., 1992, pp. 256–7). Yet, the two relatively recent non-mainstream schools of Western (American) psychology—Humanistic and Transpersonal —have not been able to appreciably loosen the strong grip of Freudian psychology on America. Its evils—narcissism, sexual libertarianism, irresponsibility, corruption—have now started invading even schools in India. So, Y-V spiritual psychology, Bharat's very own millennia-old fruit of supra-mental endeavours, remains the bulwark—both for children and adults. We must return to this core with alacrity and vigour.

Sri Aurobindo had clearly foreshadowed, many decades ago, what some Western critics are starting to admit now. Thus, replying to a letter from a disciple he wrote (Aurobindo Sri, 1987, p. 6):

> 'Your practice of psychoanalysis was a mistake...The psychoanalysis of Freud is the last thing that one should associate with yoga. It takes up a certain part, the darkest, most perilous, the unhealthiest part of the nature, . . . isolates some of its most morbid phenomena, and attributes to it and them an action out of all proportion to its true role in the nature.'

This is an irrefutable critique of modern, secular, psychotheraputic remedies for mental ill-health, including stress. Spirituality has been exiled from them.

APPENDIX

This Appendix has two parts:

(A) Extracts from some great thinkers and contemporary magazines etc. covering a period of 110 years are given in A. They correctly reveal the roots of the poison-tree of stress.

(B) A list of some verses from the Bhagavad Gita are given in B which clearly express how stress can be managed or prevented so far as it springs from internal, controllable psychological causes.

(A) EXTRACTS FROM SOME THINKERS, REALIZERS AND CONTEMPORARY MAGAZINES

(a) *Vivekananda* (1896):

'The more I study the more I find the idea of competition to be wrong ... the day will come when men will study history from a different light and find that competition is neither the cause nor the effect, simply a thing on the way, not necessary to evolution at all.'

(b) *Mowerer* (1948):

'Many sources of present evidence indicate that most neurotic human beings suffer not because they are unduly inhibited as regards their biological drives, but because they have disavowed and repudiated their own moral cravings.'

(c) *Akhilananda* (1951):

'The majority of people in post-renaissance Western civilization adopt the method of competition for their personal and public life ... let us analyze the psychological effect of the spirit of competition based on rights and privileges on the individual and society.'

(d) *Tillich* (1955):

'Of all illnesses, mental illness is by far the most widespread in the USA. What does this mean? There maybe something in the structure of our institutions which produces illness in more and more people ... the unlimited ruthless competition which deprives everybody of a feeling of security, makes many in our healthy nation sick; not only those who are unsuccessful in competition, but also those who are most successful.'

(e) *Time* (June 6, 1983):

'Our mode of life itself, the way we live, is emerging as today's principal cause of illness. The upheaval in society's most basic values adds greatly to the general level of anxiety.'

(f) *Fortune* (April, 1986):
'These superficially successful people, particularly the new breed of careerist, success-oriented men and women 25 to 47 years old, are among the most damaged victims of what I term modern madness, madness that derives from a invisible link between careers and emotions.'

(g) *Newsweek* (March 5, 1995):
'Americans are fried by work, frazzled by lack of time, technology hasn't made their life better. No wonder that a quarter of them say they are exhausted. They need to chill out before they hit the breaking point.'

(h) *Sunday Morning Post* (Hong Kong) September 10,1995:
'Hong Kong is such a commercial city. Speed is important for efficiency, effectiveness. People work under competition: there must be pressure.'

(i) *India Today* (March 13, 2006):
'Not in touch with the ground realities, they set very high standards and goals for themselves. And to achieve these, they push themselves hard, sometimes over the edge. In most cases, the difference between high expectations and ground realities creates stressful situations for both the employer and employee.'

(B) THE GITA ON STRESS AND SAMATWA*

II. 38   *Sukhe-Dukhe Same Kritwa Labha-Labhau Jaya-Ajajau*
      ('Make grief and happiness, loss and gain, victory and defeat equal
      to thy soul.')

II.50   *Yogah Karmasu Kausalam*
      ('Yoga is skill in works.')

II. 56   *Dukhesu Anudvignamana, Sukhesu Vigataspriha*
      ('Mind is undisturbed in the midst of sorrows and amid pleasures.')

III.30   *Nirashi Nirmamobhutwa,Yyuddhasya Vigatajwara*
      ('Fight, free from desire and egoism, and delivered from the fever
      of the soul.')

---

* All English translations are from Sri Aurobindo's *The Message of the Gita*, Pondicherry, Sri Aurobindo Ashram, 1977.

IV.20 *Tyaktwa Karmaphal-asangam, Nitya Tripto Nirashrayah*
('[Abandon] all attachments to the fruits of work, [be] ever-satisfied, without any kind of dependence.')

V.03 *Yo na Dwesti, Na Kankshati, Nirdwandwo hi Mahabaho*
('Who neither dislikes nor desires, ... free from the dualities.')

X.II *Yo na hrisyati, na dweshti, na shochati,*
Na kankshati, shubha-asubha parityagi.
('He who neither desires the pleasant, ... nor abhors the unpleasant ..., who has abolished the distinction between fortunate and unfortunate happenings...')

XIII.19 *Tulya ninda-stutir-mauni*
(Treating blame and praise to be equal, in silence),

XIV.24 *Sama dukkha swastha, sama loshtra kanchnati*
Tulya priya-apriyo, dhirastulya ninda atmastuti.
('He who regards happiness and sufferings alike, gold and mud and stone as of equal value, to whom the pleasant and the unpleasant, praise and blame are equal things.')

Sustainable Economics
'Spirinomics' in Hindu Thought and Experience

This chapter presents the Hindu view of the economic function at some length. It begins by denying the common perception that Hinduism has not given economic activities their due place. Next, it draws attention to some major ancient texts showing the character of the Hindu perspective about economic functions. This is followed by quotes and interpretations of the views of several modern Indian savants on the subject. Then the chapter proceeds to marshal the extra-orbital views of several Western authorities, not professional economists, about the dangers springing from the reckless economism of our times. This is succeeded by references to globalization and its consequences for the long-term cultural and social viability of a diverse cosmic-human habitat. Lastly, the future direction for a wholesome 'Spirinomics' flowing from essential Hinduism, is indicated.

Most authorities in Oriental studies tend to agree that Hinduism represents the longest unbroken culture and civilization, though it may not be the earliest (Basham, A.L., 1999, p. 2). This implies that the economic function must have played an integral part in the total scheme of life as conceived by it. Rigorous examination reveals that the Hindu worldview with respect to the economic function has been practical yet sublime, logical yet noble. Thus, explains Bose (Bose, A.C., 1979, p. 244):

' ... the Vedas accept earth and material existence to the fullest extent, but subject them to the fundamental moral and spiritual laws. Here lies the difference between the positive and 'this-worldly' and active outlook of the Vedas, and the exclusively ascetic, negative and inactive attitude of certain post-Vedic cults....'

This holistic, therefore, sustainable, keynote could be extended (Pusalkar, A.D., 1965. Vol. , p. 654)—

'Wealth, however, was never regarded as an end in itself, but as a means to an end. Contrary to common notions, they condemned asceticism and held those seeking to embrace the ascetic order without discharging their duties liable to punishment.'

Both the above statements are identical in spirit. They view material wealth as a support only to attain a higher goal in life. Not only that; those who wanted to embrace asceticism straightway were considered guilty of dereliction of their respective secular duties as son/daughter, husband/wife, father/mother etc. They invited censure from society. This *prioritized harmony* between the 'here' (*aihik*) and 'here after' (*paramarthik*) is the fundamental factor behind the endurance of the Hindu culture.

That material well-being was always accorded due importance for a well-appointed life, and not considered to be antithetical to achieving spiritual goals, has been substantiated by Sri Aurobindo further (Sri Aurobindo, 1975, p. 63).

'... ancient Indian thought admitted that material and economic capacity and prosperity are a common though not the highest or most essential part of the total effort of human civilization. In that respect India can claim equality with any ancient or mediaeval country. No people before modern times reached a higher splendour of wealth, commercial prosperity, material appointment .... That is the record of history, of ancient documents ....'

In addition, Sri Aurobindo also asserts clearly that the economic function was never neglected in ancient India. This truth explains why Bharatvarsha and the Hindu culture have attracted endless greedy invasions.

Once again, returning to the 'this-worldly' versus the 'other-worldly' debate, Sarkar has opined (Sarkar, B.K., 1985, p. 6)—

'Rather it is in and through the positive, the secular and the material that the transcendental, the religious and the metaphysical have been allowed to display themselves in Indian culture-history.'

Sarkar too re-emphasizes that, instead of considering the desire for a decent material life as a hurdle, it was viewed as an enabling factor for fulfilling the supra-material aspirations of life. But for this priority to the *supra-material* in the total scheme, a merely matter-centric Hinduism could have perished due to material decline caused by external invasions and internal neglect in certain epochs in her very long history. Nonetheless, here is a profound message of history: rich Rome is ruined, great Greece is gone, excellent Egypt is extinct, beautiful Babylon is buried – yet Hindu culture is alive still.

However, some mainstream economic historians attribute the cause of India's poverty in recent centuries to her 'other-worldly' temperament, supposedly espoused by Hinduism. This argument is derived primarily from a narrow interpretation of the philosophical concept of *mayavad* (illusionism) propounded by Shankaracharya in the 8th century AD. Since this material world is illusory, a human being's primary aim of life should be to attain permanent bliss and joy (*moksha*) which is independent of the fluctuating and fleeting material-sensual satisfactions. Accordingly, the economic function becomes marginal, with no serious thought or effort behind it. Much earlier to Shankaracharya, Buddhism too had advocated *shunyavad* (nihilism) which had tended to induce large masses in society to adopt to monkhood. However, these two philosophies never comprised the core of the Hindu worldview.

THE SACRO-SECULAR SYMBIOSIS – A FEW SALIENT IDEAS
The upshot of the above initial clarifications is that the Hindu culture was fashioned by the ancient socio-centric *rishis* (seers) to function like a pair of scissors with two blades: *pursuit of the supra-material or sacred, with the support of the material or the secular*. This pairing maybe called *sacro-secular symbiosis* (Chakraborty, S.K., 1993. pp. 173–4). This perceptual vision and amplitude of Hinduism in positioning the economic functions or the *secular* dimension is best captured through the following classification (Pusalkar, A.D., op. cit., p. 655)—

The comprehensiveness of the ancient Hindu mind, which identified such an ensemble of economic functions, is noteworthy. They wisely realized that generation of wealth without proper allocation would spell lopsided economic growth without social harmony. Hence, care was taken to channelize wealth for the allround healthy development of society.

Against the backdrop of the above *trans-economic scheme*, it will now be helpful to understand how the sacro-secular symbiosis had been attempted since the days of the Vedas.

(A) The *Rig-Veda* (3000 BC or earlier), the oldest sacred text in the world, contains the following verses which capture the spirit of the sacro-secular approach towards the economic function in Hinduism (Bose, A.C., op. cit., p. 249)—

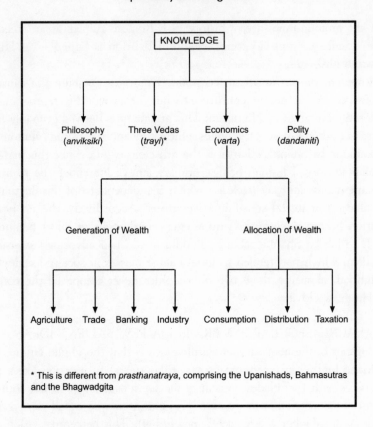

* This is different from *prasthanatraya*, comprising the Upanishads, Bahmasutras and the Bhagwadgita

(i) Let a man think well on wealth
And strive to win it by the path of
Law and by Worship:
And let him take counsel
With his own Inner Wisdom,
And grasp with Spirit still greater ability.

(ii) O God! Bestow on us the best treasures:
The efficient mind, and spiritual lustre,
The increase of wealth, the health of bodies,
The sweetness of speech and fairness of days.

The following points emerge from the two verses quoted above—

• Only honest acts should underlie generation of wealth.
• Worship and prayer of the Cosmic is advised.

- If dilemmas or conflicts arise in the pursuit of wealth, then one's conscience or spiritual power should be employed. In other words, the sacred goal cannot be undermined in the pursuit of secular wealth.
- While praying to the Divine for good health, spiritual upliftment, efficient mind etc., increase in wealth is also sought.

Thus, in both the verses the secular pursuit of wealth has been yoked and subjected to the sacred. For, this is the way to wholesome social and human development—as the *rishis* had declared on the basis of time-transcending, supra-mental vision (*trikalajna*).

(B) In the *post-Vedic* period upto the time of the Buddha, the concept of wealth was further elaborated (Mahadevan, T.M.P., 1958, pp. 163–6, 179–80). The most notable development during the period was the formulation of a comprehensive scheme encompassing the four goals of human life (i.e. *purusarthas*) namely—

(D) *Dharma:*   rectitude, righteousness, morality, ethics etc.
(A) *Artha:*   pursuit of wealth or money
(K) *Kama:*   fulfillment of legitimate desires with moderation
(M) *Moksha:*   permanent emancipation into the state of eternal Consciousness and Bliss

Of the four goals of life, D-M are considered to be the base and apex respectively. The A-K are the intermediate levels in the structure of social life of householders (*grihastha*). Thus, ethics forms the very foundation of material existence. Wealth thus generated is then sanctioned to fulfill legitimate earthly desires with moderation. Thus, universal insistence on ascetic life was ruled out. Yet the final goal for all did lie in the attainment of *moksha*. Therefore, in this scheme of existence, opportunity had been provided for those who wished to skip the second and third goals to pursue *moksha* directly. Renunciants belong to this category.

The following philosophical keynotes of the economic function emerge from the framework of *purusarthas*—

- D-M provide solid embankments on two sides to tame the turbulence associated with the intoxication of A-K.
- There is no indication to suggest that wealth creation was discouraged, or satisfaction of (needs) worldly desires was frowned upon.

• Like in the Vedic period, here too A-K were not considered to be ends in themselves, but as facilitators towards *moksha*. While this was true for the majority in society, the renunciants consciously curtailed their dependence on A-K to the barest minimum, at times to the extreme of the total abnegation. They provided role models for the laity. Nevertheless, *moksha* was held as the common potential destiny of all human beings, whether a householder or a renunciant.*

Another two-dimensional concept emerged during this period. These two dimensions were—

(Ab) *Abhyudaya:* material development
(Ni) *Nihsreyasa:* supreme good, above petty goods

Ab embraces both A-K. Correspondingly, Ni comprises D-M. The lesson is—pursue Ab without losing sight of Ni. The latter acts as the pole star.

The frameworks of *purusarthas* and Ab-Ni have been put into widespread practice, albeit in varying degrees, at different times right upto this day. They were not just theoretical constructs like Plato's 'philosopher-king'. The following narratives demonstrate the integration of these frameworks in education for social life—

(i) The *Katha Upanishad* contains dialogues between Yama, the King of Death, and Nachiketa, a mere boy. Of the three boons sought by the boy from Yama, the last one related to the knowledge of existence after death. Yama tried to deflect him from this query by promising all kinds of wealth, progeny, women, long life etc. Indeed, all that comprised A-K were offered to him. Yet an unrelenting Nachiketa responded by uttering (Gambhirananda, S., 1980, pp. 24–5),

'Man is not to be satisfied with wealth'. Now that I have met you, I shall get wealth. I shall live as long you will rule it. But the boon that is worth praying for by me is that alone.'

---

* Sri Aurobindo's Integral Yoga, however, gave a radical turn to this mainstream Hindu psycho-philosophy. His sadhana had aimed at Divinising and Supramentalising this very terrestrial life and consciousness.

This shows that even a young boy like Nachiketa had the strength of character to prioritize D-M over A-K. This stand of Nachiketa demonstrates the principle that in Hinduism the economic function is not allowed to over-rule the spiritual aspiration of human life. The Upanishadic *rishi* produces a telling effect by putting across to us the above principles through the words of a boy.

(ii) In the *Mahabharata*, the biggest epic of the world, the third section in *Sabha Parva* provides an elaborate description of the palace of the Pandavas. Some of the verses are quoted below (Lal, P., 2005, pp. 18–19):

> It covered an area
>   Of five hundred square cubits;
> It was beautiful to see;
>   It shone with the radiance
>
> Of fire, with the radiance
>   Of the sun, with the radiance
> Of the moon; its splendour shamed
>   The rays of the sun ...
>
> With the finest craftsmanship
>   On jewelled walks and portals
> In paintings and luxuries –
>   It was Viswakarma's handiwork!
>
> Soft breezes stirred the flowers
>   In the pool; all around it
> Were slabs of expensive marbles,
>   Inlaid with pearls.
>
> Many kings, seeing it for the first time,
>   So richly decked
> With stones and pearls,
>   Mistook it for land, and fell in.

The above stanzas indicate the height of both technical excellence and material affluence achieved in the bygone era. At the same time, towards the end of the *Mahabharata*, after victory, these very Pandavas renounced secular life in search of *moksha* (*mahaprasthan*—the great departure).

(C) Kautilya's *Arthashastra* is one of the most important administrative and economic treatises of the post-Buddhist era (about 300 BC) (Sastri, K.A.N., 1967, Vol. II, p. 107). Two of the salient features pertaining to the economic function furnished in the book are (Rangarajan, L.N., 1992, pp. 13–4)—

(a) The term *artha* used by Kautilya has a broader meaning beyond personal wealth. In this sense Kautilya's *artha* seems to be more all-embracing than A in the D-A-K-M framework. In the latter the *individual* is the prime focus, the *society* follows. In the former this *priority* appears to be reversed. In fact, Kautilya talks only of D-A-K or the three *purusarthas*.

(b) Unlike in the Vedic or post-Vedic period, Kautilya's *Arthashastra* recognized the crucial role played by the state or government for the material *well-being of the nation* and its people. For example, it includes guidelines on foreign policy, taxation, revenue collection, budget, accounts, defence etc. In the earlier two phases the emphasis was exclusively on individuals, guiding them how and why they should mould their lives for ethical wealth generation.

(c) Kautilya is silent about M. Since he was focusing on the King's role, this silence is understandable. However, with D at the base of A-K, the door to M is not shut. Heroes in epics like the *Ramayana*, the *Mahabharata*, kings like Chandragupta, Harshavardhana and others have upheld the goal of M by departing for *vanaprastha* after handing over the reins to able successors.

The following passage enunciates a major duty to be pursued by the king (Ibid., p. 149):

'Hence, the king shall be ever-active in the management of the economy. The root of wealth is [economic] activity and lack of it [brings] material distress. In the absence of [fruitful economic] activity, both current prosperity and future growth will be destroyed.'

This quote reinforces again the basic proposition here that Hinduism has never been adamantly ascetic in principle. While discharging his duty on the economic front, the following guiding principles of administration are expected to be adhered to by the king: *to run a diversified economy actively, efficiently, prudently and profitably* (Ibid., p. 74).

One cannot help but appreciate the farsight of Kautilya in gauging the benefits of 'diverse' economic functions. It is equally true that while economic functions were encouraged, the king was expected to act with 'prudence' which is the cornerstone of *dharma*. This is how Kautilya had formulated the scope of *sacro-secular symbiosis* at the state level.

(D) The *Bhagavad Gita*, containing the gist of the Vedas and the Upanishads, also re-emphasizes the principle of *sacro-secular reciprocity* between Devas (beings higher than man in the scale of evolution who are in charge of cosmic functions) and mankind. The following verses elaborate this process of mutual exchange (Sri Aurobindo, 2003, pp. 86–7)—

- With sacrifice the Lord of the creatures of old created creatures and said, By this shall you bring forth (fruits or offspring), let this be your milker of desires. (3.10)
- Foster by this the gods and let the gods foster you; fostering each other, you shall attain to the supreme good. (3.11)
- Fostered by sacrifice the gods shall give you desired enjoyments; who enjoys their given enjoyments and has not given to them (in return), he is a thief. (3.12)

The fundamental law conveyed through these verses is that all the basic requisites (like water, air, light, minerals etc.) for the performance of economic function are bestowed upon us by what we may call *Devas* or Gods. In Hinduism the many Gods and Goddesses mean the supra-human or Cosmic powers and forces of Nature. Personification helps humans to relate to these Cosmic powers with humility. Appropriating these Cosmic gifts, the human world creates utility through multifarious ways of conversion. Hence, human beings should gratefully offer their works and worship to these Cosmic agents or Gods.* This could also be done by physical acts of sacrifice (*yajna*), with fire (*agni*) as the central deity. Thus propitiated, these very powers of Nature would nourish humanity with more wealth. It is in this way that the *sacred cosmic dimension* is married with the secular economic function. The snowballing ecological problems due to aggressive economic activities can be addressed only by restoring the above sacro-secular symbiosis. The economic function in Hinduism has always maintained

---

* This is inner psychological *yajna*, done continuously through all work humans perform.

fidelity to this holistic truth. It is only now that a major departure from this is being enforced on it – the ethos of domination over Nature, not one of humble and grateful interdependence.

Similarly, the sage of the *Isa Upanishad* advises (Gambhirananda, S., 1983, p. 4)—

> 'All this—whatsoever moves on the earth—should be covered by the Lord. Protect (your Self) through that detachment. Do not covet anybody's wealth.'

Thus, caution has once again been sounded not to exalt the pursuit of A-K by succumbing to the wrongful envy of someone else's wealth. International GDP or per capita income rankings, countrywise, is a dangerous violation of this eternal principle. Because of this, materially-obsessed national minds succumb as servants of *artha* and *kama* only. For the individual, pursuit of Supreme Good (or Self) as the true goal vanishes altogether. Not only does *moksha* become impossible for him, even *dharma* or ethicality in secular affairs is gravely jeopardized.

It is therefore relevant to conclude this section by suggesting an important connection between the 'four-goal' system explained above and the two other quartets for the conduct of life and society i.e. four stages (*ashrams*) of life and the four classes or functionaries (*varnas*) in society. The 4-ashram system accords pride of place to the householder or *grihastha ashram*. Yet, in principle, it is not supposed to intrude into the first, third and fourth stages (*brahmacharya, vanaprastha* and *sannyasa*). Thus, it is only the second *ashram*, the householder stage, wherein A-K goals have their true and full scope. Similarly, in the 4-class system, the *brahmins* in principle are expected to be almost wholly free from embroilment with A-K, the society supporting them. *Kshatriyas* too are to be incidentally engaged in A-K. Truly, it is the *vaishyas* who have the prime role in A-K matters for society as a whole. But today all these principles are being flung overboard. Greed for money and sensual pursuits have started invading the first *brahmacharya* stage itself. Similarly, *brahmins* and *kshatriyas* are getting as much mired in A-K as *vaishyas* or *shudras*. No supra-economic saving outlook underpins the present mode of economic and financial activities. According to some alarmed observers things have come to such a pass today that almost 90 per cent of world economy is mere money churning, with the 'real' economy becoming a minuschile. This topsy-turvy portion started in 1971 when Richard Nixon delinked the dollar from the gold standard, and made it a floating currency (Harman, W. and Porter, M., 1997, pp. 61–2).

MODERN INDIAN SAVANTS ON THE ECONOMIC FUNCTION

So far the ancient Hindu outlook about the economic function has been highlighted. In this section observations by some of the greatest contemporary Indian minds on the subject shall be presented. They are some of the best flowers of the *sanatan* Bharatiya culture. They had both thought and lived Hinduism and other cognate psycho-philosophies in their varied aspects. Their chief contributions had poured out during the second half of the 19th century and the first half of the 20th century. They were also adequately familiar with the Western culture. Moreover, having studied and/ or worked there for long periods, the bulk or portions of their writings are available in English.

(A) *Rabindranath Tagore*—

(i) 'Our *Laxmi** is not the goddess of the cash balance in the bank: she is the *symbol of that ideal plenitude* which is never dissociated from goodness and beauty.' (Tagore, R., 1988, pp. 66)

(ii) 'In the old time when commerce was a member of the normal life of man, there ruled the *spirit of Laxmi*, who with her divine touch of humanity saved wealth from the unseemliness of rampant individualism, mean both in motive and method.' (ibid., p. 71)

(iii) 'In former times the intellectual and spiritual powers of this earth upheld their dignity of independence, but to-day, as in the fatal stage of a disease, the influence of money has got into our brain and affected our heart.' (Ibid., p. 67)

Tagore, reminds us that the Hindu concept of wealth bore the signet of Divine sanctity. It is also noteworthy that prayers for goddess Laxmi's blessings for wealth generation has been a part of domestic life in our society. We have seen our mothers performing this puja every Thursday evening. Tagore had prophesied way back in 1920 about one of the greatest problems of modern society: *dictation of terms by money power over the spiritual and intellectual capacities of man.* This indeed is a reflection of the unrecognized perversion now possessing our minds.

---

* The Hindu goddess of abundance and fortune.

(B) *Swami Vivekananda—*

(i) 'In the West they are trying to solve the problem *how much a man can possess,* and we are trying here to solve the problem on *how little a man can live....* if history has any truth in it, and if my prognostications ever prove true, it must be that those who train themselves to live on the least and control themselves well will in the end gain the battle.' (Vivekananda, S., 1993, p. 199)

(ii) 'Whenever any religion succeeds, it must have economic value. Thousands of similar sects will be struggling for power, but only those who meet the real economic problem will have it. *Man is guided by stomach.*' (Vivekananda, S., 1960, Vol. I, pp. 454–5)

Vivekanada's words are striking. He articulates two worldviews which are diametrically opposite. With anticipatory reference to rapacious greed and consumerism propelled by contemporary economic activities, he had predicted them to be unsustainable. He believed that the philosophy of 'plain living and high thinking' is the answer. Later in the chapter we shall find that point (i) was a perfect forecast (made in 1897) of the entropy problem.

Vivekananda's second quote is a seeming contradiction to the first one. But the latter had been uttered in the specific context of the-then poverty among large masses in India. It was the agonized outburst of a soul bleeding for the poor. But he could also see far beyond the immediate present. So, present inequitous poverty must be solved, but not at the cost of man's holistic future destiny – this is his message.

(c) *Mahatma Gandhi—*

(i) 'I offer the economics of God as opposed to the economics of the Devil which is gaining ground in the world-to-day. The latter aims at or results in concentrating a million rupees in one man's hands, whereas the former in distributing them among a million or thousands;...' (Gandhi, M.K., 1998, p. 34)

(ii) 'True economics never militates against the highest ethical standard,...An economics that inculcates Mammon worship,...spells death.' (Gandhi, M.K., 2001, Vol. III, p. 54)

(iii) 'The real value of acquired wealth depends on the moral sign attached to it, just as sternly as that of a mathematical quantity depends on the algebraical sign attached to it.' (Gandhi, M.K., 2001. Vol. V, p. 275)

Although much in the same spirit as the preceding savants, Gandhi has been more down-to-earth. He understands that all of us may not be successful in winning wealth. But those who will be successful should act as trustees, and plough-back as much wealth as possible to the masses. The secret behind ancient India's richness and minimal poverty was this ideal of *sacred trusteeship*. Self-centered pursuit of wealth will invite inequity of wealth distribution which is immoral. Only the spirit of trusteeship lends moral sanction to wealth generation. These remarks were made in the 1930's. Could this be a benchmark for self-introspection by those Indian graduates who are now walking away with jobs paying Rs 5 lacs per month or more in their mid-twenties, or Indian MP's who legislate Rs 65,000 per month (excluding allowances) for themselves – in a nation where 30 per cent people live on Rs 3,600 per year?

(D) *Sri Aurobindo*—

(i) 'A *full* and well-appointed life is desirable for man living in society, but on condition that it is also a true and beautiful life. Neither the life nor the body exist for their own sake, but as vehicle and instrument of a good higher than their own. They must be subordinated to the superior needs of the mental being,....' (Sri Aurobindo, 1985, p. 73)

(ii) 'All the economic development of life itself takes on as its end the appearance of an attempt to get rid of the animal squalor and bareness...It is pursued in a wrong way, no doubt, and with many ugly circumstances, but still the ideal is darkly there' (ibid., p. 155).

(iii) 'The aim of...economics would be not to create a huge engine of production, whether of the competitive or the cooperative kind but, to give men—not only to some but all men each in his highest possible measure—the joy of work according to their own nature and free leisure to grow inwardly ...' (ibid., p. 241).

Aurobindo too does not negate the desirability of a well-appointed life. But he emphasizes that there should be a still higher goal of life which is intrinsically ennobling and joyous. Wealth to him symbolizes Divine power. Man being its custodian, should mentally offer it to the Divine before utilizing it. Otherwise, it will soon regress towards 'economic barbarism' (Ibid, p. 72). 'Free leisure to grow inwardly'—modern economics is hostile to this human right.

(E) *S. Radhakrishnan—*

(i) 'The Hindu code of practice links up the human world of natural desires and
social aims, and the spiritual life with its discipline and aspiration on the other.
It condemns only natural existence which is unrelated to the background. Such
a life...dissolve(s) into emptiness...' (Radhakrishnan, S., 1957, p. 79)

(ii) 'Unfortunately at the present day in almost all parts of the world the strain of
money-making has been so great that many people are breaking down under
it...Hinduism has no sympathy with the view that 'to mix religion and business
is to spoil two good things.' (Ibid., p. 110)

Radhakrishnan, a philosopher and one of the past Presidents of India,
reiterates that a materialistic life led without any higher aim has been looked
down upon in Hinduism. However, while doing so, the fulfillment of
mundane needs has never been denied. It is also noteworthy that as far
back as in 1926 he had expressed his anxiety about single-minded
pursuit of money, making people psychologically more brittle. Thus, like
the above quartet, he too approves the 'sacro-secular symbiosis' thesis of
this chapter.

(F) *Swami Nikhilananda—*

(i) '...*Hinduism has never condemned a rich and full life in the world* or extolled
poverty as a virtue in itself—though the case is different with monks, who
voluntarily take the view of mendicancy.' (Nikhilananda, S., 1968, pp. 25–6)

(ii) 'It was *India's fabulous wealth that invited foreign invaders*, ... Religion has never
been the cause of India's poverty; it is indifference to religious precepts that
has been largely responsible for her general backwardness' (ibid., p. 26).

(iii) 'The history of India shows that when the country was *spiritually great* it was
also materially prosperous and culturally creative' (ibid., p. 14).

Nikhilananda, who had been the head of the Ramakrishna Vedanta Centre
in New York, re-asserts in point (i) the aspect emphasized by Sri Aurobindo
in point (ii) above. He also adds a new dimension while analyzing the causes
of India's poverty: non-adherence to D in the pursuit of A-K. Both foreign
exploitations and internal dereliction from D had led to economic decline
of varying degrees at different times. The third point above is a masterly
appraisal of the central, symbiotic drift of the Hindu culture in India.

(G) *Ananda K. Coomaraswamy*—

(i) 'Thus the ideal society is thought of as a kind of co-operative work-shop in which *production is to be for use* and not for profit, and all human needs, *both of the body and the soul*, are to be provided for.' (Coomaraswamy, A., 1989, p. 6)

(ii) 'On the one hand the inspired tradition rejects ambition, competition and quantitative standards; on the other, our modern 'civilization' is based on the notions of social advancement, free enterprise (devil take the hindmost) and production in quantity. *The one considers man's needs,...the other considers his wants.*' (Ibid., p. 7)

Coomaraswamy, (the renowned art critic and philosopher) upholds the view that traditional society (which includes Hinduism) encouraged economic practices with the purpose of nourishing body, mind as well as the soul. That apart, social advancement by performing economic function was defined in terms of fulfilling man's essential needs, and not his unlimited wants. Indulgence was a taboo.

SOME EXTRA-ORBITAL VIEWS FROM THE WEST

Some of the extra-orbital views from the West on the philosophy of economic functions will now be considered. Their views have also been sampled because, hailing from rich western nations as they are, such opinions may appear more acceptable to the present readers. Although they represent the best minds, yet none of them is a professional economist. Therefore, they have been able to take a more detached view of the consequences of the economic function than that of mainstream economists. It will also be explored if their assessments and remedies are in alignment with the spirit of the ancient Hindu framework (D-A-K-M) for economic functions. Such opinions will cover a period spanning 1912 to 2006 in order to capture the evolutionary trend of the critical western thought-process. The extra-orbital views of Indian savants cited above will also find authentic corroborative echoes in what follows.

(A) *R.H. Tawney (1926)*—

(i) Tawney, having observed the domination of 'economic egotism' in modern societies, had averred in 1926:

'Such societies may be called acquisitive societies because their whole tendency and interest and preoccupation is to promote the acquisition of wealth' (Tawney, R.H., 1942, p. 32).

(ii) 'Society ... must rearrange its scale of values. It must regard economic interests as *one element in life* ... the instrumental character of economic activity is (to be) emphasized by its *subordination* to the social purpose for which it is carried out' (ibid., p. 191).

Eighty one years since Tawney had written these words, the universal mania for acquiring money, as speedily as possible, has become awfully acute. Therefore, his concluding words are a faithful echo of the Hindu worldview about *subordinating* economic activities to higher social and spiritual causes.

(B) A. *Carrel* wrote in 1935:—

(i) 'Economists would realize that human beings think, feel, and suffer, that they should be given other things than work, food, and leisure, that they have *spiritual as well as physiological needs*. ... Economics would no longer appear as the ultimate reason of everything. It is obvious that the liberation of man from the materialistic creed would transform most of the aspects of our existence. Therefore, *modern society will oppose with all its might* this progress in our conceptions' (Carrel, A., 1961, p. 142).

(ii) 'When *our activity is set toward a precise end*, our mental and organic functions become completely harmonized. The unification of the desires, the application of the mind to a single purpose, produce a sort of inner peace. Man integrates himself by meditation, just as by action' (ibid., p. 263).

From the tenor of Carrel's observations, who was a Nobel Laureate in Medicine, it is evident that by 'activity' he meant the economic function, and by 'precise end' implied a transcendent goal of life. His implicit opinion is that economic activities and higher goals in life are essentially contradictory. Harmony can be established between the two if economic philosophy admits its neglect of the urge for fulfillment of spiritual goals as well. But he expresses his doubt if modern society would permit such a favourable environment. Carrel's misgiving, as events now show, was not a fantasy.

(C) P. *Sorokin* was sounding these warnings in 1958—

(i) 'The widespread notion that an improvement of economic conditions necessarily leads to a corresponding ennoblement of human conduct is largely a *myth*' (Sorokin, P.A., 1962, p. 80).

(ii) 'They may remain materialistic and mechanistic within the legitimate limits of these aspects of the Infinite Manifold. ... they should clearly emphasize their partial and *subordinate* role, that there are non-material, non-mechanistic, rational, and super-rational aspects transcending the material appearance...' (ibid., p. 110).

Sorokin (a social scientist) thus asserts that improvement in economic conditions will not automatically restore the sacred aspect of life. In other words, conscious acknowledgement and effort are called for appreciating the supra-material aspects of integral life. He even goes to the length of stating that materialistic (A-K) pursuits should remain subservient to the trans-material aspects of true human development (*moksha*). Otherwise, he apprehends, man would remain confined to a sensate worldview. Refinement of human conduct will then remain a far cry.

(D) E.F. *Schumacher* had thus pointed out the malaise of economics in 1973—

(i) 'The hope that the pursuit of goodness and virtue can be postponed until we have attained universal prosperity and that by the single-minded pursuit of wealth, without bothering our heads about *spiritual and moral questions*, we could establish peace on earth, is an unrealistic, unscientific, and irrational hope' (Schumacher, E.F., 1997, p. 28).

(ii) 'The modern economy is propelled by a frenzy of greed and indulges in an orgy of envy, and these are not accidental features but the very causes of its expansionist success' (ibid., pp. 26–7)

(iii) 'Needless to say, wealth, education, research, and many other things are needed for any civilization, but what is most needed today is a revision of the ends ... which accords to material things their proper, legitimate place, which is *secondary and not primary*' (ibid., p. 276).

Schumacher believes that single-minded pursuit of wealth will not by itself pave the way for peace and happiness. He too feels that since economic functions have enabled some nations to become materially affluent, it is now all the more important for them to get re-connected to their spiritual bearings. Otherwise, it will only accelerate misery. In this he agrees with Sorokin. Thus, all the four authors quoted so far happen to concur with the pristine Hindu scheme of priorities i.e., the material aspects of life (A-K) should only be a support to the higher order goals (D-M).

(E) A. *Toynbee* had reflected thus in 1976—

(i) 'Present-day society sees success and happiness in terms of ever-increasing economic affluence. This objective is not only economically unattainable but also *spiritually unsatisfying*. It does, however, provide an incentive for exertion and zest for work.' (Toynbee, A., 1987, p. 103)

(ii) 'I agree that we ought to aim not at gross national product but at gross national welfare. My tests of welfare would be...the *average per capita spiritual welfare*,...the *average standard of self-mastery*, which is the key to spiritual welfare....The last test gauges the extent to which the society has succeeded in giving *spiritual welfare* priority over material welfare.' (Ibid., p. 106)

Toynbee, a great historian, admits the futility of the attempt to seek happiness through economic affluence only, at the cost of the spiritual aspiration. He too unambiguously prioritizes the importance of gross national welfare over gross national product i.e. the *sacred over the secular*, as a correct approach for evaluating society's quality level. Thus, once again, Toynbee's stand rhymes well with that of the preceding thinkers.

(F) J. *Rifkin* had sounded, in 1981, clear caution about secularity:

(i) 'Having removed God from the affairs of people – as Bacon had removed Him from nature – Locke was left with human beings, all alone in the universe. No longer was the human being considered as part of a *divinely directed organism*' (Rifkin, J., 1981, p. 24).

(ii) 'Believing that men and women are basically egoists in pursuit of economic gain, Smith's theories subordinate all human desires to the quest for material abundance to satisfy physical needs. There are *no ethical choices* to be made, only utilitarian judgements exercised by each individual pursuing self-interest' (ibid., p. 27).

(iii) 'The illusion of material progress is exemplified over and over again in every major economic and social activity simply because *the second law* is swept under the rug ... we have convinced ourselves that we have made tremendous progress ... On closer examination such claims turn out to be *pure bunkum*. The debunker turns out to be the second law.' (Ibid., p. 137)

(iv) 'Speeding up the physical flow doesn't insure greater spiritual development; quite the contrary. *Transcendence* comes out of quietude and the recognition of the beauty in 'being,' not out of discord and the travails of 'doing' (ibid., p. 253–4).

Rifkin holds a few western philosophers responsible for dissociating modern economics from the Divine. He regards Adam Smith as equally instrumental in encouraging exclusively utilitarian judgments in the realm of economic functions. Thus, interpreting progress from the perspective of economic growth only brings us face to face with the 'second law' (that is *entropy*). Rifkin mirrors Vivekananda's mystic grasp of the problem in scientific terms.

This law needs a little amplification. From thermodynamics we learn: The total energy content of the universe is constant and the *total entropy is continually increasing.* This implies, 'Every time something occurs in the natural world some amount of energy ends up being unavailable for future work' (Ibid., p. 35). That is, at the time of conversion of energy from one state to another, some amount of it becomes *unusable*. Therefore, the greater the rate of conversion of energy, the higher the rate of entropy. Hence, rapid economic progress, pursued through increased exploitation of non-renewable sources of energy within a closed earth-system, is eventually bringing forward a state of unusable energy only. To decelerate the pace of entropy, which is otherwise inevitable, he suggests a look *within* to find the true meaning of happiness and development. This matches well with the Hindu tenet that 'objective entropy' can be prevented or remedied only by cultivating 'subjective affluence' i.e., Spirituality.

To be more explicit, the Buddhist dictum, 'a desire conquered yields more satisfaction than a desire gratified' may be recalled here. This should be complemented by the Vedantic theory of higher Self or *paramarthik vyaktitwa* which, by definition, is *poorna*. That is, the Self is whole and full in and by itself. But the lower self or *vyavaharik vyaktitwa* is deficit-driven, interminably. The 'Self' represents the ascetic end of the sacle, the 'self' the acquisitive. The deadly threat in objective entropy compels the recovery of the subjective Vedantic theory of higher Self. There seems to be no other route to real freedom and development—even survival.

(G) *D. Bohm* had these frank thoughts to share in 1994—

> 'We try to produce situations, such as acquiring wealth—people will make a lot of
> *money* to show that they are really great people. They make far more money than
> they need for whatever they want to do. *They keep on making money.* And if the
> mere making of money isn't enough, then they *buy* all sorts of things—far more
> than they need—to show that they are great people.' (Bohm, D., 1994, p. 165)

Bohm, a Nobel physicist, laments the modern-day tendency to judge
greatness on the basis of how much money a person has amassed, for
example, the ranking of world's richest persons. He points to the
displacement of higher goals of life which can foster a sense of proportion
in wealth acquisition. Vivekananda had, a century ago, foretold Bohm's
critique: 'Isn't it man that makes money? Where did you ever hear of money
making man?' (Vivekananda, S., 1960, Vol. VI, p. 455). Bohm has followed
suit by calling the bluff in regarding that money is the cause of greatness,
and man the effect. A humane outlook would place man before money.
Spirituality could follow then.

(H) *J. Carroll* felt sadly compelled to admit in 1993—

(i) '*Humanism* sought to turn the treasure laden galleon of Western culture around.
It attempted to replace God by man, to put man at the center of the universe,
to deify him. Its ambition was to found a human order on earth,...*without any
transcendental or supernatural supports*—an entirely human order.' (Carroll, J.,
1993, p. 2)

(ii) 'So the humanist fathers put their founding axiom: man is all-powerful, if his
will is strong enough he can create himself....He is creator and creature in
one' (ibid., p. 3).

Through Carroll's remarks rings the warning that an attempt to establish 'a
human order on earth', exclusively through the pursuit of economic activities,
bars our openness and access to the transcendental. He attributes this
mentality to the modern man's self-magnification – in the name of
humanism.

(I) *D.C. Korten* had bluntly told in 1998—

(i) 'Modern economics turned the Hobbesian ideology of rational materialism into
an applied science of human behaviour and social organization that embraces

hedonism as the goal and measure of human progress, and absolves the individual of responsibility for moral choice' (Korten, 1998, p. 27).

(ii) 'Life's song calls us to engage fully the wonder, joy, and love of life *inherent within our being*. ... The song of money calls us to experience life through the pursuit of material diversions...' (ibid., p. 36).

Korten, airs a sentiment akin to that of Bohm. But he is more critical. He considers adoption of hedonism as the key to human progress a faulty step. This makes man morally irresponsible and also snatches away the inner rhythm of life. He echoes the Vedantic *poornatwa* of man. Korten's last sentence is reminiscent of Tagore's statement (in 1916) about the philosophy of his school at Shantiniketan: 'Wealth is a golden cage in which the children ... are bred into artificial deadening of their power'. (Tagore, 2002, p. 131)

(J) *S. Davis and C. Meyer*, writing in 2000, opined—

'Not long ago, a lawyer brought this home to us by saying, 'No matter how much or little you make, it's still only walking-around money.' The statement is both arrogant and accurate. His remark underscores the increased importance of *'unearned' income*...that wealth accumulates in the form of financial assets, and the more those shares and other securities appreciate in value, the more wealth is created, not as earned, but as unearned income' (Davis and Meyer, 2000, p. 10).

Thus, Davis and Meyer too have chastized the money obsession of the economic function by calling it 'unearned income'. Essentially it means creation of artificial income by speculating in the stock market. This does not add anything to the real economy.

(K) *B. Hudson* has followed up the above train of thoughts in 2003—

(i) '... modernist optimistic idea that science and rational government can deliver security, prosperity and general welfare has been replaced by a *pessimistic awareness* of the ills brought about by the scientific-rational endeavour' (Hudson, 2003, p. 43).

(ii) '*Risk society* means that risk-thinking has become not only pervasive but also routinized: it is a part of everyday thinking processes of individuals in their private and organizational lives' (ibid., p. 44).

The essence of Hudson's argument is that science and technology on the one hand, and business and economics on the other, constitute a vicious spiral. They have been mutually reinforcing each other. The psychological impact of this marriage of convenience on the human mind is one of mounting insecurity and threat.

(L) *W. Rowland*, in 2003, joined his mind to those above—

(i) 'Progress is on the march. At the same time there is an undeniable melancholy at the core of it all. Something seems amiss. For one thing, we are making a mess of the planet. For another, the eternal goals of justice and equity seem to be receding, and at an accelerating rate. Not just progress, but meanness, obsessive self-interest, callousness towards others increasingly reflected in our public institutions, seems to be on the march. *Mental illness and spiritual malaise are endemic.*' (Rowland, 2003, p. XX)

(ii) 'The trouble with corporations is that they were designed to reproduce only one aspect of the multifaceted human psyche – in a word, *greed*.' (Ibid., p. XX)

Rowland endorses the same viewpoint as that of the other fellow-westerners quoted above. Although he agrees that on the material front there has been progress, the underlying driving force has been greed. This has shattered the ethical-spiritual and mental health aspects of human beings.

The major points emerging from the above views and concerns are summarized below—

(a) There is an intrinsic dormant urge in humans for the fulfillment of spiritual goals, which are higher than merely material sustenance. But this urge is smothered by modern economics.

(b) Measurement of development in terms of gross national product should be cross-checked against gross national welfare which includes spiritual welfare.

(c) Methodical attempts to learn and develop spiritual awareness is a pre-condition for wholesome management of economic affluence.

(d) Greatness of a man is wrongly assessed in terms of material wealth, and not his character wealth.

(e) Hedonism has devoured morality and ethics.

(f) It is essential to understand and appreciate the inevitability and consequences of entropy. Therefore, tempering the one-track economic function with a taste and search for intrinsic, higher Self *poornatwa* or wholeness is imperative. This human right must be restored urgently.

Evidently, some of the perceptive contemporary westerners, who have been able to scan from beyond the orbit, are also deeply worried about the skewed temper of the modern economic function. Their unanimous verdict is that pursuit of *economic activities without a spiritual anchorage* will be unsustainable. Thus, their opinions reinforce the same worldview as propounded and practised in Hinduism for several millennia. In other words, D and M have to set the limits for A and K. Many Indian savants and thinkers have been regularly fore-telling what thinkers from the West are now admitting.

GLOBALIZATION AND HINDU ECONOMIC PHILOSOPHY

It will now be indicated how the economic function fuelled and dictated by globalization fares with respect to the D-A-K-M framework of Hinduism. Here are some of the latest facts from the *Human Development Report* of 2005:

(i) 'For most of the world's poorest countries the past decade has continued a disheartening trend: not only have they failed to reduce poverty, but they are falling further behind rich countries. ... In 1990 the average American was 38 times richer than the average Tanzanian. Today the average American is 61 times richer' (Human Development Report, 2005, p. 36).

(ii) 'Most developing regions are falling behind, not catching up with rich countries. ... Absolute income inequalities between rich and poor countries are increasing even when developed countries have higher growth rates – precisely because initial income gaps are so large' (ibid., p. 39).

(iii) 'Measured in 2000 purchasing power parity terms, the cost of ending extreme poverty – the amount needed to lift 1 billion people above the $1 a day poverty line – is $300 billion. Expressed in absolute terms, this sounds like a large amount. But it is equivalent to less than 2 per cent of the income of the richest 10% of the world's population' (ibid., p. 19).

It is important to note from above that although the era of globalization has been marked by advancement in technology, trade and investment originating from the affluent nations, yet the key indices measuring human development have fallen relatively far behind in the poorer parts of the world. The emerging picture is far from encouraging. First, the Report testifies to the fact that the rich are becoming richer and the poor poorer by the day. Although it is true that many developing countries are registering higher growth rates, but those of the developed countries are higher still. Second, this inequality can be substantially mitigated if the world's richest 10 per cent population have the heart to share even 2 per cent of their income in philanthropy. But the reality is not as noble as that. A Shylock-mentality seems to underlie all aid negotiations. As the Mother of Sri Aurobindo Ashram at Pondicherry explains (through the monologue of an industrialist) (The Mother, 2005, pp. 18–19):

'And what have I contributed to humanity? Men travel more easily. Do they understand each other better? Following my example, all sorts of labour-saving gadgets have been mass produced and made available to an increasing number of customers. How far has this done anything more than to create new needs and a corresponding greed for gain?...I feel that there is a secret yet to be discovered; and without this discovery all our efforts are in vain'.

It seems the Mother could anticipate fifty years ago the role that might be played by today's globalization. Although globalization is being pushed through in a calculated and comprehensive manner, yet the 'secret' to be discovered, as confessed in the monologue, is still elusive. By 'secret' she implies a Consciousness in humans which can appreciate that the spirit of D-M, of higher or *poorna* Self, has to govern the motives of A-K. Leading nations and their leaders are accountable for this turn-around.

One of the causes behind the above problem is the acceleration of a 'sensate culture' (quoted earlier) implemented through globalization. A sensate society holds the following maxim: *more is less*. However, as mentioned above, the basic sacro-secular, sustainable philosophy of Hinduism is: *less is more*. This view was echoed in the words of Vivekananda (quoted earlier) where he had compared the two different worldviews about managing society. But the storm of globalization is crushing this enduring and sustainable basis of the economic function of Hinduism. With greater entanglement in complex external life, the higher goals (D-M), which intrinsically encourage living on less, are disappearing faster. Almost nine decades later Rifkin has endorsed this capital insight of Vivekananda. The former has put it succinctly (Rifkin, J., op. cit., p. 255),

'The more energy each of us uses up, the less is available for all life that comes after us. The ultimate moral imperative, then, is to *waste as little* as possible. By so doing we are expressing our love of life and our loving commitment to the continued unfolding of all of life.'

Harman corroborates this sacred logic in his own language (Harman, W., 1997, p. 142):

> 'Progress is the driving force behind all the assumptions at the heart of our economy-dominated society. Material progress assumes that what we have is *never enough*.'

Thus, the modern man, shedding his hubris, should be grateful to the primitive man who had conserved this earth for the former to blow up in a mere four secular centuries. The Hindu view of the economic function therefore receives both *scientific and social validation* from these extra-orbital thinkers of the West. The 2005 UNDP Report, highlighting the consequences of the worldview upholding 'more is less', had been anticipated by a few others also in the following terms:

(i) 'In 1750 the per capita incomes of what are now called developed countries and underdeveloped countries were equal. In 1930, the developed per capita incomes were four times higher. By 1980, they were seven times higher' (McLaughlin, 1998, p. 22).

(ii) 'Today, industrial civilization has increased the reach of human beings, at least the wealthier peoples, far beyond their own lands to the entire world. Tropical forests in Brazil have been razed to grow soyabeans which are fed to cows in Germany ... This artificial ecosystem has increased Germany's carrying capacity but drastically lowered it for the one million displaced forest settlers' (Hawken, 1993, p. 25).

(iii) 'The buy-now-pay- later epidemic has caught on. An entire generation of consumers is living life close to the edge, spending more than they earn. Now, with the economy taking a turn for worse, they are a step closer to the precipice' (Carvalho and Prasad, 2001, p. 39).

In search of 'more', masked in the guise of choice and capability, powerful economic entities (that is the corporate houses) are marginalizing the indigenous people. Not only that, consumers are also being increasingly seduced to purchase on credit. This has legitimized greed with unhealthy social and moral implications. Most importantly, and dangerously, the so-called developmental agenda is eliminating the saving 'spiritual choices and capabilities' of humanity.

Besides, India has special psychological reasons to be cautious and on-guard against the above influences. The nation's subconscious preserves the memory of the impoverishment and exploitation of her wealth during two centuries of British colonization. Globalization of today is after all a strategy originating from the wealthier nations. Massive R & D investments lead to large-scale industry, followed by mass production which requires huge markets worldwide. Thus, the norms of sustainable living in mature cultures like India are being pushed aside. In any case, let us have a glimpse of some data from Dutt about the colonial period (19th century) which bear the same character as mentioned by the three writers quoted above.

(i) 'Every nation reasonably expects that the proceeds of taxes raised in the country should be mainly spent in the country. ... But a change came over India under the rule of the East India company. They considered India as a vast estate or plantation, the profits of which were to be withdrawn from India and deposited in Europe.' (Dutt, 1989, I, p. XXV)

(ii) 'The East India Company's trade was abolished in 1833, and the Company was abolished in 1858, but their policy remains. Their capital was paid off by loans which were made into an Indian Debt, on which interest is paid by Indian taxes. The empire was transferred from the Company to the Crown, but the people of India paid the purchase money. The Indian debt which was £51,000,000 in 1857, rose to £97,000,000 in 1862 ... in 1902 (it) amounts to £200,000,000.' (Ibid., p. XXV)

(iii) 'Given these conditions, any fertile, industrious, peaceful country in the world would be what India is today. If manufacturers were crippled, agriculture over-taxed, and a third of the revenue remitted out of the country, any nation on earth would suffer from permanent poverty and recurring famines. ... If India is poor today, it is through the operation of economic causes.' (Dutt, 1989, II, p. XII)

Against this backdrop, India's renewed brush with the globalization gospel of 'more is less' is no less perilous. It follows up the trail of two centuries of economic terrorism in the colonial era which, in turn, was preceded by six centuries of armed terrorism by many invader groups.

Another reason why it is hard to take globalization at its face-value is the advocacy by some economists for breaking-down the supposed cultural barriers prevailing in enduring traditions. This position ignores that such worldviews have been much more holistic than the one-sided materialism of globalization. Let us sample a recent book (Roy and Sideras, 2006, p. 8):

'...Globalization does and will pose cultural challenges. But it would be to the advantage of a developing country to accept these challenges, as the greater diversity in culture and social tradition created with the interaction of foreign cultures and people can enrich local societies and cultures. Since, in developing countries, culture consisting of many centuries-old greatest hindrance to their development.... they need to shed some aspects of their culture which are not conducive to economic growth and development, as well as absorb those aspects of foreign culture which are pro-growth and development. ... For the first time in the international economy, a global society has emerged ...'

Roy and Sideras advocate their path for economic development of the developing countries with great audacity. They argue for globalization as the panacea for many of the ills which are plaguing developing countries due to their respective age-old traditions and cultures. They add further that the process of globalization will revitalize such societies by removing cultural impediments!

A reputed economist like Stiglitz, though more moderate, also defends globalization as an all-round positive approach for development.

(i) 'Globalization can be reshaped, and when it is, when it is properly, fairly run, with all countries having a voice in policies affecting them there is possibility that it will help create a new global economy in which growth is not only more sustainable and less volatile but the fruits of this growth are more equitably shared' (Stiglitz, J., 2002, p. 22).

(ii) 'I believe that globalization can be reshaped to realize its potential for good and I believe that the international economic institutions can be reshaped in ways that will help ensure that this is accomplished. But to understand how these institutions should be reshaped, we need to understand better why they have failed, and failed so miserably' (ibid., p. 215).

The above quotes reflect Stiglitz's optimism. However, it is well-known that every package of change in the past has been preceded by many similar pious hopes, of which the IMF, WB, WTO etc. are good examples. Stiglitz himself has acknowledged this in his book. Therefore, there is no convincing reason to be hopeful that successive rounds of cosmetic changes in these institutions and their policies will make things better. Above all, the most important *philosophical underpinning of sustainable holistic development cannot be anything but local*. Thus, material globalization will always be an unsustainable strategy for reducing poverty, promoting economic equality and maintaining cultural diversity. Two concrete examples maybe cited. In the cultural sphere, the mushrooming of call-centres (or BPOs) in India has made sexual permissiveness acceptable so-long as it motivates the young workforce. On the economic front, small scale units are dying out because they are no match for the MNCs who come to or penetrate India armed with advanced technology. Large numbers of such units have been forced to close down due to liberalization and removal of import quotas.

However, if we pay careful attention to the 'Report of the World Commission on Culture and Development' on *Our Creative Diversity* in 1995, it appears that economic experts are continuing to be oblivious of several fundamental principles of human development. Here are a few excerpts from the above Report,

(i) 'Clearly, there was a need to transcend economics, without abandoning it. The notion of development itself had broadened, as people realized that economic criteria alone could not provide a programme for human dignity and well-being' (Report of The World Commission on Culture and Development, 1995, p. 8).

(ii) 'The logic of rejection...to diminish each society's faith in its own resources and to threaten the diversity of cultures that is vital to the well-being of the human race' (ibid., p. 9).

(iii) 'The challenge is to promote different paths of development, informed by a recognition of how cultural factors shape the way in which societies conceive their own futures and choose the means to attain these futures' (ibid., p. 11).

Evidently, the intra-orbital, parochial perspective of economists and businessmen seem incapable of taking into account the many subtleties of human existence in a world of varied cultures. So, it is indispensable to listen respectfully to the voices of wise caution about the character of the economic function that has been overwhelming the world for the last one and half centuries. There is indeed a strong case for the economic function to turn towards *Spirinomics*, away from Capinomics or Communomics. Y-V Hinduism had worked out its basic blueprint with thorough anticipation and comprehension of the Whole. Volumes of *niti shastra* and *dharma shastra*, grounded in Y-V psycho-philosophy, have woven the highest and deepest principles into every detail of personal life, community life and public administration. It is not for nothing that the Hindu culture and economics of Bharatvarsha has continued unbroken for over seven thousand years. The world will be saved from death if it can climb down to the at-one-time-much-derided 'Hindu rate of growth'. That will be the beginning of 'Spirinomics' (Chakraborty, S.K., 2003, p. 136).

'TAKING CULTURES' AND LOST PARADISE

Yet, many people nowadays ask a legitimate question: Why then is corruption (which is monetary unethicality) today so pervasive and uncontrollable in Indian society: It is indeed both embarrassing and difficult to answer this charge. The following responses may be submitted:

(a) Corruption afflicts mostly the urbanized, organized, secure and educated sections of the population. They are usually the mutual perpetrators (Chakraborty and Chakraborty, 2006, pp. 56–8). The simple, uneducated or semi-literate people e.g. taxi drivers, rickshaw pullers, fishermen, ploughmen, street corner shopkeepers, domestic helping hands and the like are appreciably more clean and honest. They are normally the one-sided victims. They are also the majority -fortunately in a way!

(b) This difference may be explained by the fact that, consciously or unconsciously, the non-competitive, grassroots population is in much closer practical touch with several salient tenets of the Y-V ethos. Their daily lives are largely governed by such derived traditional rules of conduct. The sacred has not yet been demolished by the secular in their existence, as it has been for the liberated urbanites.

(c) Corruption plagues the country not because of our *shrutis* and *smritis*, Epics and Puranas, but because our privileged, politicized, higher echelon functionaries are systematically uprooting the rich ethical consciousness imbedded in our people.

(d) We already have a plethora of superimposed 'legal systems' and 'institutional systems'. Yet, in the absence of a vibrant, personalised 'belief system' coursing through our veins, corruption is not going to reduce. The key components of such an indigenous *'belief system'* should be as follows:

- Fear of the omni-seeing God.
- Karmic (Cosmic)law of inexorable retribution (*ritam*)
- Man-made laws are circumventable, not the karmic law.
- Party-less, democratic governance by people of high character.
- A live and active sense of shame vs. honour (i.e what adjectives will be ascribed to me behind my back?)
- Abandonment of the poisonous notion that no other existence precedes or follows this specific human life. There is/are after-life/after-lives where no corruption will be left unaccounted for.
- Love and reverence for the nation's honour and prestige.

At the end of his keynote address at a national conference on 'Challenges of Change', the Director of a reputed all-India centre for management education ended on this brave-new-world-note: 'The Future is India's. By 2050 India's economy would be equal in size to that of the USA'. This pronouncement was the finale of a standard package of power-point, all-purpose slides. Just to mention one or two arguments made in the presentation e.g., 'Natural resources? No issue. If coal or fertilizer is in short supply, they can be readily imported; Money? No issue. Any amount can be raised in a trice? So, who cares about some weird notion like global entropy hotly chasing such short-term international transfers of materials? Who again wants to realize that our domestic basic industries are being decimated by our own colluding politicians, bureaucrats and businessmen? 'Global economics' is in fact meant to force open countries like India for the sake of 'national economies' of the rich and powerful countries—who cares? Here is a drop from the ocean of deception: Rain forests along the Amazon basin are being felled at the rate of 200 football grounds every hour. Why? To grow fodder for cattle feed in rich nations (Wallace, 2007, pp. 43, 49). So much for ethics and international transparency then!

As for raising money like a song, our top-level educationists do not seem to know that by now, since 1971 when the USA had taken the dollar off the gold standard, a mere 10 per cent of the world's economy is 'real', the rest non-productive speculative currency economy only (Henderson, 1999, pp. 2–6). No wonder raising money is no issue. But towards what 'real' achievement for a nation where 30 per cent of its people are still at or below the poverty line?

The word 'nation' itself is, however, being turned fast into a dead word. For instance, an all-India professional body of long standing has been asked by the powers-that-be that the first word 'National' has to be dropped from their name if a certain new course is to be approved. The smart do-gooders of India want the country to be free from what they choose to call 'hyper-nationalism'. Signs are there that soon the 'national flag', 'national anthem', 'national song' and several more such symbols and institutions could be stripped of their 'national' character. No other country in the world, manipulated by the personal or partisan interests of its professionals and intellectuals, does such an efficient job of psychological enervation of their people. Even secular economics, not to speak of Spirinomics, will tend to be a chimera in such a dismal mental atmosphere.

Comparison with nations so disparate as China and Malaysia should put India's spiritual and secular de-nationalisation in the right perspective. So far as the West goes, we are informed that in Britain, Germany, USA etc., *leikultur*—the guiding sense—is traced to the 'dominant culture's set of values' (Saul, 2005, pp. 244–5). If *Sanatan Bharatiya* values like 'less is more' can be given a fresh stimulus, not only shall Bharat serve her all-round well-being; it will also transform crafty globalism into true universalism.

CONCLUSION

It is worth comprehending that from the time of 'knowledge is power' to that of the 'invisible hand', of the 'acquisitive society' to 'affluent society', of the 'predatory society' to that of 'narcissistic society', and now to 'risk society' – the day of reckoning for us may not be too distant. The deluded modern mind is tending towards suicide. The ruling 'greed-speed' alliance should be governed by the 'sacred-secular' symbiosis. Hindu thought preserves the integral blueprint and the detailed mapping of this saving sojourn of sobriety. Sarkar (op. cit., p. 6) has put this across well by saying that all the creative writings of the Hindus:

'...have sought to realise the synthesis and harmony between the eternal antipodes...of the universe—the worldly and other-worldly, the positive and transcedental, the many and the one, science and religion...

Thus secular desires were legitimized but subjected to careful moderation.

Globalization, should it continue, and if it is to make for sanity and peace, should essentially, not cosmetically, veer towards the Spiritual. For, the universal declaration of 'Spiritual Globalization' had issued forth aeons ago from the *Upanishadic* rishi of the *Taittiriya Aryanaka:*

'*Yatra vishwam bhavati eknidam*'
('Let this world be but one nest for all birds'.)

Human Relationships in the Workplace
A Few Spiritual Clues

HORIZONTAL RELATIONSHIPS

Both the epics, *Ramayana* and *Mahabharata*, are replete with episodes demonstrating human or inter-personal relationships at their best and worst. The purest pattern of such relationships is amply displayed among Ram and his three brothers when Ram accepted the 14-year exile to the forest to honour Dasharath's promise to Kaikeyi. Complete absence of greed for power, along with complete freedom from egotism, had produced the perfect model of fraternal relationship between Ram and Bharat. Similarly, one day during their exile the Pandava brothers returned to their hut, and announced to mother Kunti about their *bhiksha* for the day. Busy as she was within the hut, without looking out, she said 'divide it equally amongst yourselves, sons'. But it was Draupadi who was with them, Arjuna having won her hands in Drupad's court. Kunti's instruction was obeyed, and Draupadi became the co-wife of all the five brothers. Here too the values of filial piety, of trust, of large-heartedness, of loyalty, of humility etc. among all the characters, including Draupadi, emerge gloriously.

On the other hand, the *Mahabharata* also weaves the web of vile and crooked interpersonal relationships between the Kaurava and Pandava brothers right from childhood days. The spiritually-grounded human values of magnanimity, transparence and patience of the Pandavas, especially of Yudhisthira (the eldest), were consistently negated by the secularly-driven dis-values of vanity, envy and greed of the Kauravas, led by Duryodhana (the eldest).

After such epic insights into human relationships, a few relevant episodes of our times may be examined—

(A) Two Sublime Examples
(i) During the infancy of Belur Math, Swami Vivekananda had announced a rule requiring waking up at 4am. It was meant for all. Swami Premananda,

a *gurubhai*, one day failed to wake up at the gong of the bell. Vivekananda asked another inmate to strike the bell beside Premananda's bed. But to no avail. Then the no-nonsense Vivekananda himself went in and broke his sleep. Later, at the tea table Vivekananda explained why it was essential that elder monks could not violate such norms for the sake of an efficient organization. Premananda realized his lapse. Repenting, he admitted his fault, and sought punishment for it. This noble gesture of his *gurubhai* moved Vivekananda to tears. He embraced a tearful Premananda and was heard sobbing, 'How could you even think that I could punish you, Baburam-da?' Swami Brahmananda (Rakhal) was a witness to this sublime drama and interceded, 'Yes, the punishment for such an offence is to support oneself by *madhukari* or *mushti bhiksha* for the day.' Swami Premananda instantly accepted the verdict (Chattopadhyay, 1976, pp. 280–1).

(ii) Sometime during 1908, when Sw. Brahmananda (Raja Maharaj) had visited south India, he had a tiff with Sw. Ramakrishnanda (Shashi Maharaj) at the Madras Math. Raja Maharaj wanted Shashi Maharaj to send Swami Vivekananda's *Inspired Talks* to the *Bombay Chronicle* for review. Shashi Maharaj thought that not many would read the *Bombay Chronicle*. Therefore, it would be adequate and effective to have it reviewed in the *Hindu*. So, the book was not sent to Bombay. Raja Maharaj did not protest, but became very grave. When Shashi Maharaj went to offer him his regular daily *pranam*, even then Raja Maharaj remained silent, absolutely aloof. Shashi Maharaj soon realized that Raja Maharaj was displeased with him. So he spoke to him with emotional intensity, 'Raja, you have such a petty mind! Is Shashi your equal that you are offended with him? If you so will, you could create hundreds of Shashi's like me. Are you not then ashamed of treating me as if I were your equal?' At these words Raja Maharaj blushed. He said softly, 'No, no – nothing to bother has happened, Shashi.' (Prameyananda, 2001, p. 99)

(B) TWO RIDICULOUS EXAMPLES
(i) The Board meeting of a large nationalized bank had just commenced. One of the Board members was also a member of the Audit Sub-Committee. A one-hour meeting of this committee had just preceded the full Board meeting. Perhaps this was a very heated process. Thereafter, this particular Board member took the full Board session by surprise by casting aspersions on the Bank's practice of inviting the General Managers to attend all Board meetings. Technically, the GMs are not Board Members. True. But the Bank's Chairman-MD explained the intention behind this long tradition: to obtain specific details on any Board agendum for greater clarity and help in decision-

making. But this Board member went on hurling insinuations at the CMD, and even said he could hit him physically! A few other dazed Board members tried to pacify him and bring about some decorum and dignity in the tense and ugly atmosphere. But nothing worked! He even announced that he might put his foot down on this practice by virtue of being a Joint Secretary of the GOI. This non-agenda item got stalemated. The rest of the Board meeting was listless. At lunch time this person absented himself.

(ii) A conscientious, caring and diligent Head of the Department in an all-India Institute had arrived at a consensus with all his colleagues together about various courses to be offered by the Department in the next semester. This consensual list was then communicated to the academic Dean's office —six weeks prior to the semester. Then suddenly, just a week before the semester, one colleague pleaded ill-health and withdrew his course. Another colleague argued that the HOD had not given anything in writing, so he was not obliged to honour his verbal promise. The simple-minded, trusting HOD was caught napping in this sudden storm. The other colleagues kept quiet. The HOD pleaded and begged of his colleagues not to create such a crisis which would damage the credibility of the department within the entire Institute community. The registered students would also suffer for no fault of theirs. He also told them that if they had any grouse against him, that should be handled separately without dishonouring the departmental commitment. But alas! None heeded to all this—even those whom the HOD was instrumental some years ago in recruiting to the prestigious Institute. Democratic (?) individualism wrecked the structure of disciplined teamwork.

Lest readers imagine that noble human relationships blossom only in sacred institutions, and not in secular organizations, we should recall the magnificient relationships between Satyen Bose and Meghnad Saha. These two had become world-class scientists, although they did not posses the latest books and equipment. They were inducted into Calcutta University by its Vice Chancellor, Ashutosh Mukherjee. As students they used to compete in the class for years for the top position. Yet, during their long research and teaching careers they worked with perfect mutual respect and whole-hearted cooperation in all aspects. It was a life-long bond for both, though at a later stage Saha had entered public life as an independent MP. (Salvi, 2002, pp. 24–35)

A Brief Analysis of A and B

The first pair of examples in (A) demonstrate how spirituality, when it penetrates into the very marrow of role players, fosters 'nobility', 'dignity' and 'generosity' (NDG) in the workplace. The second pair of examples (B) shows how mere formal education and cleverness leads to or manifests as 'pettiness', 'smallness' and 'meanness' (PSM). While Vedantic spirituality (*dvaita, vishist-advaita, advaita*) admit intellect and reason as valid capabilities, yet it decidedly goes beyond into the realm of *chittasuddhi* or *antarshuddhi*. For example, the classic response of Mahavir Hanuman to Sri Ram about the former's attitude towards the latter illustrates the whole range of Vedantic *chittasuddhi*: When in the *dvaita* mood, Ram is Lord, Hanuman is servant; when in *vishista-advaita* mood, Ram is whole, Hanuman is part; when in *advaita* mood, Ram and Hanuman are One. The Bose-Saha pair is an excellent example of superlative *budhivritti* and noble *hridayvritti* (i.e. *chittashuddhi*) working in wholesome harmony.

What is the difference in the hub of the wheel in a sublime workplace on the one hand, and that of a ridiculous workplace on the other? It is ego, *ahankara*. This is the greatest polluter, contaminator of the heart – the seat of emotions in our being. All the *shadaripus*,[*] *asuri sampats*[**] are emotional spokes which converge on the hub of *aham* (ego). Contemporary education is universally aggravating egoistic individualism, the 'unripe ego'. It begins in infancy at home, and continues throughout the person's life. Emotional purification through assiduous culture of *daivi sampats*[***] does not figure at all in the educational agenda. Within the heated milieu of competitive careerism, personality development and ego inflation are often becoming synonymous. Swami Vivekananda had insisted upon confidence – but not in the PSM-ruled, deficit-driven self, but in the NDG-dominated, *poorna* SELF. A lawn will invariably get dirty in a short time if it is left unattended. To clean it up, to make it green and flowery will require conscious and hard labour. So is the case with the human heart. 'Ripe ego' will require culturing on lines quite different from those for the 'unripe ego'. In fact, 'unripe ego' does not need culturing. It is just there. Human Values (HV) culture, flowing directly from the spiritual hub of *ego renunciation*, will be needed for the former. For the latter, respective professional skills will be enough. But these sharp skills, when applied through dis-values (DV's), cause perversion in the workplace. 'Behavioural unethicalities' like backbiting, sycophancy, deceit etc. go on snow-balling. This is what had happened in the second set of

---

[*] *Shadaripus* — six internal enemies like bust, anger, greed, delusion, vanity and envy.

[**] *Asuri Sampats* — demoniac qualities (Gita, chapter 16)

[***] *Daivi Sampats*— divine qualities (Same)

incidents. Intellect and reason were used in malafide ways. And such degrading inter-personal exchanges are ever on the rise.

VERTICAL RELATIONSHIPS

So far a few common but critical aspects of horizontal relationships only have been touched upon. Vertical relationships are of course equally important. It is the leader's role which is of prime significance here. Swami Vivekananda, himself a born leader and institutional-builder, has formulated this principle as the basis of leader's relationships with his colleagues and team-members (Chakraborty, 2006, p. 249):

> 'It is absolutely necessary to the work that I should have the enthusiastic love of as many as possible, while I remain entirely *impersonal*. Otherwise jealousy and quarrels will break up everything. A leader must be *impersonal*'.

The concept of 'impersonal love' is unique. Its essence is *impartiality* and *fairness* in the leader's dealings with his co-workers. 'Impersonal' does not imply cold aloofness or unconcern or apathy. In a very large and complex social mosaic like India's, unlike in homogeneous small societies as Japan or Sweden, the task of a leader in maintaining all-round trust and credibility is a difficult one. Caste, religion, region, language —all such factors provide a fertile soil for partiality, favouritism, bias, prejudice etc. to thrive. They all feed the lower self of the leader. It is that aspect of his personality which is chronically deficit-driven, hence insecure. So he needs his *coteries* and *cliques* to survive and hang on to power. A few get 'included', and the rest feel 'excluded'. This destroys trust and cohesion, breeds conflicts and demoralization. This is the warning sounded by Vivekananda in the quoted statement.

To be able to function with 'impersonal love', the awakening of the Higher Self in the leader is indispensable. Its essence being the settled state of *poornatwa* felt within, insecurity does not haunt the leader any more. Narcissistic addiction to power and pelf having been put on the leash, the Higher Self leader functions with great ease and self-assurance, earning the respect and loyalty of all. The lower self dealings of Dhritarashtra along with Duryodhana were the cause of the Mahabharata war. His sentimental love was personal. On the other hand, the Higher Self behaviour of Buddha towards his errant son Rahula was the cause behind the dignity and honour accruing to Buddhist institutions for several centuries. Buddha's sternness towards Rahula constituted 'impersonal love'.

So far as *followers* are concerned, their vertical relationship with the leader must be founded on the acceptance and practice of this principle—to become or to deserve *to become a leader tomorrow, one must be a good follower today.* To be vain and conceited as a follower today, and then hope later as a leader to earn the loyalty and devotion of followers is an absurdity. The defence services, we are informed, adopt this attitudinal norm as the basis of vertical relationships:

- *The senior should not remember that he is the senior;*
- *The junior should not forget that he is the junior.*

This is a sound and practical method of putting leader-follower relationships on the base of reciprocal caring and respect (Chakraborty and Chakraborty, 2006, pp. 3–10 and 210–18).

Whatever has just been highlighted in the previous paragraph about follower-attitude is valid when the leader himself has, in the first palce, the capacity for impersonal love flowing from Higher Self. It cannot work when the leader is a lower-self, coterie-dependent person.

The other side of the picture also needs highlighting. We have often seen leaders close to the Higher Self-Impersonal Love category to be heckled and insulted by arrogant subordinates. Neither age, nor experience, nor the positive intentions of the leader count for anything. Many a times constructive changes for the long-term improvement of the organization or the team, mooted by such leaders, have been cleverly scuttled – in the name of democracy, freedom of speech, equality etc.

A FEW SPIRITUAL SOLUTIONS

- Swami Vivekananda had once declared, '... excess of knowledge and power, without holiness, makes human beings devils' ((Swami Vivekananda, 1962, Vol. I, p. 425). More than hundred years later our workplaces richly (!) deserve this scathing rebuke to a much greater degree than before. The answer is gaining *holiness*—by confronting the 'unripe ego' as practical Vedanta lays down.
- The great institution-builder that he was, Vivekananda had also thundered thus—'Learn obedience first....We are all of us self-important, which never produces any work....perfect obedience (is)...altogether lacking in us' and 'Jealousy is the bane of our national character, natural to slaves.'(Swami Vivekananda, 1962, Vol. VI, p. 349)

Thus, two signal DV's—*disobedience* and *jealousy*—have been pointed out above. They mar the worker, the workplace and work alike. They both spring from the 'lower self' or the 'unripe ego'. The secular approach to individualism cannot combat this scourge—at least not in India. It is education about the *sacred*, according to Bharat's Yoga-Vedanta tradition, which has to assume central importance. Intimations of *para vidya*[*] ought to *precede* entry into *apara vidya*.[**] The *brahmacharya ashram* was indeed meant for such infusion in the first quarter of human life. We have stinking workplaces because even a modicum of *para vidya* has vanished altogether. The joint blight of both capitalist and communist ideologies have done irreparable damage (Chakraborty, 2001, pp. 101–20).

• In the wake of the above reference to jealousy, envy etc., aphorisms I.33 and II.33 of Patanjali's *Yogasutras* are instructive. (Swami Vivekananda, 1976, pp. 148–9). I.33 educates us that *maitri* or friendliness (towards the happy), *karuna* or compassion (towards the unhappy), *mudita* or appreciation (of the virtuous), and *upeksha* or indifference (towards the wicked) would lead to peace of mind. Thus, the above four critical HV's for every workplace are to be cultured. The result is more *peaceful* workers, and therefore a more healthy, energetic and powerful workplace.

Aphorism II.33 anticipates the difficulty of cultivating the above HV's in general. So it suggests the practical psychological discipline of *pratipaksha bhavanam* – the deliberate raising of *contrary* (e.g. *maitri* vs. envy, *upeksha* vs. retaliation) thoughts.

This is no easy magic formula. But is there any other fundamental way out of unhealthy workplaces?

Swami Premananda had once (1914) given a very lucid explanation of these four *bhavanas* (in Bengali) to a small group of devotees. His own process for ego management (a persistent problem as mentioned earlier) was an exquisite *mantra* he used to mutter to himself: '*naham, naham, tuhun, tuhun*' i.e., 'not I, not I, but Thou, only Thou' (Swami Chetanananda, 2002, p. 213).

• Workplaces are becoming increasingly degenerative because of mounting *behavioural unethicalities*. Monetary unethicality is only the visible tip of the iceberg. Behavioural unethicality is the more ubiquitous, though hidden, reality. Jealousy, indiscipline, disobedience etc. have already been mentioned. To these should be added interpersonal unethicalities through DV's like duplicity, flattery, arrogance, vindictiveness, deceit etc. The *shadaripus* that grip the lower self or unripe ego, are the soil upon which

---

[*] *Para vidya* — learnings to realize the higher self
[**] *Apara vidya* — learnings to sustain the lower self

these poison plants grow with profusion. Codes of conduct or legislation cannot tackle this aspect. Cultivation of the Higher Self, the ripe ego is the true answer. *Atmany eva atmano tushtah* (one should cultivate contentment within one's *atman* or soul)— education for this perception is the real remedy (verse II.55, *Gita*).

- The first example has shown how Swami Premananda had readily admitted his mistake and volunteered to undergo the relevant punishment. Absence of this attitude is one of the biggest deficits in workplaces today. We do not accept errors or lapses. Intellect is used in all possible ways to rationalize irresponsibility. The sense of remorse, regret, repentance, shame for wrongdoings is virtually gone. Even, the simple courtesy of saying 'I am sorry' is nowadays a rarity. Why? Because it is the 'lower bird self' of the *Mundaka* and *Shwetashwatara Upanishads* which presides and rules over workplaces (verses 3.1-2, and 4.6-7 respectively). The Vedantic approach is obvious again—attaining the 'Higher Bird Self'.
- In search of solutions from Vedanta for unhealthy workplaces, serious attention may be given also to, what we may call, *prarthana yoga* (the *yoga* of prayer). Here are some moving and ardent prayers for positive, healthy leadership and teamwork from some of the *Upanishads* and the *Rigveda* (Narayana, 2005, pp. 10–11, 14).

From *Kathopanishad, Kenopanishad*
  '*Aum, saha nau avatu, saha nau bhunaktu,*
  Saha veeryam karava vahai, tejaswi nau
  Adhitam astu, ma vidwishwavahai'
  (Let us be *protected* together, let us be *nurtured* together, let us work with *energy* together, let us learn with *effectiveness* together, let us not have *friction* among ourselves.)

From *Rigveda*, X.191.4
  '*Samani va akutih, samanah hridayani vah,*
  Samanamastu vo mano, yatha va susahaasati'
  (Let there be *oneness* of your aspirations, *oneness* of your hearts, *oneness* of your thoughts – so that you work with perfect *cooperation*.)

From *Taittriya Aranyaka*, 7.I.
  '*Ritam vadisyami, satyam vadisyami,*
  Tanmam-avatu, tad vaktaram avatu
  Avatu maam, avatu vaktaram'

(Let me speak Right, let me speak Truth, Thou art please protect me, please protect the teacher.)

CONCLUSION

Bloated self-esteem and its *asuric* cohorts, afflicted with secular 'money-ism', breeds selfish *a-dvaita*: none, nothing matters except 'I'. Workplace ill-health is then inevitable. So, let us pray and strive for shrinking our egotism with the help of *daivi* or divine values. And then march towards the 'monism' of sacred *advaita*.

A Few Architects of Indian Industry
The Architecture of Their Minds

ACHARYA PRAFULLA CHANDRA RAY

Acharya Prafulla Chandra Ray was born in 1861 and died in 1944. Mahatma Gandhi had been introduced to him by Gopal Krishna Gokhale in these words (Gandhi, 1972, p. 174):

'This is Prof. Ray who, having a monthly salary of Rs 800, just keeps Rs 40 for himself and devotes the balance to public purposes. He is not, and does not want to get married.'

This happened probably around 1896. Thereafter, thirty years or so later, when Gandhiji wrote his autobiography in 1926-27, the following estimate of PC Ray was given by him (Ibid., p. 174):

'I see little difference between Dr. Ray as he is today and as he used to be then. His dress used to be nearly as simple as it is, with this difference of course that whereas it is *khadi* now, it used to be Indian mill-cloth in those days. I felt I could never hear too much of the talks between Gokhale and Dr. Ray, as they all pertained to public good or were of educative value.'

It was this Dr. Ray (Knighted by the British government, 1919) who had launched the first Indian chemical and pharmaceutical factory, utilizing indigenous natural materials, in 1892. It was called 'Bengal Chemical and Pharmaceutical Works'. Later, in 1901, it was converted into a public limited company (Chaterjee and Sen, 1986, p. 10). He had started the venture in 1892 with a capital of Rs 800 only, all from the savings out of his salary, the bulk of which he used to give away to the needy or to deserving social causes. Thus, PC Ray was probably unique among the industrial pioneers of India who, being an academic and a professor par excellence in the first instance, was also a daring entrepreneur.

Teaching, research, business, social service, literary activities – these five pillars constituted the solid base for the imposing edifice of his 84-year life. In course of time, therefore, he came to be called by various affectionate names: 'the Master of Nitrites', 'Doctor of Floods' (by the Mahatma), 'a saint' (by Gokhale), 'guardian angel of the suffering humanity' (by Ashutosh Mukherjee) (Ibid., p. 25).

PC Ray was later earning Rs 1,000 by 1914 as a Professor in the Presidency College. Moreover, he was the son of a zamindar. Yet he had always led the life of an ascetic. Out of Rs 1,000 he kept Rs 200 for himself. Thus, towards the close of his life, he had given away as much as Rs 6 lacs for noble causes (Gupta, 1966, pp. 78). He took no dividends or salaries from the companies he had floated (e.g. Bengal Potteries, Bengal Enamel besides BCPW).

This story is an eye-witness account. One morning a devoted attendant brought him a few nice, large ripe bananas. He was very happy. But moments later he asked: how much did they cost? 'Three pice, sir'. The Acharya exploded in anger at such over-spending, and refused to eat the fruit. The same day in the afternoon a gentleman came and explained to him about an important project to help some poor people. Convinced, PC Ray drew a cheque for Rs 3,000 and gave it to the visitor. The attendant was confounded about this 3 pice vs. 3000 rupees drama in the space of just a few hours (Ibid., p. 66)!

As we shall see later in this chapter, PC Ray, much like Ardeshir Godrej, had to contend with the same psychological handicap the Indian market has been prone to: their abhorrence of local products and admiration for foreign brands (Ibid., p. 33). Such was the attitude in pre-independence days. Sadly, this drawback seems to be even more severe in post-1950 India.

When he later shifted to the Calcutta University Science College, he rose to be the *acharya devoh bhavah* for a large number of world-class scientists of the next generation. The following description etches a sublime picture of the 'transformation' (a word much in vogue in leadership literature these days) he had ushered (Chaterjee and Sen, op. cit., p. 45):

'These activities made the College a temple where the people came in response to his call for work. Enthusiasm for offering money and effort ran high, youth came to uplift the condition of villages, and from far off places came votaries to have a *darshan* of this selfless *sannyasi*.'

How many high-profile business leaders of today can even dream of attaining such inspiring heights?

Yet, in his autobiography, written when he reached seventy years, he confessed that 'he was open to the reproach of egotism' (Ray, 1932, p. 541). Let us listen to Acharya in his own words:

- 'Mine has been a dull, humdrum and routine-regulated school master's life. I have no sensational tales of adventure to tell, no thrilling hair-breadth escapes to narrate, no cabinet secrets to divulge. ... I thought however that a plain unvarnished narration of my uneventful career, which has run its noiseless tenor, might convey some lesson to my countrymen, especially to the younger generation' (ibid., p. 540).
- 'I confess I am a strange contradiction. Although I am generally credited with being an industrialist, yet from the dawn of my intelligence the ephemeral character of the phenomenal world has haunted me, and a disregard for worldly effects has become my second nature' (ibid., p. 541).

The attentive reader will not fail to note how strong a fidelity the above character traits of PC Ray bear with the age-long *rajarshi* model of Indian leadership. A later chapter in this book on Kautilya-Kalidasa-Harshavardhana will reveal the unbroken line of such *rajarshi* leaders upto the days of PC Ray and his tribe. And even later to this day.

PC Ray-the-*rajarshi* was firmly anchored in the 'sacred', while sailing his life-boat in the stormy 'secular' waters of life. So, anyone who approached him for blessings, the Acharya invoked the benediction of God (Gupta, op. cit., p. 58). Later in the chapter we shall hear again his complete trust and surrender to Providence in all his works.

Let it be noted also that *non-attachment to secular wealth* for himself had never come in the way of devoting his whole life to the *augmentation of the nation's wealth*. This indeed is *nishkam karma* at its best. What a reversal of this ideal we see all around us today! Thank God, those were the 'primitive' days when human cleverness had not devised 'modern' methods to rank and lionise the richest or wealthiest people in cities, countries and the world! What a travesty of even humanism!

ARDESHIR GODREJ

Ardeshir Godrej was born in 1868 and died in 1936. He had begun his career as a lawyer, but left it soon after losing his very first case in Zanzibar. He refused to twist the truth to favour his client (Karanjia, 1997, pp. 1–2).

Ardeshir's first attempt in the new pasture of industry was to make surgical instruments. But the chemist's firm wanted to market them under a 'foreign' brand name which would sell better to local doctors. He would not pocket this insult. So the first foray into industry was also a failure (Ibid., pp. 24–5).

He next ventured into locks in the year 1897 and gradually expanded into a whole range of world-class security equipments (Ibid., pp. 27–30). 'Ardeshir was the first to invent and put on the market a lever lock without springs. This was the earliest of the thirty six Godrej patented inventions' (Ibid., p. 32). When it next came to soaps, Ardeshir succeeded in producing stable toilet soaps from vegetable oils instead of animal fats. He launched first the 'No. 2' soap. After perfecting the results of further experiments, 'No. 1' soap with a lingering rose perfume was introduced. Releasing No.1 after No. 2 was a subtle marketing tactic since people would think that if No. 2 was so good, then No. 1 must be even better. Rabindranath Tagore wrote: 'I know of no foreign soap better than Godrej, and I have made it a point to use Godrej soaps' (Ibid., pp. 49–50)

Here are a few intimate portrayals of Ardeshir, the-man-within, from Karanjia:

- 'By all accounts he was a lonely man, given to plain living and high thinking, ... A recluse, who inhabited a solitude and always kept his distance ... He exuded the confidence of one who had the measure of his task. But he showed no pride in his achievements, and seemed not to consider himself in any way an exceptional human being. He was only doing his duty as an Indian, doing his best for India' (Ibid., p. 58).
- 'Ardeshir believed in simple, unostentatious living ... He would take public transport or walk to his destination, using a car only late in life at Pirjosha's insistence. A man of considerable culture and a voracious reader, particularly of books on literature and philosophy ...' (Ibid., p. 61).
- 'Ardeshir was religious. Every morning he spent a few moments at the Vatchagandhi Agiary on Hughes road. But he was truly religious in the sense that he lived his religion, particularly in the practice of philanthrophy' (Ibid., p. 61).

Thus, much like PC Ray, Ardeshir also possessed the key qualities of a *rishi* in good measure. Self-reliance for India was the most important, overriding goal of Ardeshir's industrial career. He wanted always to 'show Indians the way to do things for themselves' (Ibid., p. 74). This was as much the central theme of Acharya Ray's dedicated life. Of course, as a teacher, he had also a great deal of concern for the youth of the country.

JRD TATA

JRD Tata was born in 1904 in Paris, and died in 1993 in Geneva (Lala, 1995, p. 3). Lala informs us that JRD once told him: 'I've made sure that I don't have much money'. Only at forty, in 1944, he gave a part of his wealth to the JRD Tata Trust. Every penny of the Trust came from him. Money was never the driving force of his life—Lala remarks (Ibid., p. 6). This illustrates once again one of the *rishi* principles: money is only a means , not the end. JRD put his money in trust, but did not trust money. *Artha anartha moolam* (money is the root of evil)—as the wise proverb goes.

During the reply speech at a reception given to him on being awarded the Bharat Ratna in 1892, JRD remarked at one stage (Lala, 2002, p. 183):

'An American economist has predicted that in the next century India will be an economic superpower. I don't want India to be an economic superpower. I want India to be a happy country.'

Today such a statement, fifteen years after it was made, must be sounding outlandish, even heretical. But let the leaders of today, whether in industry or academics or politics, do some soul-searching. Without any trace of visible spiritual proclivity, such speaking-from-the-heart by JRD is in full consonance with the Spirit of Bharatvarsha. For, the boy Nachiketa had understanding and guts to tell Yama (the Lord of Death) (Swami Gambhirananda, 1980, pp. 24–5)—

'na vittena tarpaniyo manushya'

Wealth or money power does not yield happiness for mankind. Not only is this temper revealed in JRD's comments on the economist's prediction, it finds further extension in his wise observation, 'If prosperity comes it makes one more selfish' (Lala, op. cit., p. 129). This truth is self-evident through processes like globalization master-minded by prosperous nations. At the other end, this is equally true at the individual level e.g. the great public dispute of 2005–6 between the two owner-brothers of India's most formidable private industrial house.

Let us return to the Bharat Ratna award again. When advance news about this event reached JRD, he is reported to have mentioned to Ratan Tata: 'Can't we do something to stop it?' (Ibid., p. 106) But the award nonetheless came to him, he did not run after it. When this was officially confirmed to JRD, he exclaimed: 'No more! No more!' (Ibid., p. 21) On the contrary, today even academics are known to indulge in wire-pulling to secure awards such as Padma Shri etc.

JRD had a strange fancy: he wanted to die outside India. He did not want to be a 'bother' to people. Though he was humble, he was conscious of his eminence. Death in India would entail a lot of 'trouble' to many (ibid., pp. 119, 169). He actually did die in Geneva. Such characteristic distaste for being fussed about speaks of non-attachment or *nishkam bhavana*. There is something yet more significant to share which adds lustre to this trait of inward autonomy in JRD.

When in 1983 Lala had proposed the possibility of a biography, he replied lightly: 'Can it not wait till I step down from my chairmanship of companies?' (Ibid., p. 184). It was learnt later from other senior colleagues that JRD wanted nothing to be published about him before his death. Like the facts mentioned in the preceding paragraphs, this one too is a clear proof that JRD was altogether free from narcissism—a common affliction of most leaders today.

Another feature of JRD's mind-mansion could be highlighted. He believed in *reincarnation*. He argued: 'I can't believe that a man is born to live for a second of a lifetime. I hope to be reborn in this world' (ibid., p. 129). The writer of a letter to an English daily, a few days after JRD's death, wrote that he had recently heard JRD expressing his wish to be born again – and in India. For, India, to him, was such an interesting country.

Finally, for the time being, a brief insight into ethics for business is in order. In response to the issue of relatively smaller growth in the size of the house of Tatas in the 1960's and 1970's JRD said (Lala, 2005, p. 176):

> 'I have often thought about that. If we had done some of the things that some other groups have done, we would have been twice as big as we are today. But we didn't, and I would not have it in *any other way*.'

Thus, we find that Ray, Godrej and JRD had all been able to subordinate all the fundamentals of business to a spiritual adventure which Sri Aurobindo had specified clearly (See first para of chapter nine). Spirituality had set the limits to greed, growth and profits. Spirituality was not reduced to the level of an instrument subordinate to the bottomline.

VERGHESE KURIEN

Dr. V. Kurien's autobiography shows how ethico-moral competence, as a foil to professional competence, is not an exercise in fanciful idealism. He emphasizes the point, early in the book, and correctly at that, that integrity unto one's own self is a pre-condition to integrity in dealings with others (Kurien, 2005, p. XII). Probably the most telling example of this principle in action was in his confrontation with Jagjivan Ram, a heavy-weight central minister and astute politician of his times (Ibid., pp. 165–6). The latter had summoned Kurien to help set up a private dairy with funds drawn from the cooperative dairy system. He refused to oblige, and therefore had to bear the brunt of the minister's wrath. But he had the requisite ethical stamina, so did not buckle.

Two fundamental philosophies could govern our lives. One emphasizes that an individual should run after name and fame. This may be called 'ambition'. The other prefers name and fame to run after an individual who concentrates fully on duties at hand. This is 'dedication'. For those inspired by the latter, the life of Kurien could serve as a model. In a letter (in the Prologue) to his grandson he wrote (Ibid., p. XII):

'To be quite honest, service to our nation's farmers was not the career I had envisioned for myself. But somehow, a series of events swept me along and put me in a certain place at a certain time when I had to choose between one option or another. I was faced with a choice that would transform my life. I could have pursued a career in metallurgy and perhaps become the chief executive of a large company. ... Yet, I chose none of these because somewhere, deep down, I knew I could make a more *meaningful contribution* (emphasis added) by working here in Anand, Gujarat.'

The message above is that it was not a calculated move by him to earn more money or position. It was an intuitive decision impelled by a higher cause. Reward and fame followed him in due course.

In the same letter, reflecting on the values which stood him in good stead, he held 'personal integrity' to be most important. He has stressed (ibid., p. XIII):

'I have often spoken of integrity as the most important of these values, realizing that integrity – and personal integrity at that – is being honest to yourself. If you are always honest to yourself, it does not take much effort in always being honest with others.'

He follows it up later in the book with two more values (ibid., p. 216)—

(a) to lead by personal example

(b) respect for time

Kurien has amply demonstrated the above values in his career and life. One such incident occurred in connection with the mopping up of the mess (corruption) in the Delhi Milk Scheme within forty-two days, and making it a new brand (Ibid., p. 88). He did this even at the risk of making enemies in Delhi's corridors of power. Thereby, he initiated a complete turnaround in just six weeks, leading from the front.

There is yet another important learning from the same Prologue/letter. He reflected (Ibid., p. XIV),

'Yet, there is little correlation between circumstances of people's lives and how happy they are. Most of us compare ourselves with someone we think is happier...But when we start looking closely we realize that what we saw were only images of perfection. And that will help us understand and cherish what we have, rather than what we don't have.'

This is a more sound and realistic principle of happiness. It is indeed true that a major cause of unhappiness is comparison with others in terms of what we do not have (money, fame, status in organization etc.), instead of what we have and others do not. Of course, it is not clear why the phrase 'image of perfection' has been used. Instead, 'image of happiness' would have been the appropriate expression. One should learn to feel happy by comparing oneself with persons less fortunate than oneself—who are more numerous than the few who are more so.

It is a common Indian belief that the higher Divine Will works for our good, though we may not be able to comprehend or evaluate it properly in the immediate. Kurien's life has been no exception. In no uncertain terms he expressed his displeasure on being deputed by the Government of India to the National Dairy Research Institute at Anand. He had big dreams of leading a luxurious life, and in no way Anand suited his temperament. He hated Anand (Ibid., p. 20). But he had to accept the posting because the government had spent for his higher education in the USA. As destiny would have it, he came in contact with, and was intrigued by a band of tenacious dairy farmers and their leader—Tribhuvandas Patel (Ibid., pp. 22–3). Gradually he fell in love with Anand. He quit the government job and joined the Kaira Milk Cooperative. The rest is history. Now he wants that even his body be cremated in Anand only (Ibid., p. 36). This evolving sequence of events shows that the grand design of Providence cannot usually be comprehended through secular rationality only. Kurien apparently, unlike PC Ray, possessed no such outlook on life.

The chapter on 'History in the Making' refers to an interesting incident involving a *chhaya jyotishi* who had predicted a phenomenal rise in Kurien's career (Ibid., p. 26). He, although a non-believer in occult matters, admitted that this prophecy had indeed turned out to be true. However, he also added that it was, '... one of life's curious accidents' (Ibid., p. 27). Such a remark about the *jyotishi's* accurate prophecy smacks of uncharitableness towards a capacity which is as thorough as any other. Rather, this experience in Kurien's life substantiates what has been said in the previous paragraph: the inscrutable Providential umbrella overhanging our terrestrial affairs.

There is an English phrase 'living for others' which has been called in the *Bhagavad Gita* as, *sarva bhuta hite ratah* or *lokasmagraha* (III.20—engaged in the well-being of everyone and everything). Kurien's philosophy of life epitomizes this. He avers, '... but if you work for others, there is a deeper sense of fulfillment, and if things are handled well, the money too is more than adequate (Ibid., p. 28). The last part of the statement refutes a common argument that a life lived for an ideal necessarily implies sacrificing material goals. Similar views have been echoed by him elsewhere also like:

- 'I chose to remain in Anand, as an employee of farmers, all my life' (ibid., p. 81).
- '...an employee of farmers has to please only the farmers' (ibid., p. 100)

Nowhere has it appeared that Kurien had been a discontented man, not satisfied with his life and its myriad circumstances.

At one place Kurien provides sound insight into cohesive teamwork. Three men were at the helm in running the Kaira Cooperative: Tribhuvandas Patel (the person representing the dairy farmers), Mr. Dalaya (a colleague of Kurien) and Kurien himself. However, as Kurien added, the three had, '...distinctly different...manners and skills'. Yet they formed a cohesive team because of, '...tremendous respect for the integrity and the strength of the other two' (Ibid., p. 37). This enabled them to find solutions amicably, instead of falling apart over different viewpoints they had. This quality is called *mudita* in Patanjali's *Yogasutras*.

Kurien had no hesitation in exposing the business motives of the MNCs. Generally bureaucrats and leaders in India, for their own reasons, are found to ignore or join the dirty games played by many MNCs. But he bluntly observed, '...the technical advice of 'experts' is all too often dictated by the economic interests of the advanced countries and not by the needs or ground realities in developing countries' (Ibid., p. 42). Later in the chapter 'From organization to Institution' he highlights another incident: a heated altercation with the chairman of Nestle whose dealings were bordering on bullying tactics commonly adopted by the MNCs. Kurien retorted (Ibid., p. 44):

'I've been in this game for fifty years and I know your modus operandi well ... You want to buy him (Kurien himself) out, which is what you'd normally do. But you can't buy me out ...'

Whenever situations demanded he used to rise to the occasion and face it resolutely. He observed, '... with adequate support, confrontation at the right time pays off' (ibid., p. 50). Accordingly, he had confronted the UNICEF when it was wanting to dictate terms over the kind of powder plant the cooperative desired, although its role was to offer financial assistance only.

The ruling gospel—'fast and heady wins the race'—in the corporate sector has been contested by Kurien in terms of long-term sustainability. He believes that the philosophy of the Cooperative is to progress in a 'slow and steady' manner (Ibid., p. 75). Patience has been his watchword. However, he candidly admitted that the advantage with the co-operatives lay in the fact that they had no compulsion to placate either the shareholders or any boss by making profits their *raison dé etre*.

Obsessive love for power is widely prevalent among individuals and groups. So, whenever there is a remote possibility of losing grip over it, the wielder of power feels threatened. This is exactly what had happened after Lal Bahadur Shastri, the-then Prime Minister of India, expressed his intention to Kurien thus (Ibid., p. 100):

'The Government of India will give you a blank cheque, you may create any body, any structure you want, provided you will head it. Please replicate Anand— throughout India...whatever you need for it, the Government will provide.'

On the basis of this proposal it was decided to establish the National Dairy Development Board (NDDB). However, it met with stiff resistance as the bureaucrats belonging to the Ministry of Food and Agriculture felt that this proposal was unfair and an insult to them. He therefore confronted them. Afterwards Kurien, probably hinting at this group of bureaucrats, had observed, (Ibid., p. 129)

'...it was power that we exercised prudently over those who tried to expand our country's imports unnecessarily;...by their corrupt practices (they) held the country back from true development.'

Nowadays the phrase 'holistic approach' is in wide circulation. However, what it means to be holistic is not often well-understood. The success of Operation Flood, which had ushered in the White Revolution in India, may throw some light on it. When the idea of Operation Flood was floated, it met with criticism from certain quarters who questioned its feasibility. Kurien realized that in part this was honest criticism because India could never afford to provide one acre of green grass to each cow or buffalo for it to give 40 litres of milk each day (Ibid., p. 139). This prompted him and his team of researchers to research on animal feed, health and nutrition. Such an integral approach enabled them to ensure, '...that our milk production should come from fodder and feed which man could not eat,...(and which) was produced in the process of producing food for human beings'. Thus, it was proved to the detractors that the NDDB was formed, not for dairy development through milk production only, but also for 'holistic' development through proper care of allied aspects like animal husbandry, feed, fodder etc.

SOME COMPARISONS

It is not uncommon for autobiographies to be affected by self-projection, even egotism, in varying degrees. One of the frequently used words in *I Too Had A Dream* is 'pride'. No doubt Kurien's book is a standing proof of how one can be unflinching in matters of ethics, unrelenting in the cause of the farmers, unbending in dealing with obstructive bureaucrats, and unremitting in love for the nation. Yet, in his claim to be a non-believer e.g. his dismissal of the faultless accuracy of the *jyotishi's* predictions about his glorious career, while recounting so many illuminating career episodes, one looks in vain for the gentle touch of humility. Even the letter (Prologue) to his grandson carries the flavour of self-glorification (e.g. the award of Padma Vibhusan), bordering on pride. In contrast, as already stated, when advance news about the award of Bharat Ratna (1992) reached Bombay House, JRD asked Ratan Tata if this ceremony could not be stopped! When the award did reach him he had exclaimed 'No more, No More' (Lala, op. cit., p. 106, p. 21). This demonstrates very well the *sattwic, nishkam karma* (detached involvement) model of leadership.

Acharya (Sir) Prafulla Chandra Ray, a DSc from Edinburgh, had been the pioneering author of *Hindu Chemistry*. His autobiography (1932) contains the following testament ((Ray, op. cit., p. 541)):

> 'Whatever field I have ploughed I have ploughed as an humble instrument in the hands of Providence. My failures are my own…But my successes, if any, are to be attributed to the guidance of the All-knowing who chose me to be His humble instrument.'

PC Ray did believe in the occult (which means invisible, yet real), the Spiritual, the Divine wholeheartedly. So did Godrej and JRD, though to a lesser degree. And they had also battled against odds no less tough than Kurien did – especially in pre-independent India ruled by the British. The following words, as an interesting contrast, are reported to have been uttered by Jawaharlal Nehru about Kurien (Kurien, op. cit., p. 53):

> '…Jawaharlal Nehru turned to me, embraced me and said, "Kurien, I'm so glad that our country has people like you—people who will go ahead and achieve even that which seems unachievable."'

Similar references to Presidents, other Prime Ministers, Chief Ministers etc. are also frequent. And the book seems to mention no 'failures' at all. The comparatively brief account of facts about Ray, Godrej and JRD in the earlier sections, however, mark a noble departure from the tendency of self-praise by their junior pioneer, Kurien.

The preface of M.K. Gandhi's *Autobiography* (1925) also reflects his honest reservations about adopting the western custom of self-narration. He too had been an profoundly believing man, and used to feel quite uncomfortable about being called 'Mahatma'. The mystic, yet socially engaged Rabindranath Tagore's *Jeevansmriti* (1912) also abounds with the utterly simple truths and facts of his life till the age of 51. The Nobel Prize was still a couple of years away. Confrontations and accolades, battles and victories – all were left to others to discover and write. Infact, initially he was angry with a renowned publisher for even suggesting to him to write about his own life. And he too had lived for eighty years.

The examples of Ray, Godrej, JRD, Gandhiji and Tagore show that it is perhaps safer to leave the task of recounting and evaluating a great man's life and achievements by independent biographers. The autobiographies by the sacred trio of pre-independence India, Tagore-Ray-Gandhi, through their choice of themes and style of expression, constitute an object lesson in the art of writing without the jarring intrusion of the self. This is spiritual value-orientation at its practical best.

As for the IRMA events of 2005 (regarding its Chairmanship), we may once more recall the pristine principle of *vanaprastha* (not to be taken literally). The far-and-high-sighted *rishis* of Bharatvarsha understood human character much more holistically than modern intellect can. After all they were holy, so holistic. One of their modern-day representatives, Swami Vivekananda, had spoken these words to an elite Los Angeles audience in 1900 (Swami Vivekananda, 2005, p. 7):

'The bee came to sip the honey, but its feet stuck to the honey pot and it could not get away. Again and again we are finding ourselves in that state…Work, constantly work; but be not attached, be not caught. Reserve unto yourself the power to detach from everything, however beloved, however much the soul might yearn for it, however great the pangs of misery you feel it you were going to leave it…'

Yet again, the events associated with JRD's removal from Chairmanship of Air India (1977) by Morarji Desai carries a sublime lesson for adorable leadership. The GOI did not show the minimum courtesy of directly informing JRD about its decision. It was PC Lal, his successor, who told him about the falling axe. A wounded JRD responded to the Prime Minister by sending a touching yet dignified letter. No campus dramas or court room public displays of dirty linen. A sound philosophy of life does matter in the end (Lala, 1992, p. 211).

Verse X.41 of the *Bhagwad Gita* (*Vibhuti Yoga*) pronounces the following conclusive, holistic and sacred law for all men/women of action:

Yad-yad vibhutimat sattvam srimad urjitam eva va|
tad-tad eva 'vagachcha tvam mama tejomsasambhavam||

(Verse X.41)

'Every such being as is glorious, brilliant and powerful, know that to be a part manifestation of My Glory'.

The problem lies in the inability and disinclination of the secular, non-believing ego to cultivate this disposition. Sci-tech victories of mankind have considerably inflated his ego, cutting him loose from all sense of the One, Ultimate, Consciousness. And a common result of such magnified I-ness is our pronounced tendency towards narcissism. The *Gita* has warned us repeatedly about this danger lurking round the corner. For instance, earlier in verse III.27 the secular Arjun has been warned by the sacred Krishna:

Prakrteh kriyamanani gunaih karmani sarvasah|
ahamkara vimudhatama kartaham iti manyate||
'The fool, whose mind is deluded by egoism thinks 'I am the doer'. Truly it is only the active part of the being, constituted of *gunas*, which works.'

Sri Aurobindo has captured this very truth in his aphorism (Sri Aurobindo, 1991, p. 45):

'Do not claim to possess the Power that should possess you'.

One way or the other, the *rajarshi* leader model has been practised more deeply and authentically by Ray, Godrej and Tata, than by Kurien. Kurien has adorable no doubt been convincingly successful. But Ray-Godrej-Tata were close to perfection—*sansiddhi*.

Leadership Truths
Kautilya, Harshavardhana, Kalidasa

In one of his letters to a disciple Sri Aurobindo had propounded the yoga of business with spirituality in these words (Aurobindo, Sri, 1991, pp. 6–7):

'I do not regard business as something evil or tainted, any more than it is so regarded in ancient spiritual India. If I did, I would not be able to receive money from X or from those of our disciples who in Bombay trade with East Africa; nor could we then encourage them to go on with their work but would have to tell them to throw it up and attend to their spiritual progress alone. How are we to reconcile X's seeking spiritual light and his will?... Even if I myself had had the command to do business, as I had the command to do politics, I would have done it without the least spiritual or moral compunction. All depends on the *spirit in which a thing is done*, the *principles on which it is built*, and *the use to which it is turned*'.

This triune law of 'spirit-principles-use' had been crystallized by Sri Aurobindo a little later in the same letter by extracting the essence of the Gita (Ibid., p. 7):

'Krishna super-imposes a higher law...that work must be done *without* desire, *without* attachment to any fruit or reward, *without* any egoistic attitude or motive, as an offering or *sacrifice* to the Divine'.

This masterly articulation of the spiritual art of work (including business) can be treated as the *benchmark* to judge the present-day dominant wave in the realm of the economic function. On the whole, the general picture here is just the opposite of what the above two quotes convey:

• Burning desire, greed at the centre, as the hub.

- Compulsive attachment to personal and corporate gain/rewards as the key driver.
- Bloated egotism, via ranking of all varieties, at a premium.
- The Divine rejected as mere fantasy; even if accepted, worship regarded as an exercise in bargaining for secular ends.

When, therefore, the themes of spirituality and business and all other activities are sought to be tied together, one should *first* become conscious of the polarization between the two. The correct perspective to begin the task of linking the two has to be—

Spirituality is the end, not the means

Business and economics cannot turn to Spirituality and treat it as yet another instrument or resource to bolster its all-consuming goal of the bottom line. Even the apparently wider multiple stakeholder concept or sustainable development rhetoric is far from visualizing business as a spiritual adventure. Anticipating this as it were, Gandhiji, had declared (Gandhi, 2001, vol. V, p. 276): 'I venture to think that the scriptures of the world are far safer and sounder treatises on laws of economics than many modern textbooks'. Secular texts will not do. Sacred texts must show the way.

Picking up the leads given by Sri Aurobindo and Gandhiji, this chapter will present some gleanings from a few sacred texts and lives about how *all* social functions – government, education, family, economics, defence, international relationships etc. – in Bharatvarsha had been firmly rooted in the *Rajarshi* model for all walks of life. Although the *Rajarshi* model had been worked out for Kings, its keynotes and principles are valid for leaders of business and other human institutions also (Chakraborty and Bhattacharya, 2001, pp. 131–231).

KAUTILYA—THE SPIRITUAL PRAGMATIST[*]
Kautilya's *Arthashastra* is a fruitful starting point. This pioneering, comprehensive classic is usually dated around 4th century BC. Kautilya was the mentor of Chandragupta I. Together they had founded the Maurya dynasty, and had built the first empire in Bharatvarsha. It may be noted

---

[*] At an International conference on the Gita at Singapore (September, 2007) we heard that studying Confucius is mandatory for all civil servants in communist China. Whither secular India regarding Kautilya?

that shades of the preceding epic duo of Krishna-Arjuna are reinforced in the historical pair of Kautilya-Chandragupta. Here the details of political and other aspects of efficient administration of an empire given in the Arthashastra are set aside. Only the principles and guidelines laid down for the grooming of a prince and the conduct of a king are sampled. They will show what timeless fundamentals underlie spiritually-grounded leadership, and hence spiritually-guided secular institutions too—business not excluded. Rangarajan's comprehensive recent translation of the *Arthashastra* has been the major source for extracting the relevant points (Rangarajan, 1992).

Section III.ii of the *Arthashastra* contains 'categorical imperatives' for the 'good conduct' of a 'wise' and 'just' King. At the very start Kautilya prescribes the exercise of vigilant control over the six internal enemies in all humans (*shadaripus*)—

lust	anger	greed
delusion	vanity	envy

This basic *self-governance* mandate receives ubiquitous recognition in the vast corpus of Bharatiya *shastras* or sacred literature. Although emphasis on self-restraint may appear to be a negative beginning, yet it is entirely realistic. One has to clean up the stinking mess in a plot of land before planting fragrant flower saplings upon it. Kautilya supports his prescription by adducing historical evidence of rulers who had managed gloriously by obeying this ground rule, and those who had perished due to indulgence in the *shadaripus*.

Only such a disciplined king gains true knowledge, becomes wise, and treats justly all his people. Thus he becomes a *rajarshi*. He is an organic, intrinsic synthesis of the *sage* with the *emperor* – the sage-emperor. The greatest asset and reward of such a *rajarshi* is the loyalty and trust of his people. These ideals constitute the perennial nucleus of Bharat's conception about leadership in all spheres.

In section III.iii Kautilya highlights the need for a king to be 'energetic'. For, if he is lax or 'lazy', his subjects will drain the state's wealth or his enemies will cause his downfall. That is to say, the King's role calls for the activation of the *rajasic guna* (dynamism), and subjugation of the *tamasic guna* (sloth) (Ibid., pp. 144–6, 147–9). So far so good. But we know from the Gita-psychology that '*kama esha krodha esha rajo guna samudbhava*' (lust and anger, and hence immorality or unethicality or evil or sin, all spring from *rajo guna*) (Chakraborty, and Chakraborty, 2006, pp. 196–201). Could

Kautilya have been ignorant about this problem? No, for as the two previous paragraphs have mentioned, *strict self-control* has been laid down as a pre-condition for the exercise of dynamism. Such careful moderation in the satisfaction of normal desires (*kama*) implies an ever-awake *sattwa-guna* vigilance on the part of the king (or leader).

Kautilya proceeds further to reveal his penchant for minute details. (It will be useful to remember here that he was acting as the guru or mentor of Chandragupta-the-first – the great empire-builder of the pre-Christian, post-Buddhist era). The twenty four hours cycle for the king was divided into sixteen slots of one and a half hours each.* And for each slot specific duties had been enumerated (Rangarajan; op. cit, pp. 147–9):

RAJARSHI PROCESS
DAY
- First 1½ hrs. after sunrise: Receive reports on defence, revenue and expenditure.
- Second 1½ hrs. after sunrise: Public audiences, to hear petitions.
- Third 1½ hrs. after sunrise: [Personal – bath, meal and study].
- 1½ hrs. before noon: Receive revenue and tribute; appoint ministers etc. and allot tasks.
- First 1½ hrs. after noon: Write letters, confer with councilors, receive secret information.
- Second 1½ hrs. after noon: [Personal – recreation, time for contemplation]
- Third 1½ hrs. after noon: Inspect and review forces.
- 1½ hrs. before sunset: Consult with Defence Chief.

The day shall end with evening prayers

NIGHT
- First 1½ hrs. after sunset: Interview with secret agents.
- Second 1½ hrs. after sunset: [Personal – bath, meal and study].
- Three hrs. before and first: [Retire to the bed chamber to the sound of 1½ hrs. after mid-night music, sleep].
- Second 1½ hrs. after mid-night: [After waking to the sound of music, meditate on the work to be done].
- Third 1½ hrs. after mid-night: Consult with councillors, send out spies.

---

* A few slots in the night have been clubbed. Therefore the two lists below put together show fourteen slots only.

- 1½ hrs. before sunrise: [Religious, household and personal duties, meetings with his teacher, purohita, personal physician, chief cook, and astrologer]

At daybreak he shall cicumambulate a cow,
its calf and a bull and then proceed to his court

A searching examination of the above 24-hour plan for the King (and his modern equivalents in government, business etc.) will show how without assiduous control of the *shadaripus,* such a scheme cannot be implemented. Therefore, the *secular duties* of a king's role have been carefully punctuated with *sacred processes* and agents:

Study	Contemplation
Prayers	Music
Religious duties	Teacher
Purohita	Astrologer etc.

These are the elements which constitute the *rishi* dimension. Besides, for the modern protagonists of time-management, the Kautilyan blueprint must have a few salutary lessons to offer. Systematized, focused and exalted energy in the king is the result of such a regimen.

It is relevant here to anticipate and tackle a widespread conventional belief (or superstition?) of today—such prescriptions smack of feudal authoritarianism which stultifies personality development. This viewpoint does not stand the scrutiny of history. Nor is it psychologically sound. The logic of license implies that character development requires no investment. But we cannot get something for nothing. Being technically skilled and verbally smart is simply not enough for leadership roles. Self-restraint of lower impulses and instincts (*sanyam*) conserves pure energy for wholesome functions. This is a perennial fact of the animate world. The consequences of flouting this message had been tellingly demonstrated by the decline and fall of the Roman empire (and many more). Several others today may meet the same fate.

The *spiritual pragmatism* of Kautilya, as we would choose to characterize it, has been expressed well by Rangarajan (Ibid., p. 33):

'The Arthashastra is essentially a treatise on the art of government and is, by nature, *instructional*. It seeks to instruct all kings, and is meant to be useful at all times wherever *dharma* is held to be pre-eminent. Because it is instructional, its basis is the *practice* of government'.

At times, during current discussions on corporate governance, only one Kautilyan tactic is mentioned, rather casually: *sama*, *dama*, *bheda* and *danda*. Sometimes it is also referred to while discussing management of teams. In both cases such allusion to the quadruple tactic is torn out of its original context of political statecraft. It is forgotten or ignored that Kautilya insists first upon the king or leader being a *rajarshi*. Then only, given the appropriate circumstances, any one of these methods may be employed by the 'legitimate', not 'careerist' leader (Ibid., p. 158). Thus—

- Towards those among the above who are discontented, conciliation shall be attempted (*sama*).
- The contented or happy among those who are dependent on the king for money etc; or those who help the king in adversity or prosperity; and those who repel enemies will be given gifts of appreciation (*dana*).
- And different categories of discontented people shall be prevented from making mutual alliances by sowing dissensions among them (*bheda*) (ibid., pp. 113–5).
- If conciliation fails, then these discontented people shall be handled through punishment (*danda*).

But if organizational leaders dismiss all the salient pre-conditions of the *rajarshi* model, and resort to just the above quartet for clinging to power, then leadership reduces itself to mean organizational politics. This is debasing secular pragmatism, not Kautilya's ennobling spiritual pragmatism. The *Arthashatra* furnishes a comprehensive list of wrongs that a *rajarshi* must avoid to check impoverishment, greed and disaffection among his subjects. Here are a few of them (Ibid., p. 159)—

- Ignores the good people and favours the wicked.
- Neglects the observation of the proper and righteous practices.
- Suppresses *dharma* and propagates *adharma*.
- Does not punish those who ought to be punished, but punishes those who do not deserve to be.
- Indulges in wasteful expenditure and destroys profitable undertakings.
- Antagonizes the wise elders by lying and mischief; etc.

Leadership today in government departments, business houses, educational establishments etc. is throwing up the above ruinous lapses with alarming frequency. Democracy based on party politics, and on winning elections through manipulable or purchasable votes, seems incapable of throwing up a Kautilyan *rajarshi* leader. Yet that is the need of the hour.

It is also important to note that Kautilya had analysed the guidelines for appointing ministers laid down by many illustrious predecessors. He had arrived at the conclusion that each guideline was meritorious in the right context, and these right contexts were outlined by him. But his final recommendation was loud and clear: '... in any case anyone who is appointed as a councilor must have the *highest personal qualities*' (Ibid., p. 197). How do modern organizations measure up against this timeless benchmark?

The same individual who was Kautilya, the King's mentor, had also functioned as Chanakya, the people's guru. In this broad-band role, Chanakya's maxims provide the entire society with rules and principles which are capable of nurturing the continued emergence of *rajarshi* leaders in all walks of life. A few such maxims follow (Subramanian, 1980, p. 49, p. 50, p. 59, p. 134):

1. 'One should earn wealth as if one is immortal'.
2. 'The wealthy are respected by all'.
3. 'Cunning accompanies courtesy'.
4. 'The ruler should not be like the subjects. The people should however be like a good ruler. The ruler powerfully influences the entire people towards righteous action or the opposite'.
5. 'The ruler is responsible for the people's sin, the priest for the ruler's sin, husband for the wife's sin, and the teacher for the student's sin.
6. 'Performance of one's duty leads to heaven and eternal bliss. By violation of duty and consequent confusion people come to ruin'.

Brief interpretations of these maxims are in order. The profound principle in the first rule is that wealth should be earned with great *patience*, never in a hurry. This abiding attitude will ensure ethics in the pursuit of *artha*. To reach the top rank as fast as possible, as is the prevailing order of the day, one is quite likely to resort to means fair or foul. The second generalization about respect attaching to wealth must be read in conjunction with the first rule. That is, wealth secured by unethical means in haste does *not* command respect. This too is a widespread phenomenon at present. The third counsel serves as a caution for the simple-minded people who could be deceived by outward show of courtesy by a cunning fellow. This is one facet of prudence in social dealings.

Maxims four and five clearly define the cause-and-effect connection between the character of the ruler (or leader) and that of the citizens (or members). It is common these days to hear that after all the society is so degraded, so how can we have upgraded leaders? Chanakya, however, made no mistake on this vital cause-and-effect sequence. The ruler/leader *cannot* seek shelter for his shortcomings behind the veil of society's blemishes. The responsibility is laid squarely on the shoulders of the former for degeneration of the latter. The fifth maxim repeats this cause-and-effect sequence in a wider set of relationships within society e.g. priest-king, husband-wife, teacher-student.

The maxim about performance of *duty*, by each role in society, has today become an obsolete principle. There is talk only of rights everywhere. Naturally, in the long run such societies will throw up leaders who will not heed to their duties, but pursue their rights, whatever they may be. This is already happening e.g, the blatantly self-serving decisions by Indian M.P.s. Why not? After all, in a secular world of instant gratification who cares for heaven and eternal bliss!

Kautilya's 'spiritual pragmatism' for leaders has to be evaluated in the light of the priority given to being moral and just, self-less and self-controlled, and then only to be followed by '*sama-dama-bheda-danda*', or sending of spies and other administrative, or political tactics as and when the situation calls for them. Even when he functions as Kautilya, he asserts that *artha* could sometimes precede *dharma* and *kama* (Rangarajan, op. cit., p. 145), for the latter are dependent on the former. Yet, functioning as Chanakya he insists that wealth (*dhan*) can be preserved only on the basis of *dharma* (*vittena rakshayet dharma*) (Kirtipal, 2003, p. 114). The 'garden metaphor' has also been employed by Kautilya to communicate the message of 'spiritual pragmatism' (Sil, 1985, pp. 95–6):

'That ruler stays long in power who acts like a skilled gardener: rehabilitating the uprooted, nursing the blossoming, stimulating the weak, bending down the excessively tall, enervating the excessively strong, dividing the united, pruning those with thorns, and protecting those who have come up by themselves'.

There are eight processes in the above quote—four positive and four negative. They should be used carefully after proper diagnosis of the relevant key characteristic revealed by different members (managers, councillors etc.) working with and for the king. Obviously, a weak, characterless, self-seeking ruler cannot demonstrate such capability even for a day. Sri Aurobindo's statement of the three fundamentals of leadership in business quoted earlier (the spirit, the principles and the use) calls for *rajarshi* grooming of the leader, with an adequate grasp of the perfectionist role of a 'skilled gardener'. Self-discipline is the hub of such a role. It is important to listen to Kautilya on this starting point once more at the end (Rangarajan, op. cit., p. 142):

'Discipline is of two kinds—inborn and acquired. There must be an innate capacity for self-discipline...instruction and training can promote discipline only in a person capable of benefiting from them; people incapable of natural self-discipline do not benefit....one who will be a King should acquire discipline and follow it strictly in life...'

True to this *rajarshi* law of self-discipline, Kautilya or Chanakya himself retired into the forest after ensuring that Chandragupta was married, the Greeks were befriended, and internal adversaries won over. He was *strict with himself* before he could be so with Chandragupta and others.

As for the grooming of the *prince* for the role of future king, Kautilya furnishes the following scheme (Ibid., pp. 142–3):

'(as) the Prince enters the ashrama of a Brahmachari , he should learn philosophy and the three Vedas from authoritative teachers, economics from the heads of various government departments, and the science of government from not only theoretical exponents of political science but also from practical politicians. He should remain a brahmachari till he is sixteen. A prince's education does not stop with his reaching manhood and getting married. With a view to improving his self-discipline, he should always associate with learned elders, for in them alone has discipline its firm roots'.

This then constitutes an impeccable blue-print for grooming leaders who can deliver *artha-kama*, subject to *dharma-moksha*. Vote-fed, parties-based phoney democracy has become worthless because it has systematically driven 'good money' out of circulation, and swollen the ranks of 'bad money'. To gain a little of material wealth, at the cost of character, has been a bad bargain. If monarchical governance, based on such principles as Kautilya laid down, could nurture princes like Chandragupta I and II, Why not turn to them today?*

---

* Witness the sordid game now being played to foist a party president's son on this nation. Who will lead India towards kantilya? Whither our *rajarshis*?

HARSHAVARDHANA—THE REGAL RENOUNCER

The eminent historian RC Majumdar sketches the following picture of Harshavardhana, the emperor of Bharatvarsha in the 7th century AD (Majumdar, 1954, pp. 116–17):

> 'Harsha distinguishes himself almost equally in the arts of peace and war. He could wield the pen as well as the sword…literary skill of the royal author (and) high reputation as a poet…was a great patron of learning…a ruler of versatile ability and wonderful personality'.

Thus, after about eight or nine centuries of the *Arthashastra*, we get yet another (and there were many others before him) well-documented, inspiring example of the holistic, sacro-secular *rajarshi* model in action. If a monarch could perform such an all-embracing role, then for a company chairman, or a university vice-chancellor, or a government minister too this synthesis should be realizable.

K.M Panikkar, another noted historian, and once India's ambassador to China, has set Harsha against the larger canvas of Indian history (Panikkar, 1922, pp. 76–7):

> 'The reign of Harsha may thus be said to mark the culmination of Hindu culture. …it is Harsha's glory to have been the last in the long line of Hindu rulers beginning with Chandragupta Maurya in whose time India appeared to the world not only as an ancient mighty civilization, but an organized and powerful state working for the progress of humanity'.

A remarkable value-underpinning for such a complete king as Harsha was, when still quite young, his *reluctance* to ascend the throne. Considerable persuasion was needed to make him the king after his father's death (Ibid., p. 14). Non-attachment and humility were elements of character which never deserted him throughout his later career as a great king.

The most remarkable proof of Harsha's *rajarshi* leadership lay in his 'quinquennial convocation' of *tyaga* and *seva* (renunciation and service), the two strongest pillars of Bharat's *sanatan* culture and society. In our times first Swami Vivekananda (Vivekananda, 1962, vol. V, p. 228) and then Mahatma Gandhi (Gandhi, 1998, p. 71, p. 113) had unequivocally singled out as well as practised these two human values or sacred propensities for stable social development and cultural survival. Back to Harsha, we get a graphic account of his 5-yearly saga 'of perpetual giving up' (as Tagore has reminded us in our times) (Tagore, 2002, p. 69) or charity (rather *danam*) from Radha Kumud Mookerji – another stalwart of constructive history writing (Mookerji, 1926, pp. 80–2, p. 147). This event used to take place at Prayag over a 2-month period. The process began with the worship of the images of Aditya, Shiva and Buddha for the first three days. The costliest gifts were bestowed and charity given on these days. For the next twenty days selected Buddhists and Brahmins were gifted with gold, pearls, garments, food etc. The next forty days were devoted to giving alms and sustenance to the poor, the orphans, the destitutes from far and near. Even the King's belongings were given away. By the end of this *maha-yajna* in the vast 'arena of charity', all the accumulated wealth in the king's coffers used to be exhausted—so much so that Harsha had to beg a second hand garment from his sister Rajyasri at the closing hour of the event.

Both Panikkar and Mookerji agree that such magnanimity reflected the true spirit of charity, not vain-gloriousness. And that, charity on such spectacular scale by a king has no parallel in history. It was performed five times during the thirty five odd years that Harsha ruled. Calling him an unbending idealist, Mookerji offers this concluding estimate of Harsha (ibid., pp. 187–9):

'... a supremely versatile genius and complex character. He was at once a prince and a poet, a warrior and a man of letters, royal and kindly, with unbounded wealth given away in unbounded liberality, with the dignity of a paramount sovereign joined to the humility of a beggar, master of all the military as well as the fine arts, of all knowledge and virtues'.

Such leaders of today, in any sphere, as may be interested in spirituality beyond lip-service, might find it beneficial to sit down calmly and practise *dhyana* or meditation on Harshavardhan's rajarshi role – as portrayed by the three top class historians above. And if the effort is invested with sincerity and humility, and the imaginative power has not atrophied, Harsha's *rajarshi* qualities might then seep into the deeper consciousness of the seeker-leader. This *spiritual osmosis* is a reality in the realm of sacro-secular leadership development.

Whereas the books on Harsha by Panikkar and Mookerji, written in the 1920's, speak about the king with emotional fervour, a more recent work on the same character is less ardent and more restrained. The author, Devahuti, attempts a political, not historical, study of Harsha. Here are her comments (Devahuti, 2001, p. 205):

'His knowledge and understanding of various religious beliefs, his notably charitable disposition, his love of learning, his accomplishments in the fields of art and literature, all combined to enhance his worth as a king,...endowed Harsha with a poised personality.'

Devahuti thus corroborates (eighty years later) each major aspect of Harsha's character which her predecessors had identified, but on a subdued note. This suggests that the present-day intellectual mind might have become less capable of being inspired by greatness, and hence unable to inspire its listeners or readers.

It is important also to note that Kautilya's *Arthashastra*, written around 300 BC., should have served as a manual of guidance for most of the major Maurya and Gupta kings. Emperor Ashoka, grandson of Chandragupta Maurya, was an important exception as he was influenced more by Buddhist philosophy than by all-round statecraft. But he could probably afford that difference because of the strong foundations laid by Kautilya-Chandragupta. However, the likes of Chandragupta-II, Kumaragupta, Samudragupta, and Harshavardhan appear to have fallen back upon Kautilya—directly or indirectly. Of course, they also transcended the *Arthashastra* in many ways e.g., charity, literary ventures, support for educational centres like the Nalanda etc.

Sarkar reveals the all-round, long-term power transmitted by Harshavardhan's *rajarshi* leadership, not only during his own life time, but also to the later great kingdoms of the Palas, Senas, Rashtrakutas, Cholas etc. (8th to 12th centuries). Each one of these dynasties governed territories much larger than any single European country. They have been called by Sarkar the 'spiritual successors' of that great Empire-builder and statesman of the 7th century (Sarkar, 1985, p. 84).

At any rate, what leaders of today may do well to ponder and introspect is—could a multi-dimensional regal personality like Harshavardhan blossom without a thorough integration of the spiritual *rishi* element into the secular *raja* role? Is this not the perennial secret of leadership genius in Bharatvarsha?

KALIDASA—THE SPIRITUAL IDEALIST

Raghuvamsa ranks as a mahakavya (epic poem) by Kalidasa. Devadhar, an authority on Kalidasa, informs: '... Kalidasa lived in the first century before our era at the court of King Vikrama of Ujjayini who founded the Samvat era' (Devadhar, 2005, p. iii). Since the purpose here is to seek some lessons in leadership, the literary aspects of the epic are beyond our pale for now.

Yet it is useful to begin the discussion by listening to Tagore, almost two thousand years younger than his legendary predecessor, who had the rare power to seize upon the crucial theme of leadership imbedded in Kalidasa's work (Sen, 1966, p. 15):

> 'From his seat beside all the glories of Vikramaditya's throne, the poet's heart yearns for the purity and simplicity of India's past age of spiritual striving. And it was this yearning which impelled him to go back to the annals of the ancient Kings of Raghu's line for the narrative poem in which he traced the history of the rise and fall of the ideal that should guide the rulers of men'.

Tagore himself had attained a high level of positive spiritual realization. So he knows what he is saying—purity and simplicity have to go together with spiritual striving. The *raja* dimension has never been intended to eclipse or contradict the *rishi* aspect in Bharatvarsha's philosophy and practice. Rather, this tradition of synthesis proves its timeless character by recording an unbroken lofty pitch across nearly two millennia – Kalidasa to Tagore. Here is something of supreme importance for all types of contemporary leaders, certainly in India, and may be elsewhere too, for self-education.

The epic is titled after the second king in the Ikshvaku dynasty, Raghu. The very process of begetting Raghu as an offspring by his parents Dilipa and Sudakshina is in itself a great lesson in the spiritual genesis of *rajarshi* leaders. Being childless for long, this regal couple left the palace and surrendered to Vashistha, their guru, in his hermitage. By means of meditation Vashistha could discover the reason for the misfortune overhanging the disconsolate royal parents. Remedial penances and vows were instructed, which the couple devotedly followed for three weeks, staying in the ashram itself. But all was not over. A greater test of spiritual strength awaited them, centering around the protection of Vashistha's celestial cow, Nandini. The pleased Nandini at last granted the coveted boon of progeny to king Dilipa and queen Sudakshina. Thereafter, when Nandini offered her milk to the king, this was his reply (Devadhar, op. cit., p. 37):

> 'Well, mother, if the sage allows me, I will drink what will remain over after the calf has drunk, and the requirement of the sacrifice satisfied, even as I accept one sixth of the produce of the well-protected earth'.

This reply constitutes a simple yet powerful expression of the core of spiritually-grounded leadership.

Be this as it may, the birth of Raghu was possible only among *parents of the quality and calibre, purity and simplicity of Dilipa-Sudakshina*. Raghus, in other words, are not begotten by accident or promiscuity. Therefore, if we in India hope that her leaders of tomorrow should be like Raghu, then all parents in the country today ought to regard *Dilipa-Sudakshina as their model*.

Handing over the kingdom to their grown up and able son, Raghu, Dilipa and Sudakshina made for the forest to fulfill the family vow of *vanaprastha* (III.70) (ibid., p. 57). This too is a great lesson for healthy leadership—a point of culmination for the *raja* aspect, and the commencement of full-scale *rishi-hood*. Non-attachment to *artha-kama*, and attachment to *moksha* – this is the principle demonstrated by such an act.

As Raghu is getting groomed for the *rajarshi* role, even politics is being taught to him. Experts are instructing him in strategies—both fair and unfair. But Raghu would always choose the former, never the latter option (IV. 10) (ibid., p. 60).

In Verse VI.76 Kalidasa informs us about Raghu's performance of Visvajit sacrifice whereby he gave away all his wealth to his people, and reduced it to the residue of an earthen vessel. It is such conduct of Raghu-the-*Rajarshi* which, in the opinion of Sarkar, illustrates the 'synthetic...Kalidasan ideal of harmony between the positive and the transcendental, or realization of the transcendental in and through the positive' (Sarkar, op. cit., p. 15).We have found that centuries later Harshavardhan continued with this process of self-pauperisation for his people on an undiminished scale (ibid., p. 137–40).

In the eighth canto, versa 10 to 24, Kalidasa's 'spiritual idealism' attains perfection. Following Dilipa, his father's example, and the family tradition, Raghu too begins to withdraw from sense objects (*artha-kama*) and to enter life's last stage of self-control for Final Bliss (moksha). Aja, Raghu's worthy son, donned the royal mantle of earthly glory, whereas Raghu lived in a place outside the city. The earthly sojourn of Raghu closes by his mergence with the Changeless Soul through yogic ascesis.

The moral—Raghu is born of *tapasya* (ascesis), and dissolves in *tapasya*. This is the grand, final lesson of 'spiritual idealism' Kalidasa offers to today's leaders.

Raghuvamsa ends on a tragic note. The last king in this epic is Agnivarna, a veritable debauch. Verse 47 in the last (19th) canto says this (Ibid., p. 369):

'Thus, the king, enjoying the pleasures of senses and averse to duties of his kingly office, and swayed by passion, passed the seasons declared by their individual signs'.

Childless, he was ravaged by incurable diseases and met a dishonourable death. 'A widow on the throne—such is the tragic end of the illustrious race of the Raghus!' This is the cry with which Kalidasa ends the Mahakavya (Ibid., p. 730).

Even the last but one king of the line, Sudarshana (father of Agnivarna), possessed the same virtues as those of his illustrious ancestors. His retirement to Naimisa forest has the following characteristics (XIX.2) (Antoine, R., 1972, p. 210):

'There the holy bathing places made him forget his pleasure-lakes, the kusa grass covering the earth made him forget his bed, and his hut erased the memory of his palace; without any desire for result, he multiplied his austerities'.

Therefore, Kalidasa leaves us with this intriguing question: why of such a *rajarshi* father as Sudarshana was a depraved son like Agnivarna born – neither a *raja*, nor a *rishi*? Still, the principles that sustained the very long line of *rajarshi* leaders are not annulled by this solitary exception. The only black spot intensifies the lustre of the whole canvas.

CONCLUSION

The brief encounters above with Kautilya/Chanakya, Kalidasa and Harshavardhan, spanning between themselves almost a thousand years (3rd century BC to 7th century AD), reveal the unswerving fidelity of worthy leaders in Indian history to the *rajarshi* model. Rabindranath Tagore had upheld this model in several dramas and poems. One of his most sublime creations of this genre is a narrative poem, *Pratinidhi* (The Representative) (Tagore, Rabindranath, 1977, pp. 16–20). It is an emotionally vivid and inspiring account of a classic encounter between Shivaji and his guru, Ramdas. Once Shivaji spotted his guru begging on the streets of the capital. The tormented King kneeled down, offered his crown and all else at the feet of his Guru. He accepted all of this. But, in turn, bid Shivaji to rule the land as a renunciant and servant on his behalf. *He was to govern the kingdom without being a King.* Thereafter Ramdas conferred the gerua robe of a *sannyasi* to Shivaji. Of course this model has been re-lived time and again thereafter

right upto our own era. Even in business. (Chakraborty, S.K. and
Chakraborty, D., 2006, pp. 231–3, 243–7, 239–42, 277–9). So, as and when
we feel the urge to look for 'role models', these are the sources to tap. The
sitar must be played in its own specific technique and style. Superimposing
the guitar method on it will not work. We should always bear in mind the
following inspiring and indispensable insights of Vivekananda, himself a
rajarshi leader of the 19th century—

- 'The more...the Hindus study their past, the more glorious will be their future'
  (Vivekananda, 1962).
- 'If our national life of these ten thousand years has been a mistake, then there
  is no help for it; and if we try now to form a new character the inevitable result
  will be that we shall die' (Vivekananda, Swami, 1962, vol. IV, p. 324).

Will-to-Yoga, Ego and Leadership
Research or Realization?

TO BEGIN WITH

Almost two decades ago we had written a book which had two chapters (2 and 11) on 'Will-to-Yoga' as the basis for Quality-of-Work-life The latter of the two had begun like this (Chakraborty, 1989, p. 188)—

'Will-to-Yoga should not mystify us. Nor need it be viewed with awe. Will-to-yoga is anyway the non-stop refrain of our daily existence. When we seek fame, it is our will-to-yoga with fame. So is the case when we go for money or power or our lady-love. Our craving for a car, or for a "phoren" trip, or the managing director's chair—they all constitute our will-to-yogas....Without examining how lasting or satisfying the(se) 'union(s)' would be, one mistakenly assumes that the objects mentioned above can by themselves provide fulfillment.'

This little hint at the purport of Will-to-Yoga should provide a useful reference frame for what follows next.

A December 2006 'international workshop' brochure on yoga from India included the following statements—

'The large scale popularity of yoga triggered by "health consciousness" in the WEST* has invoked the dormant yoga in Indian blood....People at large are convinced that yoga works....As directed by Swami Vivekananda, to combine the best of the West with that of the East, we...are devoted to examine the usefulness of yoga...(by) exacting scientific research....there have been many studies examining the usefulness of various dimensions of yoga for clinical conditions. The key features of yoga are to relax the body, slow down the breath, calm down the mind, transform violent negative emotions to cultured, softer, positive emotions, and work in tension-free blissful awareness'.

The research and training organization launching this Workshop has high standing, is very purposive, and is quite dedicated. Yet, invoking the WEST for awakening dormant Indian interest in Yoga for physical health is not a cause for celebration. It reminds the sensitive reader of the lamentable 'dependency-conformity' syndrome among most educated Indians. For, how can subjective end-state feelings like 'fulfilment' or 'blissful awareness' be ever measured by 'exacting scientific research'?

It is a pity too that Vivekananda's name has been taken. By in all his speeches and addresses on Yoga he had hardly highlighted its peripheral physical-nervous benefits. Nor did he suggest that yoga should be subjected to laboratory tests to please scientific hubris. First rate scientists like Einsteins, Heisenbergs, Schroedingers, Carrels etc. have also never suggested that Yoga and Spirituality should pass the tests of materialistic science (see chapter 5). The purpose of Yoga, throughout the history of Bharatvarsha, has been to help humans to progress by disciplined *vi-yoga* (dis-identification) of consciousness from the body-mind encasement i.e., the *deha*, and by inspired *Yoga* (re-unification) of individual consciousness with the Spirit-essence or *dehi* or *atman* within the body-mansion. Yet, as a beginning only, Yoga with the Spirit admits the fact: *shariram adyam khalu dharmasadhanam*, i.e., for spiritual attainment a healthy body is an important condition. For, it enables easier dis-engagement from the body-sense. But that is just the first step, not meant to be overdone or to obliterate from view the true end of Yoga. The end is *dharmasadhanam*, not *dehasadhanam*.

Moreover, current interest in yoga, if appraised against the classic text in this field, Maharshi Patanjali's *Yogasutras* (also called *Rajyoga*), falls much short of its true import. Thus, from the eight-limbed (*ashtanga*) yoga system of Patanjali, only the third and fourth steps (*asana* and *pranayama*) are in vogue. The first two steps, *yama* and *niyama*, the foundations of the hierarchy, are ignored. Yet, the entire ethico-moral apparatus of leaders and team-members is constituted by the components of these two stages, e.g. truthfulness, non-stealing, continence, non-receiving, purification, contentment, mortification, study, and worship of God (Vivekananda, 1976 verses II.29–32, pp. 205–6). Skipping all that, yoga courses tend to jump straightway to *dhyana* (meditation)—the seventh step in Patanjali's system. But all the historical, literary and corporate examples cited in the earlier chapters have, to a large extent, stood firm by the *yama-niyama* requirements.

May be the *asana-pranayama* steps lend themselves readily to 'research' to satisfy 'scientific tests'!

The next few pages, therefore offer glimpses of authentic Yoga to answer the call to Spirit-centered leadership for a directionless, body-obsessed, techno-commercial culture. This last plague is inundating the globe, with irretrievable moral and ecological degradation. The world is crying for 'spiritually fit' leaders in the first place. In their absence at the helm, physical yoga for the *deha* alone will tend to be valueless. Whatever little good this process may achieve, is likely to be more than undone by the flood of techno-commerce sweeping into every nook and cranny of human existence.

YOGIC VS. ELECTRONIC CONSCIOUSNESS

Let us, therefore, go back almost a century from today (1909–10) to bathe in the light which Sri Aurobindo had showered upon this momentous subject of Yoga and leadership. He was the master theoretician of the nation's freedom movement in the pre-Gandhian phase – a man who had also mastered Western thought and history in England from the age of seven to twenty one. When he returned to India in 1893, he hardly knew Bengali or Sanskrit.

Over the last few years airports, hotels and other public or office spaces in India have been providing, freely and widely, plug-in points for recharging cell phones. This analogy, from the era of 'electronic consciousness' could be a concrete, though lower-order, way of conveying what the 'Yogic consciousness' operationally means in the sphere of higher-order psychology of the Spirit. Let us listen to Aurobindo about the import of this Yogic plug-in (Aurobindo, 1974, pp. 10–11)—

> 'Yoga is *communion with God* for knowledge, for love or for work. The Yogin puts himself into *direct relationship* with that which is omniscient and omnipotent within man and without him. He is in tune with the *infinite*, he becomes a *channel* for the *strength* of God to pour itself out upon the world whether through calm benevolence or active beneficence'.

The above definition of Yoga rests on sincere acceptance of God or Infinite, and also on faith in human capability for establishing rapport and union with it.[*] Humane, extra-orbital scientists like Einstein or Abdul Kalam or

---

[*] Step 4 of the Quality Mind process (QMP) in chapter 3 is a useful method for accomplishing this goal.

PC Ray readily tune in with this spiritual perspective. All the examples in chapter 3, in the text as well as in the Appendix, have demonstrated that such a re-union or Yoga of human consciousness with Divine Consciousness is a practical truth, a fact. But secular rationalists either reject it altogether, or fumble awkwardly while dwelling on it. Thereby they successfully deny their true *human right* to 'plug in' to the one ultimate source of Wisdom.

Why should leaders of homes, of organizations, of society be serious about Yoga as explained above? This is what Sri Aurobindo has to say in response (Ibid., pp. 40–1)—

> 'The knowledge of the Yogin is not the knowledge of the average desire-driven mind. Neither is it the knowledge of the scientific or the worldly-wise reason which anchors itself on surface facts and leans upon experience and probability.... He rises above reason to that direct and *illuminated knowledge* which we call *vijnanam*.... And this is the root difference that, while they reason, he knows'.

For leaders who are accustomed to whirl within the orbit of fragmented reasoning, with much greater velocity since the above words were written, the successive rounds of complexity, chaos and calamity over a century have yet to induce the saving *humility* essential for Yogic wisdom. Consciously or unconsciously, the *Gita*, Yoga and Spirituality are also being viewed as instruments for success along those very lines which are converging towards moral and ecological decay. Even the very few who may be harbouring a more sincere notion of Yoga etc., could still be far from appreciating what should be the quality and depth of the Spiritual agenda in human affairs. Of this intimate realm too Aurobindo draws an immaculate picture (Ibid., p. 40)—

> 'The thoughts of men are a tangle of truth and falsehood (*satyam* and *anrtam*). True *perception* is marred and clouded by false perception, true *judgement* lamed by false judgement, true *imagination* distorted by false imagination, true *memory* deceived by false memory'.

It is readily possible to substantiate each of the above four disabilities of the leadership mind by countless examples from the past century. The one omnibus instance that seems to fuse in itself all these degeneracies is the *superstition* that higher and greater doses of economics-technology-institution building will usher a golden age for the globe. To break out of this delusive charm, the Yogic process has first to be understood and then pursued from its *baseline*, its roots. Its character, as Sri Aurobindo spells out for leaders, is (Ibid., p. 40)—

> 'The more complete the *calm*, the mightier the Yogic power, the greater the force in action. *In this calm, right knowledge comes....* The activity of the mind must cease, the *chitta* be *purified*, a *silence* falls upon the restlessness of *prakriti*; then in that calm, in that voiceless *stillness* illumination comes upon the mind, error begins to fall away..., clarity establishes itself in the higher stratum of the consciousness, compelling peace and joy in the lower. *Right knowledge* becomes the infallible source of *right action*. *Yogah karmasu kaushalam*'.

Unless one is ready to embark on a determined journey for Yoga with the Spirit (not body or matter), the indispensability of adequate calmness or silence or stillness of being may escape comprehension. And since such comprehension eludes us, the common rendering of the portion of the Gita quoted by Sri Aurobindo is: 'skill in works is yoga' (verse II. 50). This is wrong, and imparts a perverse sense to the principle. A terrorist, for example, by this interpretation, should also merit the title of yogi! So might all unethically successful individuals or leaders join the club of yogis!

The other two important aspects to note from the last quote are—

- Understanding and decision-making become more and more error-free because our ego-conditioned being, in the silence of yoga, is able to open itself to (or plug into) that unconditioned, holistic Intelligence which leads the Universe.
- The individual, he/she is not left high and dry. Yoga bestows the abiding existential return of 'compelling peace and joy'. But the desire and courage to aspire for this true aim has been destroyed by the manner of existence modern society has evolved for itself.

Two increasingly stiff barriers to the above consummation must, therefore, be recognized—

- Mounting noise pollution.
- Alarming emotional pollution.

Whether it is midnight or early dawn, in the Himalayan slopes or riverside ashrams, filthy, nerve-wracking noise has become omnipresent. The mobile or cell phone menace has invaded temples, classrooms, bathrooms and so on. In such a milieu researchers should abandon futile efforts to arrive at spiritual quotient. Instead, noise quotient is a fit candidate for such measurement. The calmness-silence-stillness, which Sri Aurobindo declares as a precondition for Yoga, is fast disappearing from human habitat. We thus have a tragic paradox: on the one hand the calamitous world situation today is crying for Yogic leadership; on the other hand, money-centric careerism has become the chief enemy of Spiritual Yoga.

As earlier, mentioned the blinding storm of consumerism, often rationalized as higher standard of living and widened the range of choice, has its eye in the provocation of *shadaripus* (or seven cardinal sins) in humans. For, without greed, lust, jealousy (i.e competition), delusion, pride, gluttony etc. becoming legitimate and acceptable features of human conduct, right from little children to old people, secular commerce cannot reign supreme. Now, in all spiritual or sacred thought these primal emotional proclivities are treated as pollutants of the body-vital-mind layers or sheaths of our being. These dense and sticky pollutants prevent the plug-in process of human intellect with *supra-mental* Intelligence. Come to think of it, how is it that our vaunted rights-oriented ethos tolerates and conforms to such dictatorship of business and commerce! Be this as it may, the more humanity needs Yogic leadership, the weaker seem to become the preliminary enabling factors for such leadership to germinate and grow. No amount of smart strategizing is going to bring us any closer to this objective. Honest and humble recognition of this paradox is the first step in resolving the impasse. Any takers?

FROM POLLUTION TO PURIFICATION

It would be good, for a change, to recall the metaphor of the 'magnet-and-the-needle'. Even a child will know that if the needle is smeared with mud, the magnet will fail to attract it to itself, no matter how close the two are brought. There will be no Yoga between the two. The 'magnet' stands for God or the Divine or the Supra-mental, the 'needle' for the ordinary human mind or reason or consciousness. As long as the 'needle' (i.e. mind) is not cleansed, its Yoga with the supra-mental Spirit is not accomplished. The God-magnet is ever ready to pull the mind-needle to itself. But the latter is smeared with dirt. Hence no Yoga. With galloping pollution of the human mind, its cleaning or purification is turning harder by the day. Yet, this is the *first step* essential to our upward climb on the ladder of Yoga. (This metaphor was used with indelible impact by Sri Ramakrishna when he was teaching Yoga to the rebellious Vivekananda and other brilliant co-disciples during the early 1880's).

While dwelling on pollution-purification, some light from Sri Aurobindo's vast and rigorous analysis of the problem may be sought again (worked out during 1914–21)—

- 'An *unpurified* heart, an *unpurified* sense, an *unpurified* life confuse the understanding, disturb its data, distort its conclusions, darken its seeing, misapply its knowledge.... the progressive tranquillisation of the emotional heart (helps) for instance the purification of the understanding, while equally a purified understanding imposes calm and light on the turbid and darkened workings of the yet impure emotions' (Aurobindo, Sri, 1988, p. 295).
- 'All purification is a release, a delivery; for it is a throwing away of limiting, binding, obscuring imperfections and confusions: *purification from desire* brings the freedom of the *prana* (vital life force), *purification from wrong emotions* and troubling reactions the freedom of the heart, *purification from the obscuring limited thought* of the sense-mind the freedom of the intelligence, *purification from mere intellectuality* the freedom of the gnosis' (Ibid., p. 647 emphasis added).

The first quote above is a *normative* blueprint for the practical quest of Yoga with Spirit. For, notions of the pure and impure pertain to the domain of should/should not, not to that of is/is not. Yogic leadership has to embrace normative idealism by superseding objective pragmatism. Integral wisdom will then be recovered to replace or uplift fragmented knowledge. Sri Aurobindo delineates the harmful consequences of unpurified emotions of the heart, in the field of action, with the realistic precision of a seer who sees through—

- Confused understanding.
- Disturbed data.
- Distorted conclusions.
- Darkened seeing.
- Misapplied knowledge.

The last four centuries have been a long tale of these five mishaps, presided over by leaders under cover of misleading rhetoric and false promises. The dominant brain-centric world-view of today continues to ignore the lessons of its cumulative follies. Ancient heart-centric beliefs, though often summarily dismissed as superstitious, have not been lethal for natural ecology and human psychology. But modern brain-centric beliefs are irreparably damaging both on a global scale. Rightly have the above excerpts given priority to the 'heart', not the 'head'. All wisdom or sacred literature vibrates with this common keynote.

The second quote clarifies the four *critical freedoms* that could accrue to leaders who approach the task of self-and other-leadership by striving for purification required by Yoga—

- Freedom of the *prana* (primal life force).
- Freedom of the heart.
- Freedom of the intelligence.
- Freedom of the gnosis.

References to the leadership modes of R K Talwar, in chapter 2 and others and of PC Ray in chapter 9 have revealed the centrality of Yoga in their workings. To single out one instance from each:

(a) Ray: His regular prayer of
   'Tvaya Hrishikesha hridisthitena
   Yatha niyuktohosmi tatha karomi'
   'O! Lord, be always seated in my heart,
   and guide me in Thy appointed work'.
(b) Talwar: His discipline of
   Silence + Sincerity + No Preference = Divine Voice

Between them these two processes highlight the following signs of Spiritualised (or *Rajarshi* or Wisdom) leadership:

- Acceptance of Supra-mental Wisdom i.e., prayer to Hrishikesha, and a yearning for the 'Divine voice'.
- Prioritizing the 'pure heart' over the 'sharp brain';
- Giving a battle to 'limiting egotism'.

That both of them were able to function with a much greater degree of the 'four freedoms' than most other leaders, is proved by the quality of reactions, memories and emotions evoked in our minds by their names—during their lifetime and long thereafter. Of course this has been true of some other leaders also mentioned in earlier chapters.

YOGA IN THE GITA

It will be profitable to turn to the *Bhagwadgita* now, which has been the basic source of Sri Aurobindo's expositions, and Gandhi's, Ray's and Talwar's applications. Here are some of the key verses in the *Gita* drawing specific attention to Yogic or spiritualised leadership (even though all the eighteen chapters explain Yoga only, from various angles, as the concluding verse in each chapter declares)—

- Verse II.39: the terms *buddhiryoga* (wisdom of yoga) and *buddhaya yukto* (endued w ` ith wisdom) expressly introduce the principle of Yoga or union, probably for the first time. This *buddhi* is not what we mean by common intellect or reason. It is intellect clarified and purified of vital and mental infirmities and pollutions.
- Verse II.48: An operative definition of Yoga is contained in the key phrase *samatwa yoga uchyate* (even-mindedness is verily yoga). That is, unperturbable evenness of mind, in the midst of inevitable swings and fluctuations caused by non-controllable external variables, is the psychological goal of Yoga.

Once more a Sri Ramakrishna-imagery, that of a weighing balance or scale, is a telling way of driving the principle home. The weighing scale has a fixed central pointer turned downwards on its upper beam. The lower beam, with two equidistant pans on two sides, too has a central pointer turned upwards. If either of the pans leans high or low on its side, the upper and lower points in the beam's centre do not meet. They are not in Yoga. If only the two pans are of *equal* weight can there be Yoga between the two pointers. The upper one is God or Spirit or Supramental Wisdom, the lower one individual or egoistic mental reason or intellect. The imbalance of the two pans represents the dis-equilibrating emotional/vital reactions like excitement–depression, victory–defeat, gain–loss, praise–blame, anger–jealousy, greed–contentment etc. That is, the primal anti-Yoga forces in human nature, the *shadaripus* mentioned earlier, have to be acknowledged and handled on the way to *samatwa* Yoga by a *rajarshi* leader. Kautilya had given priority to the battle against *shadaripus* for the leader (see chapter 10). The figure below depicts the balance metaphor about *samatwa*.

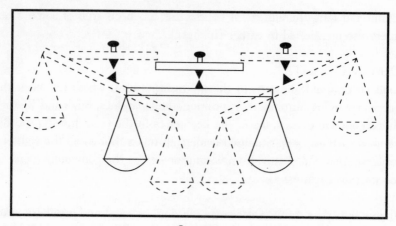

Samatwa

- Verses II. 49 and 50: Verse 49 calls Yoga achieved through the discipline of *samatwa* as *buddhiyoga*. That is, the leader's lower-order, fragmented intellect or reason would then stay poised in Yoga with the integral or Divine Intelligence. But working with egoistic motives, for personal fruits of wealth or power or acclaim, will impair *samatwa* due to the influence of the *shadaripus* triggered by such hankerings. The super-ordinate *loksamgraha* goal, the well-being of all, will recede from the leader's purview. He will turn into or remain a career-driven opportunist, with little power to inspire or command respect. The very next verse re-emphasises Yoga by the exhortation *tasmad-yogayah* i.e, therefore Arjuna learn that skill or art of working which keeps your *buddhi* in Yoga with the Divine i.e, by training it to remain internally steady in the midst of dualities in the field of external action.
- Verse IV.2: Explicit reference to *rajarshi* occurs here. (This term recurs again in verse IX.33). The true power of a Royal-Sage has for aeons been the Wisdom born of Yoga. This truth is emphasized by the teacher to the disciple. It is now being repeated for Arjuna because, in course of time, the secret art of Yoga has been lost. Perhaps it is time again, since the *Mahabharata* days, to recoup this Yoga for the leaders of today. It has suffered yet another catastrophic tumble-down since the Mahabharata battle.
- Verse VI.46: The Yogi here is considered to be better than merely the ascetic, the knower of sacred lore and the self-interested performer. The Yogi-leader functions in the midst of society, but has learnt and strives to stay clear of degrading personal motives associated with his role. The

chapter ends by calling it as an exposition of *Atmasanyam Yoga* – a pregnant phrase. This self-control nullifies ego-centric narcissism in leadership roles grounded in the *shadaripus*.

- Verses VIII.7 and 27: Verse 7 instructs Arjuna to fight while remembering (*mamanusmarah*) Him within, all the time. One may easily depersonalize 'Him', and take this to mean the Transcendental-Universal, Supra-mental Intelligence or Consciousness. Continuous awareness of Divinity within, or above, while engaged in outer work, is the direct and operative meaning of Yoga. Verse 27 at the end returns to this rule again, asking Arjuna to be *yogayukta* without break.

- Verse X.10: The above message of the feeling of ceaseless inner Yoga or union with the Supreme is repeated here. The result, gradual but sure, of such practice is attainment of *buddhiyoga*. This also harks back to the *buddhiyoga* of chapter II (see above) – Yoga with Spiritualized intellect and reason.

- Verse XVIII.78: This is the final verse of the Gita. Its import is, goodness, victory, glory and unfailing ethicality flourish whenever and wherever *Yogeshwara Krishna* and *Dhanurdhara Partha* work in unison. *Dhanurdhara Partha* is the *raja*, Yogeshwara Krishna the *rishi*. The Supreme Yogi and the Ace Archer should function like the two blades of a pair of scissors, exemplifying the *rajarshi* model.

Thus, the Gita is a meticulosuly *subjective* exposition of Yoga. And clearly it is *normative* too. The positivist or objective approach to Yoga by means of *hathayoga*, *asanas*, *pranayams* etc., which are nowadays very popular, may be good in a limited way for the physical-nervous system (*deha*) of leaders (and others too). But the substance of the Yoga-approach for inspiring leadership has to be *subjective-normative*. This is an immensely more onerous engagement. Yoga with the Spirit or *dehi*, for that is what Spirituality truly means, should not therefore be uttered glibly or lightly, as is so often being done. It has become habitual for us to hide our fear of facing our own selves by talking and acting smart. This will abort the purpose of Yoga.

THE KNOT OF THE EGO

The issue of 'ego' merits a closer look again than the passing mention of it above. Ego was created by Nature, (as mentioned in chapter 3), as a nucleus for the initial formation of an individual personality. This personality marks itself out from all else by an increasing sense of 'separateness'. But then, sticking to and accentuating such separativeness (often under the garb of personality development) as the anchor for one's entire life-span becomes anti-Yoga, both in relation to other beings and to Divine or God. This is the paradox which Sri Aurobindo had put across through an exquisite aphorism (Sri Aurobindo Birth Centenary Library, 1973, vol. 16, p. 377):

'Ego was a helper, ego is the bar'.

Career-counselling programmes, a growing craze these days, betray ignorance about this fundamental problem. For instance, children and young people both are often heard being told: 'You are special'. Such false encouragement, sooner than later, causes most of them to over-estimate themselves. The inherently limited ego becomes more inflexible, bloated and stubborn. Such individuals become internally fragile, hence susceptible to misery at the slightest shortfall in ego-massaging received by them. They also cause tremendous problems in team or group functioning. Neither can they be wholesome team players, nor inspiring team leaders. The authors have witnessed several such tragedies in organizations. Hence, Spirituality-based leadership development and teamwork must face the ego issue head-on.

This start-off ego-nucleus in the human being is raw and rough, once beautifully termed as 'unripe ego' by Sri Ramakrishna. This 'unripe ego' quickly becomes possessive, then assertive, and finally aggressive. The mainsprings of current education are all fixed in this ground. But the unheeded, yet inevitable, consequence of this process is that the person so groomed, blinded and consumed by his/her 'unripe ego', can lead neither himself nor others. Nor can he/she continue for long as a healthy team member. Chapter XVI of the Gita devotes eighteen out of the total of twenty-four verses to a vivid elaboration of what it calls *asuri sampats*, demoniacal attributes of 'unripe ego'.

Sri Ramakrishna had also spoken of 'ripe ego', as a contrast to 'unripe ego'. The 'ripe ego' learns to treat itself as an instrument, a channel for the Divine Intelligence e.g., Talwar's statement: 'I am the Mother's appointee.' The Gita also speaks of *daivi sampats* (Divine qualities) in chapter XVI. 'Ripe ego' and *daivi sampats* go together, as do the 'unripe ego' and *asuri sampats*. And these two pairs, in turn, are imbedded in *sattwa guna* and *rajo guna* respectively. Now, a few *Gita expositions* of *asuri sampats*—

- Chapter 16, verse 12: Held in bondage by hundreds of ties of expectations and wholly giving themselves upto lust and anger, they strive to amass by unfair means hoards of money and other objects for the enjoyment of sensuous pleasures'.

• Chapter 16, verse 13: They say to themselves, 'This much has been secured by me today, and now I must realize this ambition. So much wealth is already with me, and yet again this too shall be mine'.

These two sample verses mirror current reality perfectly. Leaders in government, in politics, in academics, in healthcare, in judiciary, in business etc. seem to be in a reckless hurry to prove the truth of Sage Vyasa's vintage prophecies of three thousand years ago. *Doordrishti* or far sight par excellence!

'Unripe ego', combined with the free play given to *shadaripus* and *asuri sampats*, constitute the dark backdrop against which many are attempting to talk about Yoga, Spirituality etc. But greater humility and seriousness are needed for responsible engagement with such ultimate saving principles as ends, not means. Hence also the compelling duty to turn respectfully to Sri Aurobindo and others of his ilk. They did not speak and write to flatter our 'unripe ego', nor to pander to our fancy for jargon. Genuinely activated by the Gita-call to leaders to be *sarvabhuta hite ratah* (being devoted to the welfare of all beings), they had battled their way up by covering every inch of the climb with unflinching fidelity. Repeated referral to the standards set by them is indispensable. Otherwise, we shall negate the true end of Spirituality in organizations. It will be debased to yet another means or tool.

Another critical theme associated with 'ego' is that of 'power'. Once again Sri Aurobindo has captured for us the keynote of power in a language which can hardly be surpassed (*The Synthesis of Yoga*, op. cit., pp. 164–5):

• 'All power is ultimately Divine in origin and Spiritual in nature', and
• 'You must not claim to possess the "power" that should possess you'.

Earlier chapters have already highlighted how leaders like Chandragupta, Harshavardhan, Vivekananda, PC Ray, RK Talwar, MK Gandhi et. al. had internalized and manifested the spiritual orientation to leadership power capsuled in these aphorisms.

With 'unripe ego' at its zenith now, the above insights may sound too mystical, or even senseless to most. It is because of this unrecognized infirmity in the leadership or managerial-mind that Lord Acton's warning has proved to be incontrovertible—

'Power corrupts, absolute power corrupts absolutely'.

This aphorism deserves some modification and extension in the light of the preceding analysis:

- Power in itself is neutral (both Gods and demons have done penance for power).
- But the *adhara* or instrument can be pure or profane, sacred or secular.
- Power will be frequently manifested through a secular or gredy *adhara* in corrupted ways.
- Power will be usually manifested through a sacred or holy *adhara* in exalted ways.
- Power can also intoxicate, and absolute power can intoxicate absolutely.

It is the secularly-grounded, unripe ego or *adhara* which readily succumbs to corruption and intoxication. As mentioned above, over-estimation of oneself is another great hurdle inherent in the unripe ego. This is the ego that Spirit-centered Yogi leaders have to recognize, combat and overcome.

Thereafter, the blossoming 'ripe ego' learns to revise his/her *self-perception* to that of a servant/agent/trustee/instrument of the Divine, God, Supreme (or whatever other cognate word). This type of mental orientation is called *dasoham* (I am Thy servant). Its best exemplar in Indian lore is that of Mahaveer Hanuman in his relationship with Sri Ramchandra. The fountain pen metaphor is a homely illustration of this principle. The pen cannot claim that it is writing. The truth is that it only acts as an unclogged channel for the ink to flow. It is the writer who uses the pen to express what he/she wants to. Similarly, if the human mental channel could be unclogged and purified of its *shadaripus* and *asuri sampats*, it then merges with the 'ripe ego' whose very nature is to be in Yoga with the Higher, the Divine Power. This reduces misuse-abuse, or corruption-intoxication in the handling of power.

It is useful to savour a few arresting statements of Sri Aurobindo on the implications of 'ripe' or 'Yogic' ego (*The Ideal of The Karmayogin*, op. cit., p. 11):

- 'The ideal Yogin is…(humanity's) leader in the march and the battle, but *unbound* by his works and *superior* to his personality'.
- 'He (Yogin) is in *tune* with the infinite, he becomes a channel for the strength of God to pour itself out upon the world—whether through calm benevolence or active beneficence'.

- '(He) feels himself passive, and the divine force working *unresisted* through his mind, his speech, his senses and all his organs;…he becomes *incapable* of grief, disquiet or false excitement—this is Yoga'.

The receptive reader will appreciate that such capacity as above for expressing the inexpressible can accrue only to one who has attained complete *realization* of Yoga. In the first quote the word 'personality' means the 'unripe ego' which is bound and inferior. In the second quote, to be 'in tune' is meant for the Yogin who rests upon 'ripe ego'. The third quote affirms firstly that the Divine Power finds in the Yogi-mind a free channel for its own workings. Secondly, it asserts that by taking Yoga to mean this process, the Yogin is not reduced to pulp. Rather, he exists permanently beyond the consuming sufferings invited by the 'unripe ego'. He is all bliss and joy – whether in action or not. This is very far from what is offered by the majority of money-raking yoga training businesses now on the rise.

During the period 1900-1947, all the authentic leaders of Bharatvarsha —Rabindranath, Gandhi, Vivekananda, Aurobindo, Tilak, Lajpat, Netaji Subhas, CR Das et.al.—had visioned a 'free' and 'great' India. At the end of that era of struggle and sacrifice, we may have obtained some sort of patchy political independence. But India is neither 'free' nor 'great' in that true and profound subjective sense which the above leaders had dreamed of. Instead, a crippling subjective dependency on alien ideas is the order of the day. Organizations of all varieties operating in this milieu, therefore, need a Spiritual turnaround of a more fundamental, genuine character. Its triple elements should be the ones which Sri Aurobindo had spelled out for Yoga-based leaders of a 'free' and 'great' India (Ibid., p. 17)—

- *Tapasya* – which is more than discipline; it is the materialisation in leaders by *spiritual means* of the divine energy.
- *Jnanam* – which is more than philosophy; it is the inspired and *direct knowledge* which comes out of *drishti*, spiritual insight.
- *Shakti* – which is more than strength; it is the *universal energy* which moves the stars made individual.

This triple agenda of Yogic leadership had been summed up by Aurobindo, though in the nation's context, as the birth of Ramdas and Shivaji in one body. That is, an infusion of the *rishi* into the *raja*, the seer into the doer, the sage into the king, the monk into the emperor. The 'unripe ego' cannot begin or bear this infusion. The *Gita* had sounded the relevant warning long ago (verse III.27)—

'*ahankar vimudhatma kartaham iti manyate*'

The fool, deluded by egotism, erroneously regards himself as the master, for he sees not the Master.

The way *jnanam* has been explained above recalls what is called 'intuition'. Does the Yogi-leader or *rajarshi* have anything to do with intuition? Again we have these startling enunciations from Sri Aurobindo (*The Synthesis of Yoga*, op. cit., p. 301)—

- '...real knowledge, by our very definition of it, is *supra-intellectual*'.
- 'In order to strengthen the higher knowledge-faculty in us we have to effect the ...*separation* between the intuitive and intellectual elements of our thought...
- '...we have to...cultivate the power of *intellectual passivity*'.

Just as the unripe ego is a *divider* and *separator* in man-man or man-Nature relationships, so is conventional intellect or reason in the realm of human understanding of events and problems. To the extent that expressions like 'holistic excellence', 'holistic development' or 'holistic management' do not begin with this theoretical clarity, they turn out to be platitudinous – impressive to say or hear, but insubstantial. The third and fourth steps of the Quality Mind Process (QMP) outlined in chapter 2, and numerous other cognate methods, help to fulfill the three requirements for *intuitive capability* mentioned above. This intuitive mind or intuitive reason, cultivated through the Yoga of the ordinary mind with the Universal or Super-personal Mind, asserts Sri Aurobindo, 'can do the work of the reason with a higher power, a swifter action, a greater and spontaneous certitude' (Ibid., p. 458). This is what he terms as 'pure' or 'true' intuition, to distinguish it from false claims made by demoniac, unripe egos. Distortions and contaminations of the senses and mental or vital reactions are willed out while practising 'pure intuition'. Since such 'true intuition, proceeds from the *self-existent truth* of things, is secured by that self-existent truth and not by any indirect, derivatory or dependent method of arriving at knowledge', it 'carries in itself its own *guarantee* of truth' and is sure and infallible (Ibid., pp. 459–60).

All this gives an altogether exalted sense to one of the most frequently used terms in management and leadership discourse: 'empowerment'. In the absence of this spiritual drift, empowerment is the same old wine of delegation in a new bottle. In the purely spiritual realm, *diksha* is a perennial method of empowerment of seekers by the *guru*. This method, in principle, is valid for secular leadership roles too. Only, *diksha* is replaced by inspired role-modelling. This is strongly empowering.

AT THE END

Thus, the Spirit-centered, ripe-ego *rajarshi* leader steadily empowers himself/ herself with 'truth vision', 'truth-hearing', 'truth-memory'. A visional power of truth-discernment germinates and ripens in him/her. The confused, chaotic, and terror-stricken post-modern world needs leaders of this mettle across the board. Careeristic leaders or entrepreneurs, using organizational and administrative structures for self-glory, cannot become legitimate Yogi leaders, and be of true help to the world. The 'will-to-ego' will need to be replaced by 'will-to-Yoga' if one is sincere about the spiritualised piloting of our organizations and institutions (Chakraborty, S.K., 1998, pp. 188–201). It is important to seize the fact that organizations can create careeristic managers only. But it is legitimate, ripe-ego leaders alone who can create organizations.

Much of the flowery rhetoric, the catchy jargons of the 'knowledge-era' have been proving to be unbelievably make-believe. Accelerated 'knowledge development' is not something that merits self-adulation. For, this truly means all such so-called new 'knowledge' is just like transient bubbles, invalid for both problem-prevention and problem-solution. Eternal verities had been intuited long, long ago. Leaders need to discriminate between fleeting fads and perennial truths. For that ripe-ego-based Yoga is needed. But the self-deluding *zeitgeist* of shallow scientism is now attempting to convert the supremely subjective realization of Yoga to the superficially objective research on yoga. Burgeoning 'scientific (laboratory) verification' is, in this process, bordering on topsy-turvy.

Finally, the last paragraph of the same earlier chapter, from which an excerpt was taken to start off the present chapter, also seems to hold true even today (Chakraborty, 1989, p. 201). For, it goes again to Sri Rama-krishna-parable for a verdict on research vs. realization. Let us quote it—

'A man was once very lucky to enter a large mango orchard. After entering it he began first to count the number of trees, and then the branches on those trees. He next laboured to classify them into those which were strong and straight, and those which were drooping and twirling. After that he lost himself in taking the statistics on leaves. While he was halfway through this process, the bell rang for the orchard to be closed. He had to walk back to the gate. It was only then that he realized that for the whole day he had squandered his energy on non-essentials and had missed eating the ripe, juicy mangoes on the trees!'

Afterword

The contents of this book so far may not have appealed to die-hard skeptics, nor to those who look for light only from across the seven seas, without caring for its gentle emanation from within the culture of their birth and growth. They all fail to gain from it much that is indispensable. Yet Swami Vivekananda, himself a leader, change-agent and institution-builder par excellence, had said something to this effect (around 1896-7)—*those who can dive deep into their past, can also soar high into the future.* Whence could he articulate such a fundamental insight? The following information could be one factual answer to this question.

Max Mueller had edited the 50-volume *Sacred Books of East* during the last decade of the 19th century and the first decade of the 20th. Apart from the last volume which is the index, the forty nine volumes have this composition—

- Islam   2
- Chinese   6
- Zoroastrianism   8
- Buddhism, Jainism   10
- Hinduism   23

Thus, thirty three volumes were produced in Bharatvarsha alone. And they do not include the Granth Sahib, the Ramayana and the Mahabharata, the Gita, the Srimad Bhagavatam, the Puranas, and the Tantras. This shows the virtually inexhaustible treasure of philosophy, psychology, sociology, and of course religion and spirituality, produced by the *ashramic rishis* and our householder savants. Such then is the standing ground, held firm by the one bond of Spirituality, of *all* the citizens of this land. Should one care to pause and ponder in silent reverence just over this fact, invaluable empowerment will accrue to that person.

What was the abiding purpose underlying such unrivalled *tapasya* (ascesis) by the founding leaders and managers of Bharatvarsha? The answer: To cover the entire spectrum of life with a unique range of principles and processes, structures and systems. Managing enduringly a whole culture and civilization on the basis of indestructible foundations was their him. Here history, minus politics and prejudice, offers unassailable proof.

Undoubtedly, leadership, administration, management governance and of an entire civilization were tackled in the minutest detail. From the Cosmos to Nature, from society and its institutions, organizations, homes and ultimately to the individual—these have been the successive steps of a gigantic cascade that Bharat's culture has been upholding. No matter how much denial or disdain or ignorance prevails in higher echelons about this bedrock, all varieties of common human endeavour in this country are still conducted by drawing upon this 'secret reserve'. Vivekananda had voiced this truth in his own way in the first para above. The task awaiting managers, administrators, politicians and other leaders of today is to recognize this truth explicitly, resuscitate it, and derive energy and light from it. 'Openness' cannot mean, any longer, clutching at any straw that storms in from other quarters, and remaining 'closed' to the 'core competence' (*swadharma*) of one's own milieu. This *swadharma* undoubtedly is: *leading and managing all secular activities in the light of the sacred*. One should recall Mahatma Gandhi's emphatic declaration to this effect: While I will keep all my windows open, I refuse to be blown off my feet by any and every gust of wind.

With a few rare exceptions, the Indian managerial mind and leadership consciousness, be it in industry or government or politics or judiciary or academics, draws a depressing blank in two primary respects—

- That over the long past Bharatvarsha had been a land led amply and managed soundly by holistically competent people of head and heart. Material organization and prosperity (*abhyudaya*) was surely one, but only one, of their basic concerns.
- That for the long future ahead, Bharatvarsha has an obligation to help herself and the world to govern matter-body-mind under the suzerainty of Spirit-above-Mind.

The first blank may be filled up by drawing upon a French scholar-lover of India, Michel Danino—

'At the centre of the riddle of India's ancient past lies the famous Indus Valley (or Harappan) civilization, one of the world's oldest. It was certainly the most extensive by far, since it covered today's Punjab, Haryana, Gujarat, much of Rajasthan, Maharashtra and Kashmir, the western parts of Uttar Pradesh, the whole of Pakistan, even large parts of Afghanistan and beyond. It was also perhaps the most sophisticated in terms of urbanization, industry, technology, trade and sailing. Its arts and crafts were varied and refined, while its sanitation and water management were of such a level that one wishes our municipal corporations would follow them today'. (Danino, 1999)

This assessment of Danino is, in turn, based on the most recent archaeological investigations by over a score of Western and Indian experts during the last four decades.

To fill the second void in today's Indian consciousness we turn to Sri Aurobindo, perhaps the most capacious reservoir (East or West) of immaculately expressed salered generalizations (1918, 1998)—

'Progress she (India) admits, but this (is) spiritual progress, not the externally self-unfolding process of an always more and more prosperous and efficient civilization....Spirituality is not the monopoly of India...but the difference is between spirituality made the leading motive and the determining power of both the inner and outer life, and spirituality suppressed, allowed only under disguises or brought in as a minor power.... Either India will be rationalized and industrialized out of all recognition and she will be no longer India, or else she will be the leader in a new world-phase, (and) by her example...spiritualise the human race. That is the one radical and poignant question at issue....will European rationalism and commercialism put an end for ever to the Indian type of culture?'

The empirical sketch by Danino has to be understood as a 'run up – follow through-delivery', from our cultural ethos as captured in the transcendental sweep of Aurobindo's integral vision. What change, by whom, and how and why should India lead and manage? For whom? Ought not this set of key questions dawn in the minds of today's change-agents? If not, India is, to that extent, being pitifully irresponsible, disastrously blind.

The Report of the Radhakrishnan Commission on Education, 1949, had averred thus (Chakraborty, 2006)—

(a) If we exclude spiritual training from our educational institutions we would be untrue to our whole historical development.
(b) All educational institutions should start work with a few minutes of silent meditation.

But a 'secular' Constitution was foisted on the nation the following year, 1950. Taking this cue, the above recommendations were duly dumped into the garbage bin by the designers of education for the Republic of India. The whole edifice of *deep-structure idealism*, articulated for fifty years, by Vivekananda to Radhakrishnan, was obliterated by ill-suited, borrowed gospels. [The educational outfits of the minority communities, however, enjoy full religious' freedom*]

Is it any wonder then, forty five years later (1995), to hear the Vora Committee Report to Parliament severely indicting the diabolical nexus between MP's, politicians, bureaucrats on the one hand, and mafia dons like Dawood, Memons, Iqbal etc.on the other? Even the judiciary was not spared from chastisement (Chakraborty and Chakraborty, 2006).

And it was in the same decade of the 1990s that the Indian corporate sector too bared its murky face through a series of mega scams e.g., Harshad Mehta's Bombay stock exchange swindle, the ITC scandal, the TISCO imbroglio, the UTI fraud, and so on. This then is the scale of economic filth in our contextual milieu, for considering the cleansing role of Spirituality in management and leadership. About the dirt in political leadership at all levels in the Centre and States, the less said the better.

The following few recent experiences of the authors haunt their minds—

- In 2002 one of the IIMs had invited one of the authors to deliver the Foundation Day Lecture centering on the theme of relevance of Indian ethos for management. During the question hour one student stood up and asked: 'I do not know in which country I was born in my previous birth. Nor do I know where I may be born again in the next birth. So, isn't it pointless to respect and love what you are calling "Indian Ethos" just because I am born in India this time?'
- In 2003 the apex Council of one of the most vital and prestigious professions in the country had constituted an Ethics Committee. It was headed by a former Director of an IIT. In the second meeting, even before the Committee had warmed up to its agenda, the Chairman abruptly shot out this diktat: 'While deliberating on ethical matters, at no stage shall we refer to religion'. It was a bolt from the blue. The members sat dumbfounded for some moments, and quietly left the comment at that.

---

* For example, in April 2004 we saw a large wall painting inside the ground floor corridor of a reputed missionary school in Kolkata with this]exhortation: KNOW YOUR BIBLE, followed by details of its structure. But you will not find KNOW YOUR GITA on the walls of a Ramakrishna Mission school.

- In 2004 a professor went for his first lecture to the second year MA students of Ancient Indian History. It was a reputed University of long standing. The curriculum had prescribed 50 marks for the two Indian epics, *Ramayana* and *Mahabharata*, as a part of one of the compulsory papers. The above professor was to teach this portion. He began thus: 'I do not want to waste my time lecturing on such rotten garbage'. Then he spent some minutes to abuse and insult the Epics and left the class. Students were all awestruck. And that is all they saw of and heard from him in a course supposed to be spread over thirty hours. He was a political bigwig in the system. Could anyone dream that the *Iliad* and *Odyssey* would be so contemptuously dismissed by a Western teacher in a Western University? That the Indian Epics are a hundred times richer than the Greek ones—let that be set aside for the moment.
- In 2005, a CEO was invited by one of the IIMs to deliver a certain commemorative oration. These were his opening words: 'We have had enough of poverty for 5000 years. We must get out of the rut. Therefore let us change everything – root and branch.' And lo! And behold—large sections of the audience burst into applause.

Such then is the poison of arrogant ignorance, all along the hierarchy, that is being brewed and sprayed by our hyper-rationalists and hyper-secularists. Our times are indeed out of joint! It is in this mental climate that management people and pundits are talking of Spirituality. Not wrong as such. But this must be done only after or along with an authentic grip over the characteristically Indian continuum of history and culture (of the people) – where Spirituality (*sans* imbecility) has remained the end, the *summum bonum*.

If Bharatiya culture has indeed been so sound and strong, how has it then been mauled so badly for nearly one thousand years, is materially poor today, and is ethically corrupt too?—critics persist. Four answers for them—

- The power-hungry Romans had overwhelmed and subjugated the Greeks. But none, for that reason, ever denounces Greek culture as inferior to that of the Roman.
- Which culture other than Bharat's could have or has withstood and lived on, inspite of the unprovoked and unabated cruelties, plunders and destructions by all sorts of invading cultures?
- Time is circular, as is the whole Cosmic design. Let another culture last uninterruptedly for seven millennia. Only then any valid comparison can

be done. Three or four centuries of shine and sheen are but a drop in the ocean of time.

- Pervasive corruption and unethicality are squarely attributable to the wanton neglect of the age-old religio-cultural norms and belief-systems governing our existence.

Managers and leaders in-the-making for the future, especially if they wish to be spiritually anchored, must guard their minds against assaults from yet another angle. Incalculable quantities of ink and paper have been consumed by a formidable group of academics, both Western and Indian, to depict only untouchability and dowry, superstition and idolatry, caste discrimination and women's oppression and such other abominable stuff as Hindu culture. Traditionally-designed Indian homes have a backdoor for the entry of scavengers. These academics habitually tend to behave like such scavengers – entering the vast mansion of Bharat's culture through the small and low backdoor, not by the spacious and high frontdoor. Strangely, and conveniently, such scholars gloss over the fact that every culture has its backdoor, has its stinking backyard. They do not care to ask how a 7–millennia old culture could stand or fall merely by the alleged evils (as they see it) of caste system etc.

It is worth remembering that Tagores and Vivekanandas, Gandhis and Aurobindos have also been unsparing in condemning the many apparent social evils in the degenerate phase of Indian society. But this was preceded and vitalised by their deep and unflinching love and practice of the true *sanatan* ethos of Bharatvarsha. So, they had *earned the legitimate right to chastise as well*—like parents first loving their child and, then only because of that true love, chide it too for its well-being. The class of critics alluded to above have no legitimacy from this standpoint. They deserve to be told: 'Hands off!'

All the above crucial issues have been highlighted to help the future managers and leaders to develop a correct, constructive, big-picture orientation. They must acquire such a perspective to discriminate between the legitimate and illegitimate lines of change for India.

The preceding three paragraphs are a direct outcome of the first author's experience of a so-called South Asia Conference held in the year 2000 at Edinburgh University. Plenty of patronizing, condescending and snobbish comments about various features of India's Hindu culture were showered by high-browed European and American presenters. The Indian participants were either mute listeners, or nodding consenters to what the Western academics said. Just two or three questioning types were noticed. Indian presentations were casual and trite. The largest contingent was from India, Bangladesh followed next. Intriguingly, none came from Pakistan or Nepal or Sri Lanka, So, it became clear that the latent agenda of the Conference was India-baiting. What energy and strength can such events bestow on Indian academics for giving intellectual lead today to their students who will manage and lead the country and its institutions tomorrow? It will only add one more entry to their CV. More subtly, most such Indian academics, consciously or unconsciously, would help the upstart and shallow globalist craze to swallow the dignified and deep Spirituality of India. Spirituality-as-means for techno-economic globalism poses this real peril.

For more subtle insights into the gravity of the dis-orientation afflicting the formally educated leaders-managers, we should turn to Rabindranath Tagore. He had delivered a written address while launching the Visvabharati at Santiniketan in 1919. That was thirty years earlier than the Radhakrishnan Report. Here are some samples of his critique about education, teachers, students etc. (Tagore, 1919)—

- anaemic in intellect
- never have intellectual courage
- lose the historical sense of all ideas
- borrow a foreign culture, a foreign standard of judgement
- not only the money is not theirs, but not even the pocket
- education is a chariot not carrying students but dragging them behind it etc.

He had therefore reprimanded that 'insularly modern' group of people for whom the past has been bankrupt, passing on to the present no assets, only debts. Very much in the same vein as Vivekananda, Tagore too told his audience that those who have lost the harvests of their past, have also lost their present harvest.

Today, almost nine decades after Tagore had so spoken, and nearly six decades after the Radhakrisnan Report, what is the emerging picture? Just two small but serious instances: CBSE/ICSE Boards have introduced sex education in schools (under cover of 'life skills'), and are beginning to offer courses on stock-market operations to higher classes! What standard of character in managers, administrators and other professionals might we then expect in days ahead? None but the *asuric* types, who will treat *kama* (lust) and *bhoga* (pleasure) as *parama* – the ultimate end. Even if nothing else in the *Bhagawadgita* attracts, let everyone read and reflect on at least verses 9 to 23 in Chapter XVI, and then let he/she judge, against these forecasts made three millennia ago, what the human condition today is like. And, given the current trends, what do all these bode for the future? Should Spirituality be approached for rescuing us from all this? Or, should it too be harnessed to the galloping juggernaut of human and corporate promiscuity, profligacy?

Will Spirituality boost our national ranking, our corporate survival, our individual success in this ruthless era of economic-financial globalization? This is an oft-repeated question one hears during discussions on values, ethics and now on Spirituality. The summary answer is: As an end, certainly yes; as short-term means, no. Why? Because as an end, the time horizon will be long-term. But as means, it will beat retreats too often. Chanakya's aphorisms contain many verses extolling the virtues of wealth. Yet, among them this verse too is found—

'A wise man should pursue Wealth as if he is going to live forever,
But should pursue his Spiritual vows as if he is going to die tomorrow'.

Here, perspective and priority are both unambiguous. Of course, a *rishi*-mind had been behind such perfect vision.

Corporate enterprises, especially the private ones, are obsessed with annual 'ranking', 'market valuation' and similar indices. Even corporate social responsibility is often a formality because its mention counts in ISO certifications and annual rankings by commercial media. But what about 'cultural valuation'? Here is an example from the authors' direct experience.

During the late nineteen eighties they had conducted a number of Human Values Workshops for the top and senior managers of a blue chip public sector company. It has been in the business of manufacturing and selling petrochemicals. Sometime in the late nineties it was privatized to an aggressive shooting star in the Indian corporate firmament. Somehow one of the earlier HRD managers had survived the transition and came to occupy the position of Senior Vice-President, HRD. During 2005-7 he re-called the authors again to offer similar Workshops to new groups of senior managers. This was a revealing experience. The entire 'cultural wealth' built up by the impeccably honest and high-minded public sector CMDs has been drained off in the new regime. These comments were heard during the Workshops:

- The present owners are businessmen, not industrialists.
- In earlier days we used to feel that the company is ours, now all that feeling is gone.
- Here even teachers like you are treated as 'vendors', 'suppliers'.
- Vendors, even the small ones, to this company have to chase endlessly for their dues—often for several months.
- The company township was such a warm and lovely place to live in when it belonged to the public sector. Now it wears a drab, deserted look – people are moving out.

Are administration, management and leadership not trustees responsible for the 'cultural valuation or wealth' of human institutions or organizations or systems they run? Investment in Spirituality has to be done with this motive, as an act of faith and conviction. And conviction is born in the womb of character. Short-term calculations about the bottom-line etc. should be adjusted against pristine normative standards. These latter will not necessary nullify market values or ranks. But they will remind managers and leaders that, even in the *Fortune* top 500 rankings, not many companies find a place for ten years or more. Many even collapse and die. Why?

The *Bhagavad Gita* offers the assurance of (IX.22)—

Yogakshema vahamyam

For the Spiritually committed, normatively-grounded, ethically resolute performer or worker, 'Whatever is necessary for such a person but not possessed now, and preservation of whatever he already possesses – they are both My responsibility. Therefore whatever you do, do so ethically, correctly, remembering Me as your true goal'. Spirituality in secular affairs has to mean this. This will lead to real 'corporate social responsibility'. To be settled in this attitude will take time – it is an arduous yet rewarding pilgrimage. But if the intention is firm, then again we have the Divine guarantee (the *Gita*, II.40)—

'*Swalpamapasya dharmasya*
trayate mahqto bhayat'.

That is, even a little sincere struggle along this path (of ethicality etc.) will deliver you from great dangers and perils. The authors themselves have experienced some positive proofs of this essence of Spirituality-in-practice.

Of course countless great personalities have been there, and many more unknown ones are still around, who have testified or can attest to this experiential truth. Why? Because, as Sri Ramakrisnha had said: 'The Divine keeps a watch on your inner mind, not on your outer actions only.'

The supreme problem of India today is that it is facing the 'invasion' of greedy, 'doing' cultures. They tend to show a 'good Samaritan' kind of face only to seduce other nations by their homilies. But Bharatvarsha has always been essentially a 'being-and-becoming' culture. So the clash is between two different world-views: 'doing' vs 'being'. What the majority of educated Indians cannot, or are unwilling to see is that words or phrases like 'globalization', 'cyber world', 'global village' etc. are granted only that meaning which suits the terms, conditions and ambitions of only a few nations. This disability is a betrayal of the real spirit behind the call 'arise and awake' given by the best of the country's leaders during 1861–1950 i.e. Tagore to Aurobindo, Vivekananda to Ramana Maharshi, Tilak to Bharati, Gandhiji to Netaji, Lajpat to Malviya, PC Ray to CV Raman, Jamshedji Tata to Ardeshir Godrej. India is being a betrayer of not only these great sons of Bharatvarsha. The 'insular moderns' are also badly letting down a large number of Western thinker-lovers too, who have ardently hoped India to provide remedies for the world's ills e.g. Louis Renou to Arnold Toynbee, Andre Malraux to Will Durant, Aldous Huxley to Sister Nivedita, Mirra Alfassa to David Frawley, Stafford Beer to Michel Danino, Annie Besant to John Woodroffe, JBS Haldane to Ronald Nixon (Krishna Prem). But, ironically, the doctor himself is becoming sick! What is the net result of such comprehensive derailment of post-1950 India? Just one example should suffice—the mounting craze for 'research' (i.e. 'doing') in Spirituality, instead of aspiring for 'realization' (i.e. 'becoming'). Let India do 'research' if it must. But Bharatvarsha must persist with 'realizing' the 'being'. That is to say, let India be re-born as Bharatvarsha in spirit and soul.

Research *sans* Realization will do violence to Bharat's *swadharma*, her innate law of being, her *core competence*. Again the *Gita* has emphatically cautioned us (III.35)—

'Swadharme nidhanam shreya,
parodharma bhayavaha'

Not only will Bharat be the loser; the whole world too will be at a loss. A time is sure to arrive when the research mentality will re-appraise itself, and seek for the saving alternative. Bharat should then be ready with that alternative – no 'spiritual' property rights however! Let India understand this. Let it be conscious and careful to halt its present hurry to become a cultural colony and, concomitantly, an economic one too. A true Indian (Bharatiya) manager or leader, for instance, should cultivate this kind of power: 'Mr. Change, wait a minute, What are your credentials? You sell yourself too hard. I won't buy you so readily. What are your real motives? Our past experience has been negative.'

The essence of this line of thought could be captured through the following diagram (each set of factors along the two axes are internally consistent)—

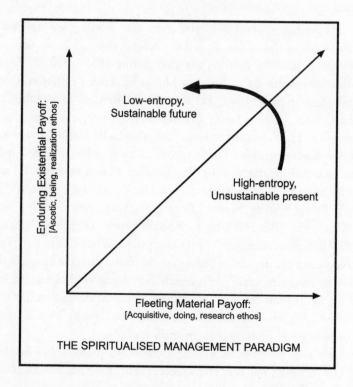

THE SPIRITUALISED MANAGEMENT PARADIGM

The purpose of bringing to the fore the above facts and ideas has been to portray authentically both the strong imperatives and stubborn impediments regarding Spirituality. Cheap euphoria has been avoided. Yet, all the positive examples highlighted in the earlier chapters, especially chapters 3, 9 and 10, should be held in the heart for positive inspiration. Moreover, the very logic of Spirituality has prompted the authors to sketch the panoramic canvas of evolutionary purpose concealed in Nature.

Management in business, or manipulation in politics has to be exceeded to bring out the real significance of Spirituality in human affairs. Genuine, exalting engagement with Spirituality—whether in business management or parliamentary politics etc.—can sprout only from a higher launching station. The above diagram is a nut-shell sketch of the stakes leaders are playing with.

POSTSCRIPT

We have the privilege of long, intimate acquaintance with an entrepreneur-industrialist of good standing. He is a rare blend of academic brilliance (mathematics, astronomy etc.) and keen industrial acumen. Besides, in his personal life he is a spiritual practitioner. *Diksha, japam, bhajan,* meditation, retreats, avid reading of spiritual literature – all find space and time in his daily life. He is nearly eighty years old, yet still fully active. Recently (August 2007) he had asked us—

'Tell me, shouldn't a student know what the latest discoveries in space are?'

We replied:

'Yes, he may know about them. But that is all extended general knowledge. If such knowledge ignores or replaces the knowledge of "inner space", and how to explore, manage and lead it, it will be a stupid bargain. The Indian student for future leadership should first understand the worth of AUM, and then only, of genome. We have to recall Vivekananda speaking thus in his 1896 first lecture on *Jnanyoga* in London (Vivekananda, 1958): 'It is grand and good to know the laws that govern the stars and planets; it is infinitely grander and better to know the laws that govern, the passions, the feelings, the will of mankind'.

As we verbally shared these reflections on space etc., there was a memory recall of some comments by RR Ernst (a Swiss Nobel Laureate in Chemistry) during a conference in 2000. He had referred to an important US government official having recently declared that 'the first settlements beyond our galaxy will have occurred by 2500. We will have left the solar system by 2200. We will have permanent colonies on Moon, Mars etc. by 2100.' Ernst's reaction was: 'If such a vision is representative for an American majority, good gracious!' (Ernst, 2001):

His second poser was:

'How then can India succeed in global competition?'

Our response was:

'Yes, today even school students are being taught to parrot such questions. Who are inviting whom into competition? What is the latent agenda? Can there be competition between a wrestler or pugilist and a singer or painter?' Hardly any voice in India seems today to be asking to what brink the world is being dragged by this hurricane of deceptive competition. Those who are at its helm know in advance the ultimate result of this process. As English dictionaries reveal, all the emotions aroused by competition are negative, unspiritual e.g. rivalry, contest, vying with, contend against, defeating etc. The title of a *Harvard Business Review* article of April 2004 was: 'Five Killer Strategies For Trouncing Competitors.' It is blasphemy to talk of spirituality in such a milieu. Yet, the simple-hearted or selfish Indian gets readily trapped in this grand strategy. One may carefully read between the words and lines of, for example, a recent UNESCO Report (UNESCO, 1998):

'... the developing countries ... need to enter the world of science and technology with all this implies in terms of *cultural adaptation and modernization of mentalities* (emphasis added).'

This contains a clear message for disempowerment from the roots for countries like India.'

He asked next:

'I have just been appointed as the Chairman of one of the IIMs. With your long experience tell me a few key points I might bear in mind in this new role.'

We replied:

'One of the most important things to be impressed upon young minds is the necessity of being firmly rooted in the core of Indian ethos. With disdain about such a sustainable ethos, the nation will be irretrievably fractured at the very base. Great world-class Indians like Tagore, Vivekananda, Gandhi, Aurobindo et. al., have unanimously and repeatedly warned this country about the perils to her destiny if India's central spiritual principle is sacrificed at the altar of secular modernization. The implanting of this 'sense of destiny' has to be done by appropriate methods, at all levels of education.'

He asked again:

'People are now saying that all the prophecies by Vivekananda's and others about India's greater future glory than her past stature were just vain hyperboles. Sixty years after independence, yet India is in a huge mess just beneath the shining veneer.'

We responded:

'Why should today's hypocritical careerists blame or discard what these utterly selfless lovers of Mother India had visioned about her in their unpolluted integral vision? Their visions had emerged out of the fundamental assumption *that a free India would belong to people and leaders of high moral-spiritual character, with minds of their own.* Have we, during the last six decades, understood, heeded or followed even a single principle or warning they had worked out for us? For example:

(a) *Tagore* (1919):
'We forget that the same weakness in our character ... which inevitably draws us on to ... imitation, will pursue us where our independence is merely of the outside.'
                    (*The Centre of Indian Culture*, Vishwabharati, 1988, p.12)

(b) *Vivekananda* (1898):
'On one side, New India is saying, "What the Western nations do is surely good, otherwise, how did they become so great?" On the other side, Old India is saying, "The flash of lightning is intensely bright, but only for a moment; look out boys, it is dazzling your eyes. Beware!
                                        (*Complete Works*, Vol. IV. p.477)
He had also given this principle:
'The national ideals of India are RENUNCIATION and SERVICE. Intensify her in these channels, and the rest will take care of itself.'
                                        (*Complete Works*, Vol. V, p.228)
(c) *Gandhi* (1930):
His code for governors, ministers, parliamentarians was:
- His private life should be so simple that it inspires respect, or even reverence.
- Bungalows and motor cars should be ruled out of course.
- The other members of his family ... should do all the household work themselves ...

- Plain living and high thinking must be his motto ...
- They may not mke private gains either for themselves or for their relatives.
- They must be humble.

(*Selected Works*, Navjivan, Vol. VI, p. 588)

(d) *Aurobindo* (1918):

He had cautioned India in 1918:

'If there is only a mechanical imitation, if there is a subordination and servitude, the inactive or weaker culture perishes, it is swallowed up by the invading leviathan.'

(*The Foundations of Indian Culture*, 1998, p.437)

So great was his concern that, much later in 1948, one year before the Radhakrishnan Report, in a message to the Andhra University, he had to remind us again:

'It would be a tragic irony of fate if India were to throw away her spiritual heritage ... we must not disguise from ourselves the fact that after long years of subjection and its cramping and impairing effects a great inner as well as outer liberation ... is needed if we are, to fulfil India's true destiny. (Quoted in Michel Danino, *Sri Aurobindo and Indian Civilzation*, Auroville Press International, 1999, p.31)

Sixty years on, liberation from servitude to the spurious modern secular temper into the freedom of the authentic ancient spiritual temper – this is the *leadership* role that still awaits acceptance by India and Indians.

Thus, citing or referring to the above counsels of wisdom from those who had embodied Indian spirituality, we informed our respected interlocutor that there are two categories of people who raise doubts about the veracity of their prognostications:

(a) those majority who tend to look upto the immediate, apparent no–fulfilment of such allegedly frothy forecasts as a ready handle to sweep them out (perhaps without ever reading them properly);

(b) those minority who ask, with pain and sorrow, how come the true and worthy visions of this great souls are taking so long to emerge on the horizon?

Hence, it is felt that the blunder lies in post-1947 India officially damning all the pre-requisites and imperatives for her to play a spiritually saving role for the country and the world.

Arnold Toynbee probably offers one of the most honest Western articulations of the Spirit-centered role of India, (in an all-embracing sweep covering management, politics, business and all else) (Toynbee, 1969):

'...it is already becoming clear that a chapter which had a Western beginning will have to have an Indian ending....In the Atomic Age the whole human race has a utilitarian motive for following this Indian way....The survival of the human race is at stake....*The primary reason is that this teaching is right – and is right because it flows from a true vision of spiritual reality.*'

'Indian ending and 'Indian way' for Toynbee surely mean the original yoga-vedanta, Hindu-Buddhist thought and culture developed in and by Bharatvarsha. This is quite distinct from cliches like 'composite culture', 'plural culture' etc. used in political, journalistic and academic circles of India. For them neither truth nor spirituality in the agendum; obfuscation is.

References

CHAPTER 1

Aurobindo, Sri, quoted by K.D. Sethna in *India and the World Scene*, Pondicherry, Sri Aurobindo Society, 1997, pp. 340-1.

Aurobindo, Sri, *The Ideal of The Karmayogin*, Pondicherry, Sri Aurobindo Ashram, 1974, pp. 10-1.

Chakraborty, S.K., *Foundations of Managerial Work*, Bombay, Himalaya Publishing, 1989, pp. 3-4.

Chakraborty, S.K., *Human Response in Organizations*, Calcutta, Vivekananda Nidhi, 1985.

Rolland, R., quoted in *The Life of Josephine Mcleod*, by Pravrajika Prabuddha Prana, Calcutta, Sarada Matha, 1994, p. 208.

Rolland, R., *Life and Gospel of Vivekananda*, Calcutta, Advaita Ashrama, 1979, p. 78.

Sethna, K.D., *India and the World Scene*, Pondicherry, Sri Aurobindo Society, 1997, pp. 340-1.

Tagore, Rabindranath, *Letters to a Friend*, quoted by D.J. Andrews in 'My Reverence for Rabindranath Tagore', *Shraddha*, Aurobindo Bhavan, Kolkata, April 2007, p. 15.

CHAPTER 2

Aurobindo Sri, *The Spirit and the Soul*, Sri Aurobindo Society, Pondicherry, 1999, pp. 11-12.

Aurobindo Sri, *What is Consciousness?* Sri Aurobindo Society, Pondicherry, 1999, pp. 5-15.

Aurobindo Sri, *An Introduction to True Spirituality*, Sri Aurobindo Society, Pondicherry, 1997, pp. 3-4.

Aurobindo Sri, *The Right Attitude in Work*, Sri Aurobindo Society, Pondicherry, 1991, p. 13.

Aurobindo Sri, *The Right Attitude in Work*, Sri Aurobindo Society, Pondicherry, 1991, p. 45.

Aurobindo Sri, *The Psychic Being*, Sri Aurobindo Ashram Trust, Pondicherry, 1989, p. 18.

Aurobindo Sri, *The Synthesis of Yoga*, Sri Aurobindo Ashram, Pondicherry, 1988, p. 342.

Aurobindo Sri, *Living Within*, Sri Aurobindo Trust, Pondicherry, 1987, pp. 134-6.

Aurobindo Sri, *The Hour of God*, Sri Aurobindo Ashram, Pondicherry, 1982, p. 47.

Aurobindo Sri, *The Ideal of a Karmayogin*, Sri Aurobindo Ashram, Pondicherry, 1974, p. 6.

Aurobindo Sri, *The Life Divine*, Pondicherry Aurobindo Ashram, 1973, vol. II, p. 857.

Aurobindo Sri, *The Human Cycle*, Sri Aurobindo Ashram, Pondicherry, 1970, p. 6.

Bass, B.M. and Avolio, B.J. (eds.), *Improving Organizational Performance Through Transformational Leadership*, Sage, Thousand Oaks, 1994, p. 68.

Bass, B.M. and Steidelmeir, K.B., *Transformation Leadership-Organizational Success*, Lawrence Erlbaum, NJ, 1998, p. 175.

Bass, B.M., *Leadership and Performance Beyond Expectation*, Free Pres, New York, NY, 1985, p. 123.

Beer, S., *How Many Grapes Went Into The Wine?*, Wiley, London, 1994, p. 321.

Burns, J.M., *Leadership*, Harper and Row, New York, NY, 1978, pp. 19-20, 428.

Burns, J.M., *Leadership*, Harper and Row, New York, NY, 1978, pp. 36-7.

Chakraborty, D. and Chakraborty, S.K., *Leadership and Motivation: Cultural Comparisons*, Rupa, New Delhi, 2004, p. 94.

Chakraborty, S.K. and Chakraborty, D., *Culture Society and Leadership*, Hyderabad: ICFAI University Press, 2006, pp. 231-33, 243-7, 239-42, 277-9.

Chakraborty, S.K. and Chakraborty, D., *Culture, Society and Leadership*, Hyderabad: ICFAI University Press, 2006, p. 243.

Chakraborty, S.K. and Chakraborty, D., *Human Values and Ethics*, Hyderabad: ICFAI University Press, 2006, p. 6.

Einstein, A., *Out of my Later Years*, Thames and Hudson, London, 1950, p. 24.

Eliot, T.S., *Selected Poems*, London, Faber and Faber, 1954, pp. 107-25

Gandhi, M.K., *Ramnaama*, Ahmedabad: Navajivan, 1977, pp. 3, 9.

Gandhi, M.K., *An Autobiography*, Navjivan, Ahemedabad, 1972, p. xii.

Gandhi, M.K., *The Teaching of The Gita*, Bharatiya Vidya Bhawan, Bombay, 1962, p. 11.

Gandhi, R., *The Good Boatman*, Viking, New Delhi, 1996, pp. 166-206.

Hammarskjold, D., *Markings*, Faber and Faber, London, 1966, p. 99.

Hawken, P., *The Ecology of Commerce*, Harper Collins, New York, 1993, p. 25.

Kalam, A.P.J., *Ignited Minds*, New Delhi, Viking, 2002, p. 76.

Korten, D., *The Post-Corporate World*, San Francisco: Berrett-Koechler, 1998, p. 27.

Quinn, D., *Ishmael*, Bantam Turner, New York, 1993, pp. 143-5, 206-7.

Russell, B., *The Future of Science*, Kegan Paul, London, 1927, pp. 58-9.

Seltzer, J. and Bass, B.M., 'Transformational leadership–beyond initiation and consideration', *Journal of Management*, Vol. 16 No. 4, 1990, pp. 693-703.

Smith, V.A., *Asoka: The Buddhist Emperor*, Arihant, Jaipur, 1988, pp. 24, 97.

Solomon, R., *Ethics and Excellence*, Oxford University Press, New York, NY, 1993, p. 111, 109.

Sorokin, P., *Reconstruction of Humanity*, Bharatiya Vidya Bhawan, Mumbai, 1962, pp. 97, 198-9.

Swami Vivekananda, *Complete Works*, Vol. VI, Advaita Ashram, Calcutta, 1962, p. 284.

Swami Vivekananda, *Complete Works*, Vol. II, Advaita Ashram, Calcutta, 1958, pp. 62-3.

Tagore, Rabindranath, S.K. (ed.), *The English Writings of Rabindranath Tagore*, (ed.) S.K. Das, Sahitya Akademi, New Delhi, 1996, p. 613.

Toynbee, A.J., *Choose Life*, Oxford University Press, New Delhi, 1987.

Vivekananda, Swami, *Complete Works*, Calcutta, Advaita Ashrama, 1969, vol. VII, p. 69.

Wilson, M., 'A letter', *All India Magazine*, February, 2002, p. 21.

CHAPTER 3

Aurobindo, Sri, *Looking from Within*, Sri Aurobindo Trust, Pondicherry, 1995, p. 58.

Aurobindo, S., *The Message of The Gita*, Pondicherry: Sri Aurobindo Ashram, 1977, p. 37.

Aurobindo, Sri, *The Message of The Gita*, Sri Aurobindo Ashram, Pondicherry, 1977.

Aurobindo, Sri, *The Message of The Gita*, Sri Aurobindo Ashram, Pondicherry, 1977, p. 254.

Baharom, H.Z., 'Views From The East: ASEAN' in *Blending The Best of The East And The West: In Management Education*, op. cit., p. 119.

Chakraborty, S.K., 'Wisdom power: beyond rational humanism', in Chakraborty, S.K. and Pradip Bhattacharya (eds.), *Leadership and Power*, Oxford University Press, New Delhi, 2001, pp. 182-204.

Chakraborty, S.K., *Wisdom Leadership: Dialogues And Reflections* New Delhi: Wheeler, 1999, p. 36

Chakraborty, S.K. and Chakraborty D., *Culture Society and Leadership*, Hyderabad, ICFAI University Press, 2006.

Fukuda J., 1994, 'Bushido: The Guiding Principles of New Japan' in *Management and Cultural Values: The Indigenization of Organizations in Asia* eds. H. Kao, D. Sinha, S. Wilpert, New Delhi: Sage, pp. 76-9.

Gandhi, M., *The Collected Works*, New Delhi: GOI Publication Division, Vol. 32, 1994, p. 125.

Gandhi, M., *The Message of The Gita*, Ahmedabad: Navajivan Publishing, 1990, p. 14.

Griffiths, B., *The Cosmic Revelation*, London: Collins, 1983, p. 93.

Huxley, A., *The Perennial Philosophy*, Flamingo, London, 1994, p. 22.

Kalam, A.P.J. Abdul, *Ignited Minds*, New Delhi: Viking, 2002, p. 5.

Kallapiran, T.R., *Thirukkural: Words of Eternal Wisdom*, Madras: Baba Pathippagam, 1995, p. 74.

Kim, D., 'Views from the East: Asian Tigers cultural Aspect of Higher Productivity: With Special Reference to the Effects of Korean Values on Business Management in Korea' in *Blending The Best of The East And The West: In Management Education* eds. Subir Chowdhury and Sangeeta Bhattacharjee New Delhi: Excel, 2002, pp. 99-100.

Pruzan, P., 'The Trajectory of Power: From Control to Self-control' in *Leadership And Power: Ethical Explorations* (eds.) S.K. Chakraborty and P. Bhattcharya, OUP: New Delhi, 2001, p. 180.

Sekhar, R.C., 2002, *Ethical Choices in Business*, New Delhi: Response, p. 39.

Shu-Cheng, C., 'The Role of Chin-Shins of Top Managers in Taiwanese Organizations: Exploring Chinese Leadership Phenomena' in *Management And Cultural Values: The Indigenization of Organization in Asia* op. cit., p. 252.

Spar, D.L., *The Baby Business*, Harvard Business School Press, 2006, pp. XI-XIII.

Srinivasachari, P.N., 1986, *Ethical Philosophy of the Gita*, Madras: Sri Ramakrishna Math, p. 74.

Tagore, R., *The English Writings* ed. S.K. Das, Delhi: Sahitya Akademi, 1996, p. 288.

CHAPTER 4

Aurobindo, Sri, *The Human Cycle*, Pondicherry: Sri Aurobindo Ashram, 1985.

Bohm, D. and Peat, F.D., *Science, Order, and Creativity*, Toronto: Bantam, 1987, p. 12.

Borsuan, C., 'Chinese CEOs' Employee Categorization And Managerial Behaviour' in *Management And Cultural Values: The Indigenization of Organization in Asia*, op. cit., p. 237.

Carrel, A., *Man The Unknown*, London: Hamish Hamilton, 1961, p. 19.

Chakraborty, S.K. and Chakraborty D., *Culture Society and Leadership*, Hyderabad, ICFAI University Press, 2006.

Chakraborty, S.K. and Chakraborty D., *Culture Society and Leadership*, Hyderabad, ICFAI University Press, 2006.

Chakraborty, S.K., *Against the Tide*, Oxford University Press, New Delhi, 2003, p. 136.

Chakraborty, S.K., *Wisdom Leadership: Dialogues And Reflections* New Delhi: Wheeler, 1999.

Chakraborty, S.K., *Wisdom Leadership*, op. cit., 1999, p. 64

Chakraborty, S.K., *Managerial Transformation by Values*, Sage, New Delhi, 1993, pp. 38-43.

Chakraborty, S.K., *Management By Values: Towards Cultural Congruence*, New Delhi: Oxford University Press, 1991, pp. 176-7.

Christopher, R.G., 1983, *The Japanese Mind*, New York: Fawcett, p. 70

Davies, P., *The Mind of God*, London: Penguin, 1992, p. 193.

Eccles, J., *The Search For Absolute Values: Harmony Among The Sciences*, New York: The International Cultural Foundation Press, 1977, Vol. I, p. 14.

Einstein, A., *Ideas and Opinions*, New Delhi: Rupa, 2003, p. 53.

Gandhi, M., *The Selected Works*, Ahemdabad: Navajivan, 2001, p. 225.

Griffiths, B., *Return To The Centre*, London: Collins, 1976, p. 58.

Hawking, S., *A Briefer History of Time*, London: Bantam, 2005, p. 142.

Huxley, A., *The Perennial Philosophy*, London: Flamingo, 1994, p. 260.

Kalam, A.P.J. Abdul, *Ignited Minds*, New Delhi: Viking, 2002, p. 5.

Komin, S., 'The Thai Concept of Effective Leadership' in *Management And Cultural Values: The Indigenization of Organization in Asia*, op. cit., p. 279.

Mukherjee, R.K., *The Sickness of Civilization*, Bombay: Allied, 1964, p. V.

Penrose, R., *Shadows of the Mind*, London: Vintage, 1995, p. 9.

Radhakrisnan, S., *Recovery of Faith*, New Delhi: Orient, 1967, pp. 9-12, 15-25, 39-41.

Russell, B., *The Future of Science*, Kegan Paul, London, 1927, pp. 58-9.

Smith, H., *Forgotten Truth: The Primordial Tradition*, New York: Harper-Colophon, 1976, p. 15.

Sorokin, P., *Reconstruction of Humanity* editors K.M. Munshi and R.R. Diwakar, Bombay: Bharatiya Vidya Bhavan, 1962, p. 43.

Tagore, R., *Personality*, New Delhi: Rupa, 2002, pp. 43-82, 119-162.

Tagore, R., *Personality*, New Delhi: Rupa, 2002, p. 58.

Toynbee, A. and Ikeda, D., *Choose Life: A Dialogue*, New Delhi: Oxford University Press, 1987, p. 35.

Vivekananda, Swami, *Work And Its Secret*, Calcutta: Advaita Ashram, 1990, p. 19.

Vivekananda, Swami, *The Complete Works of Swami Vivekananda*, Kolkata: Advaita Ashram, 1962, pp. 1, 33, 62-82.

CHAPTER 5

Aurobindo, Sri, *The Human Cycle*, Pondicherry: Sri Aurobindo Ashram, 1985, pp. 70-73, 87-93, 145-46.

Carrel, A., *Man The Unknown*, London: Hamish Hamilton, 1961, p. 19.

Chakraborty, S.K. and Chakraborty D., *Culture Society and Leadership*, Hyderabad, ICFAI University Press, 2006.

Chakraborty, S.K., *Against The Tide*, New Delhi: Oxford University Press, 2003, pp. 186-191.

Chakraborty, S.K., *Management By Values: Towards Cultural Congruence*, New Delhi: Oxford University Press, 1991, pp. 176-7.

Coomaraswamy, A., *What is Civilization?* New Delhi: Oxford University Press, 1989, pp. 4-8.

Davies, P., *The Mind of God*, London: Penguin, 1992, p. 193.

Eccles, J., *The Search For Absolute Values: Harmony Among The Sciences*, New York: The International Cultural Foundation Press, 1977, Vol. I, p. 14.

Einstein, A., *Ideas and Opinions*, New Delhi: Rupa, 2003, p. 53.

Gandhi, M., *The Selected Works of Mahatma Gandhi*, Ahmedabad: Navajivan, 2001, Vol. III, pp. 3-30.

Griffiths, B., *Return To The Centre*, London: Collins, 1976, p. 58.

Hawking, S., *A Briefer History of Time*, London: Bantam, 2005, p. 142.

Huxley, A., *The Perennial Philosophy*, London: Flamingo, 1994, p. 260.

Kalam, A.P.J. Abdul, *Ignited Minds*, New Delhi: Viking, 2002, p. 78.

Mukherjee, R.K., *The Sickness of Civilization*, Bombay: Allied, 1964, p. V.

Penrose, R., *Shadows of the Mind*, London: Vintage, 1995, p. 9.

Quoted in *Physics and Beyond*, Bombay: Bhaktivedanta Institute, 1986, p. 36.

Quoted in *Physics and Beyond*, Bombay: Bhaktivedanta Institute, 1986, p. 26.

Quoted in *Quantum Questions* edited by Ken Wilber, Boston: New Science Library, 1985, p. 43.

Quoted in *Reason, Science and Shastras* edited by N.R. Sengupta, Kolkata: N.R. Sengupta, 2003, p. 38.

Radhakrisnan, S., *Recovery of Faith*, New Delhi: Orient, 1967, pp. 9-12, 15-25, 39-41.

Russell, B., *The Future of Science*, London: Kegan Paul, 1927, p. 5.

Smith, H., *Forgotten Truth: The Primordial Tradition*, New York: Harper-Colophon, 1976, p. 15.

Sorokin, P., *Reconstruction of Humanity* editors K.M. Munshi and R.R. Diwakar, Bombay: Bharatiya Vidya Bhavan, 1962, p. 43.

Spar, D.L., *The Baby Business*, Harvard Business School Press, 2006, pp. XI-XIII.

Tagore, R., *Personality*, New Delhi: Rupa, 2002, pp. 43-82, 119-162.

Tagore, R., *Personality*, New Delhi: Rupa, 2002, p. 58.

Toynbee, A. and Ikeda, D., *Choose Life: A Dialogue*, New Delhi: Oxford University Press, 1987, p. 35.

Vivekananda, Swami, *The Complete Works of Swami Vivekananda*, Kolkata: Advaita Ashram, 1962, pp. 1, 33, 62-82.

CHAPTER 6

Aurobindo Sri and The Mother, Living Within, (ed.) A.S. Dalal, Pondicherry: Sri Aurobindo Ashram Trust, 1987, p. 6.

Aurobindo, Sri, *The Message of The Gita*. Pondicherry: Sri Aurobindo Ashram, 1977, p. 18.

Bharati, Jnanananda, *The Essence of Yogavaasistha*. 1985, pp. 115.

Burke, M.L., *Swami Vivekananda: His Second Visit to the West–New Discoveries*, Calcutta: Advaita Ashram, 1973, pp. 501-02.

Dalal, A.S., *Living Within*, Pondicherry: Sri Aurobindo Ashram, 1989, p. 44.

Lal, P., *Chhandyogya Upanishad*, Kolkata: Writers Workshop, 2002, 7.XXIII.1, p. 271.

Masson, J., *Against Therapy*, London: Harper Collins, 1993, pp. 298-9.

Morse, D.R. and Furst, M.L., *Stress For Success*, New York: Van Nostrand, 1979, p. 35.

Mother, The, *Inner Peace*. Pondicherry: Sri Aurobindo Society, 1990, pp. 39-40.

Nikhilananda, Swami, *Self-Knowledge*, Madras: Ramakrishna Math, 1983, pp. 88-89.

Pestonjee, D.M., *Stress and Coping: The Indian Experience* 2nd ed., New Delhi: Sage, 1999.

Swami Vivekananda, *Rajyoga*, Kolkata: Advaita Ashram, 1976, pp. 148-9.

Swami, Akhilananda, *Mental Health and Hindu Psychology*, New York: Harper and Brothers, 1950.

Tagore, Rabindranath, *Human Values: The Tagorean Panorama*, tras. by S.K. Chakraborty and P. Bhattacharya, New Age International: New Delhi, 1999, p. 130.

Torrey, E.F., *Freudian Fraud*, London: Harper Collins, 1992, pp. 256-7.

Vivekananda, Swami, *Raja-Yoga*, Mayavati: Advaita Ashram, 1976, p. 148.

Vivekananda, Swami, *Rajyoga*, Mayavati: Advaita Ashram, 1976, p. 178.

Waite, M., *Oxford Thesaurus of English*, New Delhi: Oxford University Press, 1995, pp. 917-18.

CHAPTER 7

Basham, A.L., *A Cultural History of India*, Oxford University Press: New Delhi, 1999, p. 2.

Bohm, D., *Thought As A System*, Routledge, London, 1994, p. 165.

Bose, A.C., *The Call of the Vedas*, (eds.) K.M. Munshi and R.R. Diwakar, Bharatiya Vidya Bhavan: Bombay, 1979, p. 244.

Carrel, A., *Man, The Unknown*, Hamish Hamilton, London, 1961, p. 142.

Carroll, J., *Humanism: The Wreck of Western Culture*, Fontana, London, 1993, p. 2.

Carvalho, B. and Prasad, S., 'The Credit Cripples' in *Business Today*, Sept., 2001, p. 39.

Chakraborty, S.K., *Against the Tide*, Oxford University Press, New Delhi, 2003, p. 136.

Chakraborty, S.K., *Management by Values: Towards Cultural Congruence*, Oxford University Press, New Delhi, 1993, pp. 173-4.

Chakraborty, S.K. and Chakraborty, D., *Human Values and Ethics*, Hyderabad: ICFAI University Press, 2006, pp. 56-8.

Coomaraswamy, A., *What is Civilization?*, Oxford University Press, New Delhi, 1989, p. 6.

Davis, S. and Meyer, C., *Future Wealth*, Harvard Business School Press, Boston, 2000, p. 10.

Dutt, R.C., *The Economic History of India*, Ministry of Information and Broadcasting, New Delhi, 1989, Vol. II, p. XII.

Dutt, R.C., *The Economic History of India*, Ministry of Information and Broadcasting, New Delhi, 1989, Vol. I, p. XXV.

Gambhirananda, S., *Isa Upanishad*, Advaita Ashram, Calcutta, 1983, p. 4.

Gambirananda, S., *Katha Upanishad*, Advaita Ashram, Calcutta, 1980, pp. 24-5.

Gandhi, M.K., *The Selected Works of Mahatma Gandhi*, Navajivan, Ahmedabad, 2001, Vol. III, p. 54.

Gandhi, M.K., *The Selected Works of Mahatma Gandhi*, Navajivan, Ahmedabad, 2001, Vol. V, p. 275.

Gandhi, M.K., *Man v. Machine*, Bharatiya Vidya Bhavan, Mumbai, 1998, p. 34.

Harmann, W., 'Sustainability' in *The New Business of Business* (eds.) W. Harmann and M. Porter, Berrett Koehler: San Francisco, 1997, p. 142.

Harmann, W. and Porter, M. 1997, pp. 61-2.

Hawken, P., *The Ecology of Commerce*, Harper Collins, New York, 1993, p. 25.

Henderson, H., *Beyond Globalization*, Connecticut, Kumarian Press, 1999, pp. 2-6.

Hudson, B., *Justice in the Risk Society*, Sage, London, 2003, p. 43.

Human Development Report, *International Cooperation at a Crossroads*, Oxford University Press, New Delhi, 2005, p. 36.

Korten, D., *The Post-Corporate World: Life After Capitalism*, Berrett-Koehler, San Francisco, 1998, p. 27.

Lal, P., *The Mahabhrata of Vyasa*, Writers Workshop, Calcutta, 2005, pp. 18-9.

Mahadevan, T.M.P., 'The Religio-Philosophic Culture of India', in *The Cultural Heritage of India*, The Ramakrishna Mission Institute of Culture, Calcutta, Vol.I, 1958, pp. 163-6, 179-80.

McLaughlin, A., 'End of Development' in *Resurgence*, Sept.-Oct., 1998, p. 22.

Nikhilananda, S., *Hinduism: Its Meaning for the Liberation of the Spirit*, Sri Ramakrishna: Madras, 1968, pp. 25-6.

Pusalkar, A.D., 'Economic Ideas of the Hindus' in *The Cultural Heritage of India*, the Ramakrishna Mission Institute of Culture, Calcutta, 1965, Vol, p. 654.

Radhakrishnan, S., *Hindu View of Life*, George Allen and Unwin: London, 1957, p. 79.

Rangarajan, L.N., *The Arthashastra*, Penguin, New Delhi, 1992, pp. 13-4.

Report of The World Commission on Culture and Development, *Our Creative Diversity*, 1995, p. 8.

Rifkin, J., *Entropy: A New World View*, Bantam, Toronto, 1981, p. 24.

Rowland, W., *Greed Inc.: Why Corporations Rule Our World?*, Arcade, New York, 2003, p. XX.

Roy, K.C. and Sideras, J., *Institutions, Globalization and Empowerment*, Edward Elgar, Cheltnham, 2006, p. 8.

Sarkar, B.K., *The Positive Background of Hindu Sociology*, Motilal Banrasidass, New Delhi, 1985, p. 6.

Sastri, K.A.N., 'Manusmriti and Kautilya' in *History of Philosophy: Eastern and Western*, George Allen and Unwin, London, 1967. Vol.II, p. 107.

Schumacher, E.F., *Small Is Beautiful*, Radhakrishna, New Delhi, 1997, p. 28.

Saul, J.R., *The Collapse of Globalism*, New Delhi, Penguin, 2005, pp. 244-5.

Sorokin, P.A., *Reconstruction of Humanity* (eds.) K.M. Munshi and R.R. Diwakar, Bharatiya Vidya Bhavan, Bombay, 1962, p. 80.

Sri Aurobindo, *The Bhagavad Gita*, Sri Aurobindo Divine Life Trust, Jhunjhunu, 2003, pp. 86-7.

Sri Aurobindo, *The Human Cycle*, Sri Aurobindo Ashram, Pondicherry, 1985, p. 73.

Sri Aurobindo, *The Foundations of Indian Culture*, Sri Aurobindo Ashram, Pondicherry, 1975, p. 63.

Stiglitz, J., (2002), *Globalization and Its Discontents*, Penguin, New Delhi, p. 22.

Tagore, R., *Personality*, Rupa: New Delhi, 2002, p. 131.

Tagore, R., *Lectures and Addresses*, Macmillan, Madras, 1988, p. 66.

Tawney, R.H., *The Acquisitive Society*, Wheatsheaf, Brighton, 1942, p. 32.

The Mother, (2005), *The Great Secret*, Sri Aurobindo Society, Pondicherry, pp. 18-9.

Toynbee, A. and Daisaku, I., *Choose Life: A Dialogue*, Oxford University Press, New Delhi, 1987, p. 103.

Vivekananda, S., *Selections from Complete Works*, Advaita Ashram, Calcutta, 1993, p. 199.

Vivekananda, S., *Complete Works of Swami Vivekananda*, Advaita Ashram, Calcutta, 1960, Vol. I, pp. 454-55.

Vivekananda, S., *Complete Works of Swami Vivekananda*, Advaita Ashram, Calcutta, 1960, Vol. VI, p. 455.

Wallace, S., 'Last of the Amazon', *National Geographic*, January 2007, pp. 43, 49.

CHAPTER 8

Chakraborty, S.K. and D. Chakraborty, *Human Values and Ethics*, Hyderabad: ICFAI University Press, 2006, pp. 3-10 and pp. 210-18.

Chakraborty, S.K., *Against The Tide*, New Delhi: Oxford University Press, 2001, pp. 101-120.

Chakraborty, 2006, p. 249.

Chattopadhyay, C., *The Reminiscences of Latu Maharaj* (in Bengali), Kolkata: Udbodhan, 1976, pp. 280-1.

Narayana, G., *Nurturing Relationship Management*, Ahmedabad Management Association, 2005, pp. 10-11, 14.

Prameyananda, Swami, *The Ideal of Service in Swami Radhakrishnananda* (in Bengali), Kolkata, Udbodhan, 2001, p. 99.

Quoted in Management by Values by S.K. Chakraborty, OUP, Delhi, 2006, p. 249 from the Complete Works of Sw. Vivekananda, vol. VIII, p. 429.

Salvi, D.M., *S.N. Bose- The Immortal Scientist*, New Delhi: Rupa, 2002, pp. 24-35.

Swami Chetanananda, *Swami Premananda's Life and Reminiscences* (in Bengali), Kolkata: Udbodhan, 2002, p. 213.

Swami Vivekananda, *Complete Works*, Kolkata: Advaita Ashram, 1962, Vol. I, p. 425.

Swami Vivekananda, *Rajyoga*, Kolkata: Advaita Ashram, 1976, pp. 148-9.

Swami Vivekananda, *Complete Works*, Kolkata: Advaita Ashram, 1962, Vol. VI, p. 349.

CHAPTER 9

Aurobindo Sri, *The Psychic Being*, Sri Aurobindo Ashram Trust, Pondicherry, 1989, p. 45.

Chaterjee, S. and A. Sen, *Acharya Prafulla Chandra Ray*, Indian Science News Association: Kolkata, 1986, p. 10.

Gambirananda, S., *Katha Upanishad*, Advaita Ashram, Calcutta, 1980, pp. 24-5.

Gandhi, M.K., *Autobiography*, Navjivan: Ahmedabad, 1972, p. 174.

Gupta, M., *PC Ray – A Biography*, Bharatiya Vidya Bhavan: Bombay, 1966, pp. 78.

Karanjia, B.K., *Godrej – A 100 Years*, Viking: New Delhi, 1997, pp. 1-2.

Kurien, V., *I Too Had A Dream*, Roli: New Delhi, 2005, p. XII.

Lala, R.M., *In Search of Ethical Leadership*, Vision Books: New Delhi, 2005, p. 176.

Lala, R.M., *In Search of Ethical Leadership*, Vision books: New Delhi, 2002, p. 183.

Lala, R.M., *The Joy of Achievement*, Viking: New Delhi, 1995, p. 3.

Lala, R.M., Beyond The Last Blue Mountain; IBH: Bombay, 1992, p. 211.

Ray, P.C., *Autobiography*, Chuckervertty and Chatterjee, Calcutta: 1932, p. 541.

Swami Vivekananda, *Work and Its Secret*, Advaita Ashram: Calcutta, 2005, p. 7.

CHAPTER 10

Antoine, R., *The Dynasty of Raghu*, Calcutta: Writers Workshop, 1972, p. 210.

Aurobindo Sri, *The Right Attitude in Work*, Sri Aurobindo Society, Pondicherry, 1991, p. 7.

Aurobindo, Sri, *Right Attitude in Work*, Sri Aurobindo Society: Pondicherry, 1991, p. 45.

Aurobindo Sri, *The Psychic Being*, Sri Aurobindo Ashram Trust, Pondicherry, 1989, pp. 6-7.

Chakraborty, S.K. and Bhattacharya, P. (eds.), *Leadership and Power*, New Delhi: Oxford University Press, 2001, pp. 131-231.

Chakraborty, S.K. and Chakraborty, D., *Culture Society and Leadership*, Hyderabad: ICFAI University Press, 2006, pp. 231-33, 243-7, 239-42, 277-9.

Chakraborty, S.K. and Chakraborty, D., *Culture, Society and Leadership*, Hyderabad: ICFAI University Press, 2006, pp. 196–201.

Devadhar, C.R., *Raghuvamsa of Kalidasa*; Delhi: Motilal Banarasidas, 2005, p. iii.

Devahuti, D., *Harsha – A Political Study*, New Delhi: Oxford University Press, 2001, p. 205.

Gandhi, M.K., *The Selected Works of Mahatma Gandhi*, Navajivan, Ahmedabad, 2001, Vol. V, p. 55.

Gandhi, M.K., *Selected Works*, Navjivan: Ahmedabad, 2001, vol. V, p. 276.

Gandhi, M.K., *My Varnashrama Dharma*, Bombay: Bharatiya Vidya Bhavan, 1998, p. 71, p. 113.

Kirtipal, C.K., *Chanakya Niti and Jeevan Charitra* (in Hindi), Haridwar: Randhir Prakashan, 2003, p. 114.

Majumdar, R.C. (ed.), *History and The Culture of Indian People*, Bombay: Bharatiya Vidya Bhavan, 1954, pp. 116-7.

Mookerji, Radha Kumud; *Harsha*, London : Oxford University Press, 1926, pp. 80-2, p. 147.

Panikkar, K.M., *Sri Harsha of Kanauj*, Bombay: DB Taraporevala, 1922, pp. 76-7.

Rangarajan, L.N., *The Arthashastra*, New Delhi: Penguin, 1992, pp. 147-9.

Sarkar, B.K., *The Positive Background of Hindu Sociology*, Motilal Banrasidass, New Delhi, 1985, p. 84.

Sen, N.B., *Glorious Thoughts of Kalidasa*, New Delhi: New Book Society of India, 1966, p. 15.

Sil, N.P., *Kautilya's Arthashastra*, New Delhi: Academic Publishers, 1985, pp. 95-6.

Subramanian, V.K., *Maxims of Chanakya*, New Delhi: Abhinav Publications, 1980, p. 49, p. 50, p. 59, p. 134.

Swami Vivekananda, *Complete Works*, Kolkata: Advaita Ashram, 1962, Vol. IV, p. 359.

Tagore, Rabindranath, *Personality*, New Delhi: Rupa, 2002, p. 69.

Tagore, Rabindranath, *Katha-O-Kahini* (in Bengali), Kolkata, Visvabharati, 1977, pp. 16-20.

Vivekananda, S.W., *Complete Works*, Calcutta: Advaita Ashram, 1962, Vol. V, p. 228.

Vivekananda, S.W., *Complete Works*, Calcutta: Advaita Ashram, 1962, Vol. IV, p. 324.

CHAPTER 11

Aurobindo Sri, *The Synthesis of Yoga*, Sri Aurobindo Ashram, Pondicherry, 1988, p. 295.

Aurobindo, Sri, *The Synthesis of Yoga*; Pondicherry, Sri Aurobindo Ashram, 1988, p. 295.

Aurobindo Sri, *The Ideal of a Karmayogin*, Sri Aurobindo Ashram, Pondicherry, 1974, pp. 10-11.

Chakraborty, S.K., *Foundations of Managerial Work: Contributions From Indian Thought*, Himalaya Publishing House, Bombay, 1998, pp. 188-201.

Sri Aurobindo Birth Centenary Library, Complete Works, Pondicherry, Sri Aurobindo Ashram, 1973, Vol. 16, p. 377.

Vivekananda, Swami, *Rajyoga*, Mayavati: Advaita Ashram, 1976, verses II.29-32, pp. 205-6.

CHAPTER 12

Aurobindo Sri, *The Foundations of Indian Culture*, Aurobindo Ashram, Pondicherry, 1998, pp. 4-5.

Chakraborty, S.K., quoted in edited volume, *Philosophy and Practice of Education for India*, Kolkata, Aurobindo Samiti, 2006, p.30.

Chakraborty, S.K. and Chakraborty, D., 2005, *Human Values And Ethics: Achieving Holistic Excellence*, Hyderabad: ICFAI University Press, 2006.

Danino, M., *Sri Aurobindo and Indian Civilization*, Auroville, Auroville Press International, 1999, p. 37.

Ernst, R.R., *Synthesis of Science and Religion*, Kolkata, Bhaktivedanta Institute, 2001, p. 544.

Tagore, Rabindranath, *The Centre of Indian Culture*, Shantiniketan, Vishwabharati, 1988.

Toynbee, A.J., Foreword to *Sri Ramakrishna and His Unique Message*, Calcutta, Advaita Ashrama, 1969, pp. viii-ix.

Vivekananda, Swami, *Complete Works*, Calcutta, Advaita Ashrama, 1962, vol. IV, p. 359.

Vivekananda, Swami, *Complete Works*, Calcutta, Advaita Ashrama, 1958, vol. II, p. 65.

Index

NAME INDEX

SUBJECT INDEX